Japanese LGBTQ+ Lives, Diasporic Voices, and Resilience

Masami Tamagawa

Japanese LGBTQ+ Lives, Diasporic Voices, and Resilience

Precarious Visibility

Springer

Masami Tamagawa
World Languages and Literatures
Skidmore College
Saratoga Springs, NY, USA

ISBN 978-981-95-3104-2 ISBN 978-981-95-3105-9 (eBook)
https://doi.org/10.1007/978-981-95-3105-9

This Springer imprint is published by the registered company Springer Nature Singapore Pte Ltd.
The registered company address is: 152 Beach Road, #21-01/04 Gateway East, Singapore 189721, Singapore

Preface

This book arose from a time of global upheaval, when the COVID-19 pandemic disrupted lives and intensified existing inequalities. For LGBTQ+ communities in Japan, the pandemic brought both invisibility and exposure—moments of enforced silence at home and increased scrutiny in public spaces. During the online survey I conducted, 137 participants left not just responses but deeply personal comments—testimonies of resilience, fear, and hope that give this book its emotional core. I am profoundly grateful for their generosity and trust.

A note to the reader: In this book, Japanese names are presented in the traditional order—family name followed by given name—unless an individual uses a different format in their own publications. All translations are my own unless otherwise indicated. Some passages contain graphic or derogatory language that may be distressing; these are included in order to reflect lived realities without sanitization.

The concept of "precarious visibility" emerged from these narratives. Visibility, often heralded as progress, can also carry risk: the risk of being stereotyped, dismissed, or even endangered. As one participant observed, "It feels like society only notices us when it's convenient, but during the pandemic we were left to fend for ourselves." Another reflected, "When the government talked about protecting families, they weren't talking about families like mine. It was like being told that our health and lives don't matter as much." These voices reveal how the politics of recognition are entangled with power, privilege, and structural neglect.

This volume complements my forthcoming book, *Queer Intimacies and Cultural Dissent in Japanese Life: Quiet Subversion* (Routledge, 2025), which examines aesthetic and cultural acts of resistance. While that book explores how queer lives subtly challenge normative structures, the present work amplifies lived voices of quiet subversion—ordinary yet profound stories of survival, care, and endurance in the face of crisis. Together, these books trace both cultural and personal dimensions of queer life in Japan, underscoring that visibility must be understood not as a static achievement, but as a precarious, contested, and often exhausting practice.

I wish to express my heartfelt gratitude to Todd Norton, my husband, for his unwavering love and encouragement throughout this journey. I am deeply indebted to Alex Westcott Campbell, my commissioning editor at Springer, whose steadfast belief in this project—despite challenges and revisions—made this book possible. Alex's understanding and patience during the transition from a SpringerBrief to a full monograph were invaluable. I also thank Divyalakshmi Ganesan, my production editor, for her attentive guidance, and the Springer team for their professionalism and support.

Most importantly, I dedicate this book to the 137 participants who shared their stories in the midst of uncertainty. A participant named Misaki captured the essence of this collective experience: "I used to feel free, but here I can't even mention my partner. I feel like I'm losing myself." It is my hope that these voices—fragile yet powerful—will resonate beyond these pages and inspire deeper understanding, solidarity, and change.

Saratoga Springs, USA Masami Tamagawa

Competing Interests The author has no competing interests to declare that are relevant to the content of this manuscript.

Contents

Chapter 1
Introduction: LGBTQ+ Lives in Japan During the Pandemic

Masami Tamagawa

Abstract Japan's LGBTQ+ community, already marginalized by legal invisibility and cultural stigma, experienced a heightened tension between recognition and risk during the COVID-19 pandemic—a dynamic this book frames as precarious visibility. The pandemic not only amplified structural inequalities—such as workplace discrimination, healthcare exclusion, and family rejection—but also created new forms of digital activism and grassroots resilience. Drawing on 137 firsthand narratives, this chapter introduces the book's central themes and theoretical frameworks, including intersectionality, minority stress, and queer resilience, to explore how LGBTQ+ individuals in Japan and Japanese LGBTQ+ migrants abroad navigated a landscape where being visible could mean both empowerment and vulnerability. By situating these narratives within broader sociocultural and legal contexts, the chapter demonstrates how the pandemic exposed systemic failures while simultaneously fostering new modes of solidarity and advocacy. Ultimately, this chapter positions precarious visibility as the lens through which the book interrogates the challenges and possibilities for LGBTQ+ rights in Japan's post-pandemic future.

> When you're out, people say you're brave. But being visible means, I always have to explain myself. It's exhausting, and sometimes it just feels safer to disappear.
>
> —Nana, bisexual woman (age 25–34), survey participant

1.1 Introduction: Precarious Visibility

Precarious visibility captures the tension between recognition and risk that LGBTQ+ individuals face in Japan, particularly during the COVID-19 pandemic. To be visible can mean affirmation, connection, and advocacy, but it can also bring exposure to stigma, discrimination, and legal exclusion. This chapter introduces the historical, cultural, and legal frameworks that shape this condition of precarious visibility, setting the stage for the narratives and analyses that follow.

M. Tamagawa, *Japanese LGBTQ+ Lives, Diasporic Voices, and Resilience*,
https://doi.org/10.1007/978-981-95-3105-9_1

Japan is often portrayed as a country that harmoniously blends technological modernity with deep-rooted cultural traditions. Yet for LGBTQ+ individuals, social acceptance and legal recognition remain limited, shaped by historical norms, conservative politics, and heteronormative family structures. While queer visibility has increased in urban centers and media, it is often tolerated only when confined to entertainment or subcultural spaces. Legal protections remain minimal, and societal expectations rooted in *uchi* (the private family sphere) and *tatemae* (public façade) enforce silence, creating a climate where LGBTQ+ individuals must carefully navigate the balance between being seen and staying safe.

The COVID-19 pandemic intensified these dynamics, bringing the tension of precarious visibility into sharper focus. The crisis disrupted daily life for everyone, but for LGBTQ+ individuals, it compounded existing injustices—familial rejection, workplace discrimination, and exclusion from healthcare—while simultaneously creating new demands for visibility in digital and activist spaces. This duality of risk and recognition defines the narrative landscape explored in this book.

Understanding how LGBTQ+ individuals navigated this precarious terrain is critical to assessing both the vulnerabilities and resilience that emerged during the pandemic. Without robust legal protections or inclusive public health policies, many found themselves marginalized by state responses that prioritized conventional family structures. At the same time, digital platforms, mutual aid networks, and grassroots activism provided new forms of connection, allowing individuals to resist erasure and assert their identities in creative and collective ways.

1.2 Looking Ahead—Visibility, Risk, and Resilience

This book examines the lived experiences of LGBTQ+ individuals in Japan during the COVID-19 pandemic through the lens of precarious visibility, a concept that highlights the constant negotiation between being seen and staying safe. The pandemic deepened legal, social, and economic inequalities, but it also revealed how visibility could function both as a source of vulnerability—exposing individuals to stigma and exclusion—and as a catalyst for resilience, community-building, and activism.

Japan stands at a pivotal moment in its treatment of LGBTQ+ individuals. While grassroots activism and growing youth support suggest a shift toward greater acceptance, significant legal and cultural barriers remain. Efforts to advance marriage equality, anti-discrimination protections, and transgender rights continue to face political resistance. The pandemic amplified these gaps, making the costs of invisibility—and the risks of visibility—more apparent than ever. Yet it also galvanized advocacy efforts, digital organizing, and grassroots networks that challenged the status quo.

By amplifying voices often overlooked in mainstream narratives, this book illuminates how precarious visibility shaped both the hardships and the creative responses of Japan's LGBTQ+ community. Beyond its academic contribution, it calls for legal and social reforms that acknowledge not only the rights of LGBTQ+ individuals but also the complexities of navigating visibility in a society where silence and conformity remain powerful norms.

1.3 Literature Review—Global and Japanese Contexts of Visibility

Building on global research and Japan-specific scholarship, this section examines the pandemic's impact on LGBTQ+ communities both worldwide and domestically. It highlights how cultural norms, legal systems, and public health policies intersected to shape the lived experiences of queer individuals during this period.

1.3.1 The COVID-19 and LGBTQ+ Communities—A Global Perspective on Risk and Resilience

1.3.1.1 Health Disparities, Social Isolation, and Queer Resilience Worldwide

Globally, the COVID-19 pandemic magnified pre-existing health disparities and social vulnerabilities among LGBTQ+ communities. Studies indicate that queer individuals experienced heightened mental health challenges, economic precarity, and social isolation compared to their heterosexual and cisgender peers (Banerjee & Nair, 2020; Salerno et al., 2020). The closure of physical community spaces—such as bars, Pride events, and LGBTQ+ centers—eliminated vital sources of affirmation and support (Human Rights Campaign, 2020).

Healthcare inequalities were further exacerbated by disruptions in gender-affirming care for transgender individuals and a lack of culturally competent medical services (ILGA World, 2021). Yet the pandemic also highlighted the resilience of queer communities. Digital platforms became essential tools for maintaining visibility and solidarity, with online Pride events, virtual support groups, and grassroots mutual aid initiatives emerging to counteract isolation (Domínguez & Waisbord, 2021).

These global patterns underscore the notion of precarious visibility: while online spaces offered new forms of recognition and connection, they also exposed individuals to harassment, surveillance, or unwanted scrutiny. This global context sets the stage for understanding Japan's LGBTQ+ experiences during the pandemic.

1.3.1.2 Japan's COVID-19 Response: Public Health Measures and LGBTQ+ Exclusion

Japan's pandemic response relied on voluntary compliance measures rather than strict lockdowns, emphasizing behavioral guidelines like sanmitsu (avoiding the "Three Cs") and the ethos of jijo (self-help). While these measures were praised for fostering collective cooperation, they also reflected cultural expectations of conformity that left LGBTQ+ needs unaddressed. Government relief programs, designed around the nuclear family model, excluded many queer individuals—particularly unmarried same-sex couples and single people (Tamagawa, 2022).

Grassroots organizations and online networks stepped in to fill these gaps, but the lack of institutional recognition rendered many LGBTQ+ individuals invisible within public health policies. This exclusion reflects the broader cultural and legal dynamics—such as wa (harmony) and *tatemae* (public façade)—that will be explored in Sect. 2.2.

1.3.2 Japan's LGBTQ+ Sociocultural Climate—Precarious Visibility in Everyday Life

Building on the global and pandemic-specific contexts discussed above, this section examines the sociocultural and legal environment that shapes LGBTQ+ life in Japan. Despite Japan's historical legacy of same-sex relationships depicted in premodern literature and art, the modern era has seen the reinforcement of heteronormative structures and family ideals, particularly through the *koseki* (family registry) system (McLelland, 2000; Kakefuda, 1992).

Japan's LGBTQ+ community exists in a social and legal climate where visibility is both constrained and conditional, creating what this book frames as precarious visibility. While queer identities have gained greater cultural recognition in recent decades—through media representation, urban queer districts like Shinjuku Ni-chōme, and local partnership initiatives—these forms of visibility are often confined to specific, socially "acceptable" spaces or roles (Lunsing, 2001; Maree, 2013). Outside of these contexts, LGBTQ+ individuals continue to face structural erasure, familial silence, and a lack of comprehensive legal protections.

The interplay between cultural expectations of wa (harmony), the public façade of *tatemae*, and institutional systems such as the *koseki* family registry creates a climate where being openly queer can lead to social scrutiny or exclusion, while remaining invisible often means a loss of rights and affirmation (Tamagawa, 2017, 2018). The following subsections explore how this precarious visibility manifests in cultural narratives of tolerance, institutional barriers, and family dynamics.

1.3.2.1 The Illusion of Tolerance and Precarious Visibility

Japan is frequently portrayed as relatively tolerant toward LGBTQ+ individuals, largely due to the absence of criminal sodomy laws, the visibility of queer celebrities in entertainment, and the global reputation of Shinjuku Ni-chōme as a vibrant LGBTQ+ district (McLelland, 2000; Lunsing, 2001). These surface-level markers of inclusion—often emphasized in both domestic media and international discourse—suggest a narrative of progress. Scholars such as McLelland (2000) and Lunsing (2001) caution, however, that the visibility of queer subcultures or media personalities does not necessarily translate into broader social acceptance or structural equality.

This illusion of tolerance is reinforced by the commodification of queer identities in entertainment and advertising, where LGBTQ+ individuals are often portrayed as harmless, comedic, or hyper-stylized figures rather than as ordinary citizens deserving of equal rights (Maree, 2013; Mitsuhashi, 2010; Fujii et al., 2011). Media portrayals of *okama* (effeminate gay men, frequently caricatured in popular culture) or cross-dressing entertainers have historically framed queer visibility as a form of spectacle rather than an avenue toward genuine social inclusion. Such depictions confine queer lives to narrowly defined and socially "acceptable" spaces, leaving little room for authentic representation.

In reality, legal protections for LGBTQ+ individuals remain minimal, and cultural expectations—such as the prioritization of wa (harmony) and the pressure to maintain *tatemae* (public façade)—discourage open discussions of sexuality and gender identity (Kakefuda, 1992; Tamagawa, 2018). This dynamic produces a condition of precarious visibility, where being "seen" often entails risk: individuals who come out publicly may face workplace discrimination, family rejection, or social isolation, while those who remain invisible sacrifice affirmation and recognition (Tamagawa, 2017).

Furthermore, symbolic gestures of inclusion, such as municipal partnership certificates, offer visibility without substantive rights, as same-sex couples remain excluded from legal protections related to inheritance, hospital visitation, and joint adoption (Horie, 2010; Tamagawa, 2022). This highlights the tension between superficial acknowledgment and structural exclusion—a recurring theme in Japanese LGBTQ+ discourse.

By foregrounding the lived realities of LGBTQ+ individuals, this book moves beyond the narrative of tolerance to reveal how precarious visibility defines everyday life in Japan. This concept provides a foundation for the analyses in Chapters 2 and 3, which explore how identity, family dynamics, and social isolation are shaped by the delicate balance between being visible and staying safe.

1.3.2.2 The *Koseki* System: Institutionalized Hierarchies and Precarious Visibility

Japan's *koseki* (family registry) system, established during the Meiji era, continues to enforce heteronormative and patriarchal family structures, privileging legally married heterosexual couples and their children (White, 2014; Chapman & Krogness, 2014). Despite postwar reforms, the *koseki* remains a legal mechanism that defines family membership in exclusionary ways, rendering LGBTQ+ relationships legally invisible.

Same-sex couples cannot be recorded as family under the *koseki*, even if they are married abroad. As a result, they are excluded from basic rights related to inheritance, hospital visitation, and parental authority (Tamagawa, 2016; Horie, 2010). Municipal partnership certificates, while symbolically important, offer no legal standing. This forces many queer couples into a state of precarious visibility—recognized socially or locally, but denied legal protection at the national level.

Transgender individuals face similar structural barriers. Until 2023, the Gender Identity Disorder (GID) Act required sterilization and psychiatric evaluations as prerequisites for legal gender change. Although the Supreme Court has ruled forced sterilization unconstitutional, the broader legal and medical framework remains restrictive and pathologizing (Human Rights Watch, 2023). This illustrates how legal "visibility" often comes at the expense of bodily autonomy and dignity.

By reinforcing a narrow definition of family and gender, the *koseki* perpetuates systemic erasure. Queer individuals who challenge these norms risk scrutiny without protection, embodying the tension at the heart of precarious visibility. These structural exclusions are revisited in Chapters 6 and 7, which explore legal reforms and advocacy efforts for marriage equality and transgender rights.

1.3.2.3 *Uchi* and *Tatemae*: Familial Silence and Precarious Visibility

In Japan, LGBTQ+ individuals often navigate cultural frameworks of *uchi* (the inner circle of family or close community) and *tatemae* (public façade), which reinforce silence around sexuality and gender identity. These norms prioritize social harmony (*wa*) and familial reputation over personal expression, leading many queer individuals to conceal their identities to avoid disrupting family cohesion (Kakefuda, 1992; McLelland, 2000).

This dynamic produces a condition of precarious visibility. Coming out may invite rejection or shame, while staying closeted results in invisibility and emotional isolation. As Tamagawa (2018) notes, familial silence often forces LGBTQ+ individuals to balance authenticity against expectations of conformity, resulting in what he calls "muted existence" within family spaces.

The workplace mirrors these dynamics: many LGBTQ+ employees choose not to disclose their identities due to fears of discrimination or exclusion, while schools and public institutions provide little visibility or representation of queer lives (Lunsing, 2001; Tamagawa, 2022).

These pressures intensified during the COVID-19 pandemic, when lockdowns forced many individuals to spend extended periods with unsupportive families, heightening both emotional strain and the risks of being outed. At the same time, digital communities became a crucial refuge for self-expression and support, offering alternative spaces where queer identities could be recognized without fear.

1.3.3 Legal and Political Dimensions—Visibility Without Protection

Japan's legal and political landscape reflects a paradox in which LGBTQ+ individuals are increasingly visible in public discourse yet remain legally unrecognized and unprotected. Unlike many Western nations, Japan lacks comprehensive anti-discrimination laws addressing sexual orientation and gender identity, and same-sex marriage remains constitutionally unrecognized. While local governments have introduced partnership certificate systems in over 300 municipalities, these remain purely symbolic, offering no legal rights or protections related to inheritance, hospital visitation, or parental custody (Tamagawa, 2022; Horie, 2010). This gap illustrates how precarious visibility is institutionalized—partnership systems allow queer couples to be "seen" at a municipal level, but without national legal recognition, such visibility is hollow and, at times, risky.

1.3.3.1 Marriage Equality and Legal Gaps

The absence of marriage equality is among the most pressing issues facing Japan's LGBTQ+ community. Although municipal partnership certificates have increased, they confer no legal status, leaving same-sex couples without rights that heterosexual couples take for granted. Hospital visitation, inheritance, and spousal tax benefits remain inaccessible, forcing many couples to rely on fragile private agreements or remain invisible in legal contexts (White, 2014). This creates a dynamic of precarious visibility where couples are symbolically recognized but lack structural protections, making their visibility largely performative and non-binding.

1.3.3.2 Political Resistance and Public Debate

Court cases in recent years have challenged the constitutionality of Japan's marriage laws, with landmark rulings in Sapporo (2021) and Nagoya (2023) declaring the current ban on same-sex marriage unconstitutional. These cases have increased public awareness and support for marriage equality, yet legislative change remains stalled. The ruling Liberal Democratic Party (LDP), citing 'traditional family values,' has resisted reforms, reflecting a disconnect between legal structures and evolving public sentiment (Yoshimoto, 2025). This political inertia perpetuates the tension between being visible in public discourse yet remaining legally invisible.

1.3.3.3 Transgender Rights and Legal Recognition

Transgender individuals face similar contradictions between visibility and legal recognition. The Gender Identity Disorder (GID) Act has long required sterilization and invasive psychiatric evaluations as prerequisites for legal gender change—policies widely condemned by human rights organizations (Human Rights Watch, 2023). While the 2023 Supreme Court ruling declared forced sterilization unconstitutional, many bureaucratic and medical hurdles remain, placing transgender individuals in a position where visibility is contingent upon conforming to outdated and harmful medical norms. This creates another layer of precarious visibility, where recognition comes at the expense of personal autonomy and bodily integrity.

1.3.3.4 The Role of Advocacy and Symbolic Politics

This section highlights symbolic politics in Japan. Section 2.4 turns to participant voices, grounding these structural observations in lived experiences.

LGBTQ+ advocacy groups such as Marriage For All Japan, Nijiiro Diversity, and Stonewall Japan have played a vital role in advancing visibility and pushing for structural reforms. However, political leaders often engage with LGBTQ+ issues symbolically rather than substantively. During the Tokyo Olympics, for example, international scrutiny prompted statements of support for diversity, but these gestures were largely performative and did not result in legislative progress (Tamagawa, 2022). Activism thus remains the primary engine for change, yet it operates within a system where queer visibility is still treated as negotiable or superficial.

Japan's legal and political frameworks thus reveal how precarious visibility operates as both a condition of recognition and a source of vulnerability. While legal debates and public discourse have gained momentum, substantive reforms remain incomplete, leaving LGBTQ+ individuals caught between symbolic visibility and structural exclusion. Section 2.4 turns to the voices and experiences of LGBTQ+ individuals themselves, foregrounding how these dynamics were lived and felt during the COVID-19 pandemic.

1.3.4 Foregrounding Lived-Experiences in a Time of Crisis

This book foregrounds the lived experiences of LGBTQ+ individuals in Japan to illustrate how the pandemic intensified a condition of precarious visibility—the constant negotiation between being recognized and remaining safe. While structural inequalities such as legal exclusion, workplace discrimination, and familial silence existed long before COVID-19, the crisis amplified these vulnerabilities by disrupting the social and economic systems that many relied on for stability. Lockdowns confined individuals to private spaces where family dynamics could be fraught, while restrictions on physical gatherings closed off vital queer spaces such as bars, Pride events, and community centers.

At the same time, the pandemic created new forms of visibility through digital platforms, online activism, and media coverage of legal and social inequalities. For many participants, being "seen" online or in public discourse was empowering, but it also brought risks of harassment, outing, or backlash. This tension underscores how visibility is not inherently liberating; it is shaped by structural power, cultural norms, and individual circumstances.

By centering voices from a diverse range of participants—including Japanese LGBTQ+ individuals, migrants, and diasporic communities—this book examines how visibility was managed, contested, and reimagined during the pandemic. These narratives reveal not only the costs of visibility but also its potential as a catalyst for community resilience and advocacy. In doing so, the book contributes to a deeper understanding of how crises reveal both the fragility and the transformative power of queer life in Japan.

1.4 Research Objectives and Methodology—Capturing Narratives of Visibility

The overarching objective of this research is to examine how Japan's LGBTQ+ community experienced and navigated the COVID-19 pandemic, with particular attention to the dynamics of precarious visibility. The study aims to understand how queer individuals managed the risks and rewards of being seen—whether in family spaces, workplaces, healthcare systems, or digital platforms—while coping with the heightened stress and isolation caused by the crisis. This project seeks not only to document these experiences but also to analyze how cultural norms, legal structures, and social expectations shaped the choices individuals made about disclosure, advocacy, and resilience.

1.4.1 Research Objectives

This study was designed with the following objectives:

- To explore how visibility and invisibility were negotiated by LGBTQ+ individuals during the pandemic.
- To examine how legal and cultural frameworks—such as the *koseki* system, family expectations, and workplace norms—contributed to the precarity of queer life in Japan.

- To document forms of resilience, activism, and digital community-building that emerged in response to these challenges.
- To foreground the voices of participants, highlighting how their narratives reflect both the risks and the transformative potential of precarious visibility.

1.4.2 Methodological Approach

This book employs a mixed-methods approach, combining quantitative data from an online survey of 137 respondents with qualitative data from in-depth interviews and online media analysis. The qualitative narratives form the backbone of this study, offering rich insights into how individuals navigated their identities and relationships under pandemic conditions. By focusing on personal voices, the study captures not only the structural challenges LGBTQ+ individuals faced but also the nuanced, everyday decisions they made about being visible or invisible in specific contexts.

1.4.2.1 Participant Selection and Representation

Participants included Japanese LGBTQ+ individuals, non-Japanese queer residents in Japan, and Japanese LGBTQ+ migrants abroad. This diverse sample allows for a comparative analysis of how visibility operates across cultural and national boundaries. For some participants, the pandemic increased the pressure to remain invisible in family or professional spaces; for others, digital activism or media appearances offered new forms of visibility that were both empowering and fraught with risk.

1.4.2.2 Data Analysis and Thematic Framework

Thematic analysis was employed to identify recurring motifs in participant narratives, such as social isolation, family dynamics, workplace challenges, healthcare access, and digital worldmaking. The lens of precarious visibility guided this analysis, allowing for a deeper understanding of how visibility functioned as both a source of vulnerability and a strategy for resilience during the pandemic. This approach highlights how participants' narratives intersected with broader legal, cultural, and political forces.

1.4.2.3 Diverse Voices, Shared Struggles

While participants' experiences were shaped by factors such as age, gender identity, socioeconomic status, and migration background, a common thread emerged: the need to negotiate visibility carefully in every aspect of life. By weaving together these voices, the study underscores that visibility was not simply a personal choice but a social and political condition influenced by structural inequalities.

1.4.3 Why This Approach Matters

Foregrounding personal narratives provides a more nuanced understanding of how crises like the COVID-19 pandemic affect marginalized communities. This approach resists homogenizing LGBTQ+ experiences and instead captures the diversity of strategies, risks, and forms of resilience associated with precarious visibility. By documenting these lived realities, the study contributes to broader conversations about queer life in Japan, policy reforms, and the cultural politics of recognition.

1.4.4 Ethical Considerations

Special attention was paid to participant anonymity, particularly given the risks associated with being outed in unsupportive environments. Pseudonyms were used, and identifying details were removed or altered. In some cases, quotes are attributed to "anonymous participant" when no identifying code was provided or when the content of the response required extra protection of confidentiality. These anonymous comments were included only when they captured sentiments expressed by multiple respondents or when they provided particularly illustrative insights. Recognizing that visibility can have real consequences—both empowering and harmful—the research process itself was guided by sensitivity to how participants chose to share their experiences, reflecting an ethical commitment to their safety and dignity.

1.5 Theoretical Implications—Intersectionality, Resilience, and Precarious Visibility

This book draws on multiple theoretical perspectives—intersectionality, minority stress, crisis studies, queer resilience, and rights discourse—to examine how the COVID-19 pandemic magnified structural inequalities for LGBTQ+ individuals in Japan. Each lens helps unpack how cultural norms, legal frameworks, and societal expectations shape the lives of queer individuals. Central to this analysis is the concept of precarious visibility, which highlights the tension between recognition and risk. The following subsections explain how these frameworks collectively inform the study.

1.5.1 Intersectionality and Layered Vulnerabilities

Intersectionality (Crenshaw, 1989) highlights how multiple axes of identity—such as gender, sexuality, race, class, and migration status—intersect to produce unique forms of oppression and privilege. For Japan's LGBTQ+ community, this framework reveals how structural discrimination compounds for individuals who are not only queer but also non-Japanese, economically marginalized, or disabled. During the pandemic, these layered vulnerabilities became even more pronounced, as visibility in one sphere (e.g., seeking healthcare or government aid) could lead to exposure or exclusion in others. This book applies intersectionality to explore how precarious visibility was not experienced uniformly but was shaped by overlapping identities and systemic hierarchies.

1.5.2 Structural Inequality and Minority Stress Theory

Minority stress theory (Meyer, 2003) provides a lens for understanding the chronic stress LGBTQ+ individuals experience as a result of stigma, prejudice, and discrimination. The pandemic magnified these stressors by forcing many individuals into unsupportive family environments, isolating them from affirming communities, or subjecting them to increased workplace vulnerabilities. Within this context, precarious visibility became a critical coping mechanism: participants often had to decide whether to disclose or conceal their identities to minimize conflict or risk. This study draws on minority stress theory to analyze how these strategic negotiations impacted mental health and overall well-being.

1.5.3 Crisis Studies and the Exacerbation of Vulnerability

Crisis studies emphasize how social and structural inequalities are intensified during moments of disruption (Tierney, 2014). The COVID-19 pandemic revealed the fragility of legal and social safety nets for LGBTQ+ individuals in Japan, while also amplifying the stakes of visibility. In emergency contexts, such as hospital visits or government aid distribution, visibility could be the difference between access and exclusion. By framing the pandemic as a stress test of existing inequalities, this book examines how precarious visibility operated during a period when both recognition and erasure carried heightened consequences.

1.5.4 *Queer Resilience and Community Activism*

Resilience, as conceptualized in queer studies, extends beyond individual coping mechanisms to include collective practices of resistance and care (Ahmed, 2006; Muñoz, 2009). The pandemic prompted the rapid growth of online activism, mutual aid, and digital community-building—spaces where queer individuals could be visible on their own terms. Yet, digital visibility also introduced new risks, from online harassment to surveillance. This section explores how resilience was often about navigating precarious visibility, using creative and collective strategies to maintain safety while challenging structural erasure.

1.5.5 *Rethinking LGBTQ+ Rights in Crisis Contexts*

The pandemic underscored the limitations of legal recognition and rights frameworks that fail to account for the lived realities of marginalized communities. Visibility in the form of partnership certificates or symbolic gestures often masked the absence of substantive protections for LGBTQ+ individuals. By situating legal rights within the broader concept of precarious visibility, this study calls for a critical rethinking of what true equality entails—beyond symbolic inclusion toward systemic change that safeguards both recognition and safety.

1.5.6 *Precarious Visibility as a Framework*

Precarious visibility draws from queer theory's critical interrogation of the politics of recognition, particularly Butler's notion of performativity—the idea that gender and sexuality are not innate but are constituted through repeated acts within social and cultural norms (Butler, 1990). In Japan, these norms are deeply entwined with heteronormative expectations of family (*ie*) and workplace conformity. For LGBTQ+ individuals, the pandemic disrupted many of these scripts, exposing how the performance of "acceptable" identities—whether in the household, workplace, or public health systems—was often necessary for survival. At the same time, these disruptions created spaces where normative performances could be subtly resisted or reimagined, especially through digital communities that allowed participants to experiment with more authentic forms of self-presentation.

Sedgwick's (1990) concept of the *epistemology of the closet* helps illuminate this tension between disclosure and concealment. For many participants in this study, being "out" was not a static condition but an ongoing negotiation shaped by family pressures, workplace hierarchies, and public stigma. Sedgwick's insights remind us that visibility is not inherently liberating—it can simultaneously open possibilities for connection and expose individuals to surveillance or rejection. During the pandemic, this dynamic was heightened, as lockdowns often forced individuals back into the domestic spaces of the closet while digital visibility expanded on social media and activist platforms.

Ahmed's (2006) notion of queer phenomenology provides another lens for understanding how Japanese LGBTQ+ individuals navigate heteronormative social spaces. Ahmed conceptualizes queerness as a matter of orientation—of which bodies and desires "fit" the paths laid out by dominant norms. Participants' narratives of healthcare encounters, workplace interactions, and family life reveal how they often needed to "reorient" themselves, finding alternative routes or creating their own pathways when institutional structures failed to recognize them. This resonates strongly with the book's concept of precarious visibility, as moments of being "seen" were always shaped by the orientations and disorientations imposed by these spaces.

Finally, Muñoz's (1999, 2009) ideas of disidentification and queer futurity highlight the creative strategies queer individuals deploy to navigate and transform oppressive structures. Many participants engaged in acts of disidentification—neither fully assimilating into heteronormative expectations nor rejecting them outright, but instead crafting hybrid forms of belonging that allowed survival and self-expression. Moreover, Muñoz's vision of queer futurity as a "horizon of potentiality" aligns with the ways participants imagined post-pandemic futures of legal recognition, chosen family, and solidarity networks, even in the face of current exclusions.

By integrating Butler's performativity, Sedgwick's epistemology of the closet, Ahmed's orientation, and Muñoz's disidentification, precarious visibility emerges as a dynamic, multi-layered framework that captures both the vulnerabilities and the imaginative capacities of Japan's LGBTQ+ community. These theoretical insights also complement the book's notion of quiet subversion, showing how understated acts of resilience and care can destabilize normative expectations while offering glimpses of more inclusive futures.

1.5.7 Integrating Quiet Subversion

These discussions of precarious visibility resonate with ideas I further develop in my forthcoming book, Queer Intimacies and Cultural Dissent in Japanese Life: Quiet Subversion. While precarious visibility underscores the risks, negotiations, and systemic constraints associated with being recognized as LGBTQ+ in Japan, quiet subversion emphasizes the subtle, culturally attuned forms of resistance that often operate below the surface of public visibility. Such resistance includes non-confrontational modes of self-expression, the maintenance of discreet but affirming relationships, and the creation of private or semi-private spaces where queer identities can flourish without the pressure of public recognition.

Together, these concepts provide a holistic framework for understanding how queer life in Japan is navigated and performed. By examining both the precariousness of being visible and the power of understated dissent, this book acknowledges not only the structural challenges but also the quiet yet transformative strategies of resilience and cultural critique that define Japanese LGBTQ+ experiences.

1.6 Overview of Key Themes—Visibility and Its Costs

The COVID-19 pandemic magnified existing inequalities for LGBTQ+ individuals in Japan, affecting every facet of daily life—from family dynamics and employment to healthcare and legal recognition. Through firsthand accounts, this book highlights five interconnected themes that reveal how structural exclusions and minority stress were intensified under crisis conditions, while also showcasing how precarious visibility—the tension between recognition and risk—shaped both hardship and resilience.

1.6.1 Social Isolation, Mental Health, and Precarious Visibility

Lockdowns and stay-at-home mandates forced many LGBTQ+ individuals to live with unsupportive or hostile family members, leading to re-closeting, emotional strain, and heightened psychological distress. Visibility within family spaces often carried the risk of rejection, while invisibility caused a loss of self-affirmation. Minority stress theory (Meyer, 2003) explains how this tension between concealment and disclosure compounded mental health burdens. To cope, many turned to digital spaces and peer-support networks, which became critical lifelines for maintaining identity and community during prolonged isolation.

1.6.2 Workplace Discrimination, Economic Precarity, and Strategic Invisibility

The pandemic exposed how Japan's lack of anti-discrimination laws leaves LGBTQ+ workers vulnerable to job loss and harassment, particularly in precarious industries like nightlife, service work, and freelancing. Many participants reported suppressing their identities to avoid workplace discrimination, highlighting how precarious visibility played out in professional settings. Economic instability intersected with gender identity and sexual orientation, amplifying stress and inequality. Grassroots organizations stepped in where state policies failed, providing financial and employment support while creating safer spaces for visibility.

1.6.3 Healthcare Inequality and Medical Erasure

Transgender individuals faced delays in gender-affirming treatments—such as hormone therapy and surgeries—due to hospitals deprioritizing non-emergency procedures. Fear of misgendering, discrimination, and breaches of privacy discouraged many LGBTQ+ individuals from seeking care, illustrating how visibility within healthcare settings often carried emotional and psychological costs. These challenges underscore the urgent need for inclusive medical protocols and the importance of recognizing how crisis conditions exacerbate pre-existing health disparities.

1.6.4 Legal Exclusion and the Costs of Recognition

Japan's legal framework, rooted in the *koseki* family registry system, continues to deny same-sex couples basic rights such as marriage, joint adoption, and hospital visitation. During the pandemic, these exclusions became painfully visible, as unrecognized partners were often barred from making medical or financial decisions for loved ones. Here, precarious visibility operates on a structural level—visibility as a couple may bring symbolic recognition (e.g., local partnership certificates) but still lacks legal protections, leaving queer families vulnerable in times of crisis.

1.6.5 Digital Activism and the Politics of Online Visibility

Despite physical isolation, the pandemic sparked a surge of digital organizing and advocacy. LGBTQ+ activists and community groups used online platforms to offer mental health resources, legal guidance, and mutual aid, transforming digital visibility into a form of collective resilience. Yet online spaces also posed risks, including exposure to harassment and surveillance, reinforcing the dual-edged nature of precarious visibility. These digital responses illustrate how isolation was transformed into a catalyst for community mobilization and public awareness.

Together, these themes show that while the pandemic exposed structural failures, it also deepened our understanding of how precarious visibility defines queer life in Japan—revealing the risks of being seen, the resilience required to persist, and the collective strength found in both silence and solidarity.

1.7 Chapter Summaries—Mapping Precarious Visibility Across the Book

This book explores how the COVID-19 pandemic exposed and intensified the legal, social, and economic challenges faced by LGBTQ+ individuals in Japan, while also documenting acts of resilience, resistance, and community activism. Each chapter examines a distinct facet of how precarious visibility—the tension between recognition and risk—shaped queer life during the pandemic, from personal experiences of isolation to structural barriers in healthcare, employment, and legal recognition.

Chapter 1—Introduction: LGBTQ+ Lives in Japan During the Pandemic

This chapter introduces the book's central framework of precarious visibility, research questions, and methodology. It examines Japan's sociocultural and legal context, highlighting systemic barriers—such as the *koseki* family registry, lack of marriage equality, and absence of anti-discrimination protections—that predate but were magnified by the pandemic. The chapter reviews global and domestic literature on COVID-19's impact on LGBTQ+ communities, situating Japan's experiences within broader discussions of minority stress, intersectionality, and queer resilience. By foregrounding firsthand narratives and theoretical frameworks, This chapter positions the pandemic as both a crisis of inequality and a catalyst for new forms of community visibility and advocacy.

Chapter 2—Defining the Community: Identity, Intersectionality, and Representation

This chapter explores how diverse LGBTQ+ identities in Japan are constructed and represented, particularly during the pandemic. It examines how precarious visibility is experienced differently across gender, sexuality, race, and class, with marginalized groups—such as transgender, non-binary, and mixed-race individuals—facing compounded forms of invisibility and stigma. The chapter analyzes both online and offline spaces as critical arenas for identity formation and advocacy, emphasizing how digital platforms emerged as vital tools for visibility, connection, and resistance during times of isolation.

Chapter 3—Social Isolation and Family Dynamics: The Pandemic's Social Impact

Chapter 3 investigates how precarious visibility shaped family life during lockdowns. Many LGBTQ+ individuals were forced to conceal their identities or endure unsupportive family environments, leading to re-closeting, emotional strain, and mental health challenges. By exploring concepts such as *uchi* (private family sphere) and *tatemae* (public façade), the chapter reveals how cultural expectations around family harmony intensified the costs of being visible, while digital chosen families and support networks became lifelines of affirmation and resilience.

Chapter 4—Work, Digital Communities, and Intersectional Challenges

This chapter examines how the pandemic heightened workplace discrimination, job precarity, and economic stress for LGBTQ+ individuals, particularly those in freelance, entertainment, or service industries. Visibility at work often came with the risk of harassment or stalled career progression, forcing many to remain strategically invisible. At the same time, digital communities became crucial spaces for advocacy, skill-sharing, and mutual aid, demonstrating how online visibility could counter isolation while also amplifying collective demands for equality.

Chapter 5—Healthcare and Mental Health: Barriers to Care

Chapter 5 focuses on healthcare exclusion and mental health struggles, particularly for transgender individuals whose gender-affirming treatments were delayed or deprioritized. Visibility in medical settings was often fraught, as participants reported misgendering and discriminatory treatment, discouraging them from seeking care. The chapter highlights how precarious visibility influenced decisions about disclosure in healthcare contexts, while also examining how LGBTQ+ organizations used digital platforms to offer mental health resources and community support.

Chapter 6—Transnational Experiences: Migration, Travel Bans, and Legal Challenges

This chapter explores how precarious visibility intersected with border closures, visa insecurity, and legal exclusion for Japanese LGBTQ+ migrants abroad and non-Japanese queer residents in Japan. Binational couples and migrants faced unique vulnerabilities, often being denied legal recognition or travel exemptions. By situating these experiences within global queer diasporic frameworks, the chapter shows how visibility and recognition were shaped not just by national policies but by transnational flows of information, activism, and inequality.

Chapter 7—Precarious Visibility and Queer Solitude: Two Lives in and Beyond Japan

This chapter presents two narrative portraits that illustrate how visibility, solitude, and resilience were negotiated during the pandemic. One focuses on navigating social scrutiny and family expectations in Japan, while the other examines the compounded challenges of isolation and legal precarity abroad. Together, these narratives highlight how precarious visibility shaped individual strategies of survival and self-discovery, revealing the intimate costs and transformative potential of living openly during a time of crisis.

Chapter 8—Rights and Recognition: Voices from the Japanese LGBTQ+ Community

Chapter 8 centers on participants' reflections on legal precarity, political representation, and cultural attitudes toward LGBTQ+ rights. Through their voices, it examines marriage equality, adoption rights, workplace discrimination, and activism, while also addressing critiques of media representation and corporate allyship. By highlighting both external structural barriers and internal community dynamics, the chapter reveals how legal struggles intersect with everyday experiences of visibility, exclusion, and resistance.

Chapter 9—Conclusion: Lessons from the Pandemic and Future Directions

The concluding chapter synthesizes the book's key insights, emphasizing how precarious visibility defines the challenges and opportunities faced by Japan's LGBTQ+ community in a post-pandemic world. It reflects on the pandemic's role in amplifying structural inequalities—such as exclusion from healthcare, marriage rights, and workplace protections—while also strengthening digital activism, grassroots networks, and advocacy efforts. The chapter calls for sustained activism, inclusive policymaking, and cultural transformation, arguing that the lessons of this crisis must shape a future where visibility no longer comes at such high personal and social costs.

Chapters 2 through 7 primarily focus on personal narratives and lived experiences, while Chapter 8 shifts to participants' reflections on legal and political dimensions, creating a transition from individual stories to structural analysis before the concluding synthesis in Chapter 9.

References

Ahmed, S. (2006). *Queer phenomenology: Orientations, objects, others*. Duke University Press. https://doi.org/10.1515/9780822388074

Banerjee, D., & Nair, V. S. (2020). "The untold side of COVID-19": Struggle and perspectives of the sexual minorities. *Journal of Psychosexual Health*, 2(2), 113–120.

Berlant, L. (2011). *Cruel optimism*. Duke University Press. https://doi.org/10.1515/9780822394716

Bowleg L. (2020). We're Not All in This Together: On COVID-19, Intersectionality, and Structural Inequality. *American journal of public health*, 110(7), 917.

Butler, J. (1990). *Gender trouble: Feminism and the subversion of identity*. Routledge.

Chapman, D., & Krogness, K. (Eds.). (2014). Japan's household registration system and citizenship: *Koseki*, identification and documentation. Routledge.

Crenshaw, K. (1989). Demarginalizing the intersection of race and sex: A Black feminist critique of antidiscrimination doctrine, feminist theory, and antiracist politics. *University of Chicago Legal Forum*, 1989(1), 139–167.

Domínguez, R., & Waisbord, S. (2021). Digital activism and the LGBTQ+ community: Visibility and resilience during COVID-19. *Social Media + Society*, 7(3), 1–10.

Eng, D. L. (2010). *The feeling of kinship: Queer liberalism and the racialization of intimacy*. Duke University Press. https://doi.org/10.1215/9780822392828

Fujii, S., Fushimi, N., & Nakamura, U. (2011, January 21). Fujii Seiji, Nakamura Usagi, and Fushimi Noriaki ga onē būmu wo kiru [Seiji Fujii, Usagi Nakamura, and Noriaki Fushimi cut down the onē boom!]. *Nico Nico Dōga* [video]. June 25, 2022, from http://blog.nicovideo.jp/niconews/ni011078.html

Horie, Y. (2010). Dōsei-kan no "kon'in" ni kansuru hihan-teki kōsatsu: Nihon no shakai-seido no bunmyaku kara [Critical consideration of "marriage" between same-sex partners: From the context of Japan's social system]. *Shakai Shisutemu Kenkyū* [Social System Research], 21, 37–57.

Human Rights Campaign. (2020). The lives and livelihoods of LGBTQ people in the COVID-19 pandemic. Human Rights Campaign Foundation.

Human Rights Watch. (2023). Japan: Supreme Court rules sterilization requirement unconstitutional.

ILGA World. (2021). The impact of COVID-19 on the human rights of LGBT people: A global report. International Lesbian, Gay, Bisexual, Trans and Intersex Association.

Kakefuda, H. (1992). "Rezubian" dearu, toiu koto [On being a lesbian]. Kawade Shobō Shinsha.

Lunsing, W. (2001). *Beyond common sense: Sexuality and gender in contemporary Japan*. London, UK: Kegan Paul.

Maree, C. (2013). *"Onē kotoba" ron* [On onē kotoba]. Seidosha.

McLelland, M. J. (2000). *Male homosexuality in modern Japan: Cultural myths and social realities*. Curzon Press.

Meyer, I. H. (2003). Prejudice, social stress, and mental health in lesbian, gay, bisexual, and transgender populations: Conceptual issues and research evidence. *Psychological Bulletin*, 129(5), 674–697.

Mitsuhashi, J. (2010, October 17). Jendā to sekushuarithi no baikai [Media concerning gender and sexuality] [Panel discussion]. 3331 Arts Chiyoda, Tokyo. June 25, 2022, from June 25, 2022 from http://akaboshi07.blog44.fc2.com/blog-entry-2346.html?sp

Muñoz, J.E. (1999). *Disidentifications: Queers of color and the performance of politics*. University of Minnesota Press.

Muñoz, J. E. (2009). *Cruising utopia: The then and there of queer futurity*. New York University Press. https://doi.org/10.18574/9780814744038

Poteat, T., Millett, G. A., Nelson, L. E., & Beyrer, C. (2020). Understanding COVID-19 risks and vulnerabilities among Black communities in America: The lethal force of syndemics. *Annals of Epidemiology*, 47, 1–3.

Puar, J. K. (2007). *Terrorist assemblages: Homonationalism in queer times*. Duke University Press.

Salerno, J. P., Devadas, J., Pease, M., Nketia, B., & Fish, J. N. (2020). Sexual and Gender Minority Stress Amid the COVID-19 Pandemic: Implications for LGBTQ Young Persons' Mental Health and Well-Being. *Public Health Reports*, 135(6), 721–727.

Sedgwick, E. K. (1990). *Epistemology of the closet*. University of California Press.

Tamagawa, M, (2009). *Rediscovering Japanese motherhood: The transformation of western feminist ideas in Japan*. LAP Lambert Academic Publishing.

Tamagawa, M. (2016). Same-sex marriage in Japan. *Journal of GLBT Family Studies*, 12(2), 160–187.

Tamagawa, M. (2017). Coming out of the closet in Japan: An exploratory sociological study. *Journal of GLBT Family Studies*, 14(5), 488–518.

Tamagawa, M. (2018). Coming out to parents in Japan: A sociocultural analysis of lived experiences. *Society & Culture*, 22(2), 497–520.

Tamagawa, M. (2020). *Japanese LGBT diasporas: Gender, Immigration Policy and Diverse Experiences*. Palgrave Pivot.

Tamagawa, M. (2022). *The Japanese LGBTQ+ community in the world: The COVID-19 pandemic, challenges, and the prospect for the future*. Routledge.

Tamagawa, M. (Forthcoming, 2025). *Queer intimacies and cultural dissent in Japanese life: Quiet subversion*. Routledge.

Tierney, K. J. (2014). *The social roots of risk: Producing disasters, promoting resilience*. Stanford University Press.

Weston, K. (1991). *Families we choose: Lesbians, gays, kinship*. Columbia University Press.

White, L. E. (2014). Challenging the heteronormative family in the *koseki*: Surname, legitimacy and unmarried mothers. In D. Chapman & K. J. Krogness (Eds.), *Japan's household registration system and citizenship: Koseki, identification, and documentation* (pp. 240–256). Routledge.

Yoshimoto, K. (2025). Anywhere but here: Discourses and representations surrounding same-sex marriage in Japanese newspapers. *Applied Corpus Linguistics, 5*(1), 100120. https://doi.org/10.1016/j.acorp.2025.100120

Chapter 2
Defining the Community: Identity, Intersectionality, and Portrayal

Masami Tamagawa

Abstract This chapter explores how members of the Japanese LGBTQ+ community define their identities, negotiate intersecting social dimensions, and experience portrayal—or lack thereof—within mainstream and queer spaces. Drawing on surveys and in-depth interviews with 137 participants, the chapter highlights the limitations of Western LGBTQ+ categories in capturing local realities, the compounded challenges of intersectionality (age, class, race, and geography), and the complexities of presence. Through the voices of participants such as Yu (JJ, 18–24), Misaki (JJ, 25–34), Emma (FJ, 25–34), and Riku (FJ, 55–64), this chapter demonstrates that identity is fluid, relational, and culturally situated. The insights presented here lay the groundwork for subsequent chapters by showing how questions of identity, portrayal, and intersectionality intersect with broader social structures. These dynamics will be examined in greater depth in later discussions of healthcare inequalities during the pandemic (Chap. 5) and ongoing legal challenges such as marriage equality and anti-discrimination laws (Chap. 8).

2.1 Introduction: Why Defining the Community Matters

Defining the Japanese LGBTQ+ community is both necessary and complex. While "LGBTQ+" has become a global shorthand for sexual and gender diversity, it is not native to Japan, and its categories—lesbian, gay, bisexual, transgender, queer—do not always align with local understandings. Historical Japanese notions of same-sex intimacy and gender variance predate Western frameworks, and many contemporary individuals continue to negotiate their identities in ways that resist or adapt these imported terms. As several participants revealed, their lived realities often cannot be neatly encapsulated by the LGBTQ+ acronym. Some found empowerment in adopting global terms like queer or pansexual, while others preferred local descriptors or rejected fixed categories altogether.

During the COVID-19 pandemic, the question of who is "seen" or "unseen" became sharper. This chapter frames these dynamics through precarious visibility—the condition of being visible in ways that bring both affirmation and risk. Public

M. Tamagawa, *Japanese LGBTQ+ Lives, Diasporic Voices, and Resilience*,
https://doi.org/10.1007/978-981-95-3105-9_2

acknowledgment of identity could foster solidarity, but it also exposed participants to misunderstanding, discrimination, or tokenization.

This chapter examines how participants define and express their identities, how these identities intersect with broader social dimensions such as class, age, and nationality, and how portrayal in media and public spaces shapes lived experiences. Intersectionality—Crenshaw's (1989) concept of interlocking systems of oppression—offers a crucial lens here. During the pandemic, these intersections became especially visible: transgender participants faced delays in medical care, non-regular employees struggled financially, and foreign residents encountered xenophobia alongside queer marginalization.

Presence emerges as a recurring theme throughout this chapter, operating as both a source of affirmation and a site of vulnerability. Who is seen, who remains unseen, and on what terms? Through the voices of individuals like Yu (JJ, 18–24), Misaki (JJ, 25–34), and Emily (FJ, 25–34), this chapter illuminates a richly textured and diverse community that challenges simplistic narratives of identity.

2.2 Gender and Sexual Identity Beyond Traditional Labels

The LGBTQ+ acronym provides a global vocabulary for sexual and gender diversity, but it does not always capture the ways Japanese individuals experience identity. Terms such as gay (*gei*), lesbian (*rezubian*), and bisexual (*baiseikusharu*) have become common in public discourse, yet they coexist with local categories like *okama* (historically referring to effeminate gay men or cross-dressers), *onabe* (masculine-presenting women), and *X-jendā* (X-gender, a non-binary or genderqueer designation). These Japanese terms carry cultural and historical connotations that often diverge from Western frameworks, and they are sometimes employed with irony, resistance, or reclamation.

For some participants, these terms are empowering; for others, they feel alien, reductive, or overly clinical. Yu, a transgender man in his early twenties, reflected on the inadequacy of bureaucratic labels: "For the government, I'm just a category—female on paper, or eventually male if I follow the rules. But gender is not just a checkbox. It's how I live, who I love, and how I want others to see me."

Kumiko (JJ, 35–44), a lesbian woman in her late 30s, expressed discomfort with borrowed terms: "I call myself a *rezubian* because people know the word, but it doesn't feel right. It sounds like something from TV or the news. My relationship isn't a stereotype—it's just life."

The wide variety of self-identifications among participants illustrates that identity is relational, fluid, and context-dependent.

2.2.1 Fluidity and Resistance

A number of participants rejected rigid categories altogether, preferring more open-ended or fluid terms such as pansexual, queer, or "Q+ (Others)." Mayumi (JJ, 45–54), a pansexual woman in her late 40s, described her approach: "I don't fall in love with gender—I fall in love with the person. People think I'm confused, but I'm just being honest about how I love."

Mirai (JJ, 18–24), a 22-year-old pansexual participant, explained how she discovered queer: "Discovering the word queer through online platforms helped me articulate my identity in ways I couldn't before., it felt like I could finally breathe. I didn't have to choose between lesbian or bi—I could just be me."

By contrast, older participants were more likely to stick to familiar terms. Hiroshi (JJ, 55–64), a 59-year-old gay man, said: "For me, *gei* has always been enough. I've used it for decades, and it still feels right."

This generational difference highlights how identity categories are culturally and historically situated, with younger participants often influenced by global discourses and online communities.

2.2.2 Asexuality and Misunderstanding

Asexual participants faced persistent misunderstanding. Emily, an asexual foreigner, remarked: "People here think asexuality is a medical condition or that I'm just shy. Even some LGBTQ+ folks don't get it. I'm tired of explaining."

Ayano (JJ, 25–34), a Japanese asexual woman, expressed similar frustration: "When people talk about LGBTQ+, they usually mean gay men. Asexuality isn't even on their radar."

2.2.3 Bisexuality, Erasure, and Stereotypes

Like asexual participants, bisexual individuals also described feeling misunderstood or dismissed, both by heterosexual and queer communities. Aya (JJ, 25–34), a bisexual woman of mixed heritage, noted: "When I'm with my husband, people assume I'm straight. When I mention past relationships with women, they act like it's just a phase."

Rui (JJ, 25–34) described feeling dismissed: "If I date a man, people say I'm not really queer. If I date a woman, I'm assumed to be a lesbian. There's no space for my full identity."

2.2.4 Cultural Norms and Family Pressures

Participants frequently spoke about cultural expectations around marriage and family life, which often clash with queer identities. Misaki, a lesbian living with her partner, shared: "My mother said, 'I hope this is just a phase.' Even in my 30s, with a stable job and a partner, I'm expected to marry a man."

Kumiko, who has not come out to her parents, explained: "They expect me to marry, and I'm not ready for that fight. I love my partner, but I also don't want to lose my family."

2.2.5 Pandemic Effects on Identity Expression

The pandemic further complicated self-expression by reducing access to queer spaces and social networks. Shun (JJ, 18–24) a gay man living in a rural area, said: "Before COVID, I could go to Ni-chōme and be free. Now, stuck at home, I have to act straight again."

For some, isolation led to moments of self-discovery. Rin (JJ, 18–24), a lesbian student, reflected: "During the lockdown, I finally found the courage to confide in someone close to me. It was scary but liberating."

2.2.6 Identity as a Negotiated Performance

Many participants viewed identity as a performative process—something enacted and adjusted based on context. Hitomi (JJ, 25–34), a transgender woman, observed: "People expect me to wear makeup every day, like I need to prove I'm a woman. It's exhausting. I just want to exist without being judged."

Such narratives illustrate Butler's (1990) idea of gender performativity, where identity is constructed through repeated acts rather than innate characteristics.

2.3 Intersectionality and Multiple Axes of Identity

LGBTQ+ identity in Japan cannot be understood in isolation from other social categories such as age, class, race, and geography. The concept of intersectionality (Crenshaw, 1989) provides a critical lens for examining how overlapping systems of oppression shape individual experiences. In our participants' narratives, these intersections frequently compounded challenges—creating layers of invisibility and marginalization—but also fostered unique forms of resilience and solidarity.

2.3.1 Age and Generational Differences

Generational divides emerged clearly in how participants understood and expressed their identities. Younger participants (18–24) were more likely to use terms such as queer, pansexual, or X-gender, reflecting their exposure to global discourses and online communities. While younger participants embraced online spaces for self-expression, older individuals like Riku (FJ, 55–64) felt overlooked in youth-centric LGBTQ+ spaces, reflecting a generational divide in community portrayal.

Ren (JJ, 18–24), a 19-year-old gay man, emphasized the role of online spaces: "LINE groups are my only safe spaces. Without them, I'd feel completely alone. It's where I can talk openly about crushes or coming out."

Rin, a lesbian student, described the same dynamic: "School is still very heteronormative. Without online communities, I wouldn't even know any other queer women."

By contrast, Riku, a 55–64-year-old gay man, felt sidelined within youth-centric queer culture: "Even in Ni-chōme, it feels like the scene is for young men. I don't see my life reflected there."

Hiroshi, also in his late 50s, echoed this sense of invisibility: "In bars, people don't look at me anymore. I feel like I've passed my expiration date. It's lonely."

These contrasting narratives highlight how generational shifts in language and presence have reshaped Japan's LGBTQ+ landscape.

2.3.2 Class and Economic Precarity

Economic status shaped how participants experienced both safety and freedom. Those in stable, well-paying jobs were better able to live openly and access LGBTQ+ spaces, while those in precarious employment felt restricted.

Kei (JJ, 35–44), a transgender woman, explained: "Without stable income, I can't continue hormone therapy. Everything feels like it's on hold. It's like my life is stuck."

Shun, a gay man working in a small company, said: "I can't risk coming out at work—if I lose my job, I have nothing. My boss jokes about gay people, and I just laugh along because I'm afraid to speak up."

Others highlighted how financial independence allowed for personal freedom. Misaki, a lesbian, noted: "Having a steady job means I can live with my partner. Some of my friends can't leave home because they depend on parents who don't accept them."

2.3.3 Gender Identity and Trans Experiences

Transgender participants faced both structural and social barriers. Access to hormone therapy and legal gender acknowledgment was often difficult, and societal expectations added pressure to "perform" gender in stereotypical ways.

Hitomi, a transgender woman, shared: "People expect me to wear makeup and dresses every day. If I don't, they question my identity. I'm tired of having to prove I'm a woman."

Yu, a transgender man, discussed how the pandemic disrupted his medical transition: "Hospitals were focused on COVID, so my appointments for hormone therapy were delayed. It feels like my life is on pause."

2.3.4 Race, Ethnicity, and Migration

Non-Japanese participants, particularly those from Asian or Latin American backgrounds, described layered marginalization. They often felt excluded not only by mainstream Japanese society but also within LGBTQ+ spaces.

Alejandro (FJ, 25–34), a gay man from Peru, explained: "Even in gay bars, I sometimes feel like a foreigner. People assume I'm just here temporarily."

Emma, a queer woman from the United States, highlighted a paradox: "I feel safer as a queer woman here, but I also feel unseen and uncelebrated."

Chun-chieh (FJ, 35–44), a Taiwanese gay man, added: "Language barriers sometimes make it hard to connect, even with other queer people. It's like there's an unseen wall."

2.3.5 Rural-Urban Divide

Urban centers like Tokyo and Osaka provide more seen LGBTQ+ communities, but for those in rural areas, presence is rare and risky.

Shun said: "There are no LGBTQ+ spaces here. I feel like I'm the only one. If I came out, it would spread all over town."

Kumiko, who lives in the suburbs, noted: "In Tokyo, you can be anonymous. In my hometown, everyone watches and gossips. That's why I only feel safe in the city."

2.3.6 Disability and Neurodivergence

Participants with disabilities or mental health conditions described heightened isolation.

Skyler (FJ, 25–34), a queer foreigner diagnosed with ADHD, said: "Working from home helped me avoid microaggressions at the office, but I became incredibly lonely when LGBTQ+ spaces closed."

Niran (FJ, 25–34), a gay graduate student from Thailand, noted: "I'm an extrovert, but Japanese culture is reserved. With COVID, I had no one to talk to. Trying to explain my feelings in Japanese makes me feel even more isolated."

2.3.7 *Layered Invisibility and Resilience*

For some participants, intersectionality meant a stacking of invisibilities—but it also spurred creative ways to find community.

Emily, an asexual foreigner, shared: "I'm unseen as an asexual person, unseen as a foreigner, and sometimes even unseen in LGBTQ+ spaces. But I've built my own network online. We see each other even when others don't."

Harry (FJ, 25–34), a mixed-race gay man, reflected: "My queerness and my mixed heritage both make me different, but they also make me stronger. I've learned to carve out my own path."

2.3.8 *Summary*

Intersectionality is central to understanding the experiences of Japan's LGBTQ+ community. Generational divides, economic precarity, racial and linguistic barriers, and geography all intersect to shape how individuals navigate visibility, self-expression, and belonging. The pandemic amplified these disparities, revealing how vulnerable some groups were while pushing others to find resilience in online and chosen communities.

2.4 The Influence of English-Language Terminology and Western Discourses

While Sect. 2.3 emphasized local identity formations, this section examines the influence of Western-derived LGBTQ+ terms and discourses in Japan. Words such as gay, lesbian, queer, non-binary, and asexual are widely known but often require translation—both linguistically and conceptually—to fit the Japanese context. Participants described how these imported categories can feel empowering, but also foreign or misaligned with cultural norms around privacy, discretion, and social harmony.

Mayumi, a pansexual woman in her late 40s, shared the burden of constantly explaining her identity: "I'm always translating myself when I say 'pansexual.'

People ask if it's the same as bisexual, and I have to explain that it's not just about two genders—it's about loving people regardless of gender. It's exhausting sometimes."

Amelie (FJ, 25–34), a bisexual woman from France, echoed this feeling of "translation fatigue": "In France, people understand bisexuality, but here, when I say baiseikusharu (bisexual), people either misunderstand or assume I'm promiscuous. I feel like I'm always educating people. Sometimes I just stay quiet because it's easier."

2.4.1 *Queer as a Political and Cultural Concept*

The term queer (*kuia*) has gradually gained traction among younger activists, academics, and online communities, serving as an umbrella term for fluid and non-normative identities. For some, like Mirai, it was liberating, while for others, such as Emma and Hiroshi, it caused confusion or seemed unnecessary.

Emma, a queer woman from the United States, explained: "In the U.S., 'queer' is empowering. It's a way of saying, 'I refuse to be boxed in.' Here, it just confuses people. They think I mean gay or lesbian. Sometimes I just say 'bi' because it's simpler."

Mirai, a 22-year-old pansexual woman, described how discovering queer online helped her: "It felt right because I didn't want to pick a label that didn't fit. Now I use it with my close friends, but I have to explain it every time."

In contrast, Hiroshi noted: "I don't see the need for another label. I'm comfortable being known as a gay man, and that's how I'll keep describing myself."

2.4.2 *Coming Out and Privacy*

Western discourses often present "coming out" as the ultimate expression of authenticity. In Japan, where *tatemae* (public façade) and *honne* (true self) guide social interactions, participants described privacy not as repression but as a form of peace and self-protection.

Hiroshi observed: "Silence isn't shame—it's peace. Westerners think you have to come out to be free, but here, privacy is also a way of living."

Riku, another older participant, added: "I don't hide, but I don't announce it either. My friends know, my family knows. That's enough. I don't need to wave a flag to prove who I am."

This cultural preference for discretion influences how presence is negotiated in both everyday life and media portrayals, as discussed further in Sect. 2.5.

2.4.3 Hybrid Identities and Code-Switching

Many participants adopted a hybrid approach, code-switching between English-derived terms and Japanese labels depending on the social setting.

Aya, a bisexual woman of mixed heritage, shared: "With my Japanese friends, I use *baiseikusharu* (bisexual). With international friends, I say queer. Sometimes I say nothing because I don't want to keep explaining."

Emily, an asexual foreigner, found that global terms often required more explanation in Japan: "Asexuality is still a new idea here. Online, especially in English spaces, I don't have to explain as much."

2.4.4 Digital Spaces as Mediators

Digital platforms such as Twitter (now rebranded as X), YouTube, and Discord have become crucial mediators for global and local discourses. Many participants said they learned new identity terms through online communities.

Emily emphasized: "Online spaces feel more validating—there's already a basic understanding of what asexuality means.. I've met other asexual people through Twitter and Reddit—it's where I feel seen."

Skyler, a queer foreigner, noted: "On Discord, I can use English terms like queer or non-binary, and people get it. Offline in Japan, I have to switch to Japanese terms or avoid the topic."

2.4.5 Westernization Vs. Local Authenticity

A few participants voiced concern that LGBTQ+ discourse in Japan is overly "Westernized" and risks erasing local histories of same-sex intimacy. Fenhua (FJ, 18–24), a gay man from China, remarked: "Some Japanese friends say being gay is a Western thing, like it doesn't belong here. But Japan has its own history of same-sex relationships."

Riku added: "The government acts like marriage equality is something foreign, something we don't need because it's 'not Japanese.' These Western terms sometimes make it easier for them to dismiss us as outsiders."

2.4.6 Summary

These tensions around identity and language are mirrored in how LGBTQ+ individuals are portrayed—or overlooked—within mainstream and queer spaces, as explored in Sect. 2.5.

English-language terminology provides a useful but imperfect lens for describing gender and sexual diversity in Japan. While global categories such as queer, non-binary, and asexual help connect individuals to worldwide communities, they can feel alien, require constant explanation, and even reinforce the perception of queerness as foreign. Participants navigated these challenges through code-switching, digital engagement, and hybrid identity practices. This tension between global acknowledgment and local authenticity leads directly into the next section, which examines how presence and portrayal manifest in Japanese media and public life.

2.5 Portrayal and Visibility

Building on the cultural tension around identity and language discussed in Sect. 2.4, this section examines how Japanese LGBTQ+ individuals are represented—or not represented—within mainstream media, urban queer spaces, and public life. For many participants, being "seen" is both affirming and problematic. While presence can validate queer existence, it often comes through narrow stereotypes or tokenized portrayals that fail to capture the diversity of real lives.

2.5.1 Urban Visibility

Urban LGBTQ+ districts such as Shinjuku Ni-chōme in Tokyo and Dōyamachō in Osaka are often perceived as safe havens for queer expression, yet participants described these spaces as both liberating and limiting. Riku, a 55–64-year-old gay man, shared: "In Ni-chōme, I can hold hands with another man and nobody cares. I feel free for a moment. But as soon as I leave those streets, I disappear again."

While Riku celebrated this temporary liberation, Emma, a queer woman from the United States, pointed out that even within these spaces, inclusivity remains limited: "When I go to Ni-chōme, it feels like everything is built for gay men. I struggle to find spaces for women, non-binary people, or just a different kind of queer culture."

For younger participants like Ren, urban queer districts were aspirational but often inaccessible: "I live outside the city, and I've never been to Ni-chōme. It's like this mythical place where you can be yourself. But I don't have the freedom to go there."

2.5.2 *Rural Invisibility*

In rural and semi-rural regions, where queer spaces are virtually nonexistent and social surveillance is intense, participants described feeling both isolated and erased. Shun a gay man, shared: "There are no LGBTQ+ spaces here. I feel like I'm the only one. If I came out, it would be all over town by the next day."

Building on Shun's sense of isolation, Misaki, a lesbian living in the suburbs, contrasted this with the relative anonymity of city life: "In the city, I can live with my partner openly. In the countryside, people watch and gossip. My friends there are terrified to come out."

Together, their experiences highlight how geography profoundly shapes presence and safety, with urban anonymity offering freedoms that rural environments often deny.

2.5.3 *Media Portrayals and Stereotypes*

Mainstream media depictions of LGBTQ+ individuals remain narrow and stereotypical, often relying on outdated tropes. Hiroshi, a 59-year-old gay man, remarked: "When there's a gay character on TV, he's either flamboyant or used as comic relief. Real gay men with ordinary lives—like me—are never shown."

For women, the issue is often erasure or sexualization. Kumiko, a lesbian, explained: "If women are shown, they're overly sexualized. You rarely see a normal, loving relationship between two women. It makes you feel like you don't exist."

Emma emphasized the lack of intersectional portrayal: "There are no stories about queer foreigners or mixed-race queer people. Non-binary folks are almost unseen in Japanese media."

Together, these accounts highlight how media presence reduces queer identities to caricatures rather than authentic portrayals—a limited portrayal that resonates with broader societal attitudes of quiet erasure rather than overt hostility.

At the same time, some participants acknowledged signs of progress. Recent television dramas, such as *What Did You Eat Yesterday?* (*Kinō Nani Tabeta?*), offered more sympathetic portrayals of same-sex couples by focusing on everyday life rather than sensationalizing sexuality. Others pointed to the hit series *Ossan's Love*, which gained mainstream popularity for its comedic yet surprisingly heartfelt portrayal of male-male romance.

Ren, a 19-year-old gay man, reflected: "I loved *Ossan's Love*—it was funny and sweet, and it felt good to see two men falling in love on prime-time TV. But it also felt like a fantasy. None of my friends' lives look like that."

Beyond individual reactions, Ossan's Love sparked public conversations about same-sex relationships in Japan, with mainstream media and social platforms debating whether such storylines signal growing acceptance or merely commodify queerness as a form of fictional entertainment. While these shows were celebrated as milestones, several participants questioned whether they translate into real-world change or simply provide a temporary form of presence divorced from the everyday struggles of LGBTQ+ people.

2.5.4 Pandemic-Era Changes

The COVID-19 pandemic disrupted traditional forms of visibility, canceling Pride parades, drag shows, and other community events. While the cancellation of these events felt like a setback for some, others found new avenues of connection and presence online. Shufen (FJ, 35–44), a lesbian from Taiwan, shared: "I was supposed to attend Pride and visit my partner, but the pandemic stopped everything. It felt like our community disappeared overnight."

Skyler, a queer foreigner, noted how online spaces became vital substitutes: "Twitter and Discord became the new Ni-chōme. We had virtual Pride events, online discussions, and just kept each other company. It wasn't the same, but it mattered."

Younger participants like Ren also found online communities to be more inclusive: "I don't have LGBTQ+ spaces near me, but I can join online groups anytime. It's how I made my first queer friends."

2.5.5 Safety and Recognition

Participants often described Japan as physically safe for LGBTQ+ individuals, but this safety was frequently dependent on remaining unseen. Emma, a queer woman from the United States, explained: "As a queer woman, I feel safer here than in the U.S. I don't fear violence. But I also feel like I don't exist—there's no acknowledgment of our relationships."

Riku echoed this sentiment, pointing out the expectation of discretion: "We're expected to act like just friends in public. It's not that we're attacked, but we're unseen."

Together, their accounts underscore the paradox of safety without acknowledgment, where being left alone often means being unseen.

2.5.6 Intersectional Visibility

Presence was not equally accessible to all. Foreign residents, asexual individuals, and non-binary people often felt excluded not only within queer spaces but also from mainstream portrayals. Alejandro, a gay man from Peru, shared: "Even in gay bars, I sometimes feel like I'm on the outside. People assume I won't stay in Japan or that I don't get the culture."

Emily, an asexual participant, added: "Asexuality is unseen everywhere. Even within LGBTQ+ groups, it's treated like an afterthought."

Their experiences highlight how intersectional identities remain underrepresented, reinforcing the critique of Japanese media raised in Sect. 2.5.3, where queer characters are often narrowly framed or reduced to stereotypes.

2.5.7 Summary

In Japan, the portrayal and acknowledgment of LGBTQ+ lives remain fragmented and uneven. Urban spaces like Ni-chōme offer fleeting moments of freedom but are heavily male-centered. Rural participants remain largely unseen, while media portrayals tend to reinforce stereotypes or ignore entire identities. The pandemic diminished physical presence in queer spaces but gave rise to digital activism and online community-building, showing that acknowledgment and queer self-expression extend beyond traditional public venues, adapting to both digital and community-based spaces. From the male-centered spaces of Ni-chōme to the selective portrayals on television, acknowledgment remains uneven, shaped by geography, gender, and cultural norms.

2.6 Conclusion: Identity as Dynamic and Intersectional

The narratives in this chapter reveal that identity in Japan is fluid, relational, and shaped by overlapping social forces. While Western LGBTQ+ categories provide a shared vocabulary, participants often found them insufficient for describing their lived realities. Instead, they navigated a dynamic process of self-definition shaped by cultural norms, personal relationships, and structural conditions.

2.6.1 Intersectionality and Conditional Visibility

Intersectionality shaped not only who was seen, but also how and under what conditions, with age, class, race, and geography often compounding marginalization. For older participants like Riku, this meant facing multiple layers of exclusion: "In Japan, being gay is one thing, but being old and gay means you're unseen twice over." Foreign residents shared similar experiences of layered exclusion, as Alejandro reflected: "During COVID, I felt like a double outsider—first as a foreigner, second as a gay man. Even in queer spaces, I sometimes felt like I didn't belong." Kumiko, a lesbian woman, pointed out how media portrayal remains skewed: "If women are shown, they're overly sexualized. You rarely see a normal, loving relationship between two women. It makes you feel like you don't exist."

2.6.2 Pandemic Disruptions and Digital Resilience

The COVID-19 pandemic intensified these dynamics, shutting down physical queer spaces while prompting new forms of online connection and introspection. Skyler, a queer foreigner, noted: "Digital spaces became our community. It's not perfect, but it's what kept us alive." While Skyler emphasized digital connection, Rin, a young lesbian, described lockdown as a catalyst for self-reflection: "to my best friend online, and it felt liberating." These contrasting experiences illustrate how the pandemic both disrupted traditional community spaces and fostered new modes of resilience and self-discovery.

2.6.3 Queer Theoretical Perspectives on Identity and Representation

The dynamics of identity explored in this chapter resonate deeply with queer theory's critique of fixed categories and its emphasis on fluidity, performativity, and resistance to normative frameworks. Butler's (1990) concept of gender performativity is particularly useful here: identity is not a stable essence but a series of repeated acts shaped by cultural expectations. Participants such as Hitomi and Yu underscore this insight, describing how they are often expected to "prove" their gender or sexuality through appearance, speech, and behavior. Their narratives highlight how Japanese social norms—especially around binary gender performance—require constant negotiation of authenticity.

Sedgwick's (1990) concept of the "epistemology of the closet" illuminates the strategic navigation of visibility and discretion. For participants like Hiroshi and Riku, choosing not to "come out" publicly does not signify repression but reflects a nuanced balancing of cultural values such as *tatemae* (public façade) and *uchi* (private sphere). Sedgwick's insight—that visibility and invisibility are not opposites but interconnected states—resonates in Japan's sociocultural context, where discretion often serves as a conscious strategy of self-protection and care.

Ahmed's (2006) notion of queer orientation adds another dimension by exploring how queerness is not simply an identity but a way of navigating space and social expectations. Younger participants like Rin and Mirai find digital platforms that "reorient" them toward supportive queer communities, while others feel "misaligned" both within mainstream Japanese society and within LGBTQ+ spaces dominated by specific stereotypes. Muñoz's (1999, 2009) concept of disidentification also applies here, as participants selectively adopt or adapt global LGBTQ+ labels, creating hybrid, context-specific forms of self-expression that neither fully reject nor wholly conform to dominant narratives.

Together, these queer theoretical perspectives enrich the chapter's central argument: that identity within Japan's LGBTQ+ community is a continuous process of negotiation, performance, and creative adaptation shaped by intersecting cultural, social, and structural forces.

2.6.4 Everyday Resistance and Care

Despite systemic barriers, participants found ways to resist erasure through small acts of authenticity and care. Misaki, who lives openly with her partner, shared: "We don't have marriage equality, but we live like we're married. We introduce each other to family and friends. It's our quiet way of saying: we exist, and we deserve happiness." Similarly, Emily, an asexual foreigner, built alternative networks: "We may be unseen to the mainstream, but we see each other. That's what matters." These narratives remind us that resistance does not always take the form of public activism—sometimes it is embedded in everyday life.

2.6.5 Intersectionality and Future Challenges

The issues of presence and intersectionality explored in this chapter foreshadow the structural challenges addressed in later chapters. Economic precarity (Chap. 4), healthcare inequalities (Chap. 5), and legal exclusion (Chap. 8) all intersect with identity dynamics, revealing how social systems reinforce or challenge queer marginalization.

2.6.6 Looking Forward

The narratives in this chapter illustrate how identity, intersectionality, and representation are always negotiated under conditions of precarious visibility. For many participants, being visible brought affirmation in some contexts but also heightened vulnerability—especially during a pandemic that magnified legal, social, and economic inequalities. The Japanese LGBTQ+ community continues to balance presence and privacy, global frameworks and local realities, often resisting erasure through digital activism, chosen families, and everyday acts of resilience.

These insights foreshadow the themes explored in later chapters, where structural issues such as economic precarity (Chap. 4), healthcare inequalities (Chap. 5), and legal exclusion (Chap. 8) intersect with the dynamics of being "seen." Ultimately, the stories presented here remind us that visibility is not simply about recognition; it is about being valued and supported, and about creating conditions where queer lives are not only acknowledged but also protected and sustained.

The following chapter builds on these dynamics, focusing on how social isolation and family expectations during the pandemic further complicated the experience of visibility and belonging.

References

Ahmed, S. (2006). *Queer phenomenology: Orientations, objects, others*. Duke University Press.
Butler, J. (1990). *Gender trouble: Feminism and the subversion of identity*. Routledge.
Crenshaw, K. (1989). Demarginalizing the intersection of race and sex: A Black feminist critique of antidiscrimination doctrine, feminist theory and antiracist politics. *University of Chicago Legal Forum*, 1989(1), 139–167.
Muñoz, J. E. (1999). *Disidentifications: Queers of color and the performance of politics*. University of Minnesota Press.
Muñoz, J. E. (2009). *Cruising utopia: The then and there of queer futurity*. New York University Press.
Sedgwick, E. K. (1990). *Epistemology of the closet*. University of California Press.

Chapter 3
Social Isolation and Family Dynamics: The Pandemic's Social Impact

Masami Tamagawa

Abstract This chapter examines how the COVID-19 pandemic reshaped the social lives of LGBTQ+ individuals in Japan, focusing on isolation, family dynamics, and the psychological toll of prolonged confinement. Drawing on first-person narratives, the chapter explores how forced cohabitation with unsupportive family members led to increased emotional distress, misgendering, and, a return to the closet. Youth and young adults who had once found independence in urban queer-friendly spaces were especially vulnerable, as they were compelled to navigate heteronormative environments that suppressed their identities. The chapter also investigates the broader mental health impact of losing access to LGBTQ+ social networks, such as bars, cafés, and community centers. These spaces, which function as critical sites of identity affirmation and solidarity, were replaced by digital platforms that, while vital, could not fully replicate the sense of belonging offered by in-person connections. Through the voices of diverse participants, the chapter illustrates how the pandemic amplified structural inequalities while inspiring new strategies of resilience—from digital peer-support networks to quiet acts of defiance within domestic spaces. These narratives underscore the need for inclusive policies and mental health support systems attuned to the realities of LGBTQ+ lives in Japan.

3.1 Introduction: The Pandemic's Social Impact on Queer Lives

The COVID-19 pandemic disrupted daily life across Japan, blurring the boundaries between private and public spheres and challenging conventional notions of safety, care, and community. For LGBTQ+ individuals, these disruptions were further complicated by what I call precarious visibility—the condition of being seen in ways that can simultaneously affirm and endanger queer lives. National public health discourse emphasized family solidarity and collective responsibility, yet for many queer individuals, "home" was not a sanctuary but a site of surveillance, misrecognition, and forced return to the closet.

M. Tamagawa, *Japanese LGBTQ+ Lives, Diasporic Voices, and Resilience*,
https://doi.org/10.1007/978-981-95-3105-9_3

This chapter examines how isolation, mental health struggles, and family dynamics intersected during the pandemic, highlighting the profound psychological and emotional toll of these conditions. Through first-person narratives, it illuminates the experiences of LGBTQ+ individuals navigating both the global health crisis and the structural inequalities embedded in Japanese society. These stories—such as those of young queer people forced to return to unsupportive parental homes, older LGBTQ+ individuals experiencing heightened loneliness, and transgender participants cut off from gender-affirming care—underscore how the pandemic exacerbated existing social fractures while also revealing strategies of resilience.

The notion of home as a "safe" space is deeply ingrained in Japanese cultural narratives, reinforced during the pandemic by government messaging that urged citizens to stay home as an act of solidarity. Yet, for many queer individuals, home was precisely where their identities were erased or misunderstood. Yu (JJ, 18–24), a transgender man in his early twenties, explained: "I had to erase who I am every day, like performing a role. It's exhausting to hear my parents call me by my old name, but I can't correct them. I don't have the energy to fight during a pandemic."

Yu's reflection vividly illustrates what Sedgwick (1990) calls "the epistemology of the closet"—a dynamic of concealment and performance that queer individuals must constantly negotiate. The pandemic intensified this dynamic by forcing many back into family settings where their identities were either unacknowledged or actively rejected.

Moreover, isolation was not merely the result of physical confinement. As Berlant (2011) argues, social and emotional well-being is sustained by "affective infrastructures"—the everyday networks of care+ and recognition that give life a sense of continuity. For LGBTQcommunities, these infrastructures often exist outside of traditional family structures, taking the form of chosen families, LGBTQ+-friendly bars, community centers, and Pride events.

With these spaces closed or restricted, many participants reported feeling as if their identities and social connections were collapsing. Misaki (JJ, 25–34), a lesbian living in a mid-sized city, described this disconnection: "I used to meet other lesbians at events in Tokyo, but with everything canceled, it felt like I didn't exist anymore. I was stuck at home with parents who don't know who I am."

The pandemic also magnified generational and cultural tensions within families. Older family members often reinforced normative expectations of marriage and childbearing, leaving queer individuals with little room for authenticity. Kumiko (JJ, 35–44), who had temporarily returned home to care for her ill father, recalled facing constant reminders of her family's expectations. Her mother would ask when she planned to "settle down" and marry a man—questions Kumiko deflected with a smile, even as the exchange left her shaken inside.

These experiences are not unique to Japan, but the cultural emphasis on harmony (*wa*) and family obligation (*oya kōkō*) often places LGBTQ+ individuals under intense pressure to conform. As Ahmed (2006) observes, the family can act as a "straightening device," orienting lives along normative trajectories and making alternative paths feel like deviations or failures.

At the same time, this chapter also highlights acts of quiet resistance and resilience. Participants developed creative ways to maintain their sense of identity and connection. From Misaki's private journaling to Kentaro's (JJ, 35–44) nightly LINE chats with queer friends, these micro-strategies reveal how LGBTQ+ individuals constructed alternative "affective infrastructures" even under conditions of constraint. The pandemic, while isolating, also prompted the forging of new digital networks and intimate practices of care that helped sustain participants' emotional well-being.

In the sections that follow, Sect. 3.1 examines the psychological toll of isolation, focusing on the loss of LGBTQ+ social networks and the mental health challenges exacerbated by the pandemic. Section 3.2 turns to family dynamics, exploring how cohabitation with non-accepting relatives created daily tensions and reinforced heteronormative pressures. Together, these sections illustrate how precarious visibility during the pandemic blurred the boundaries between personal identity and social expectations, forcing LGBTQ+ individuals to negotiate their lives within environments that were often hostile to their existence.

3.2 Social Isolation and Psychological Toll

The COVID-19 pandemic amplified the structural vulnerabilities already faced by LGBTQ+ individuals in Japan, especially in terms of mental health, social belonging, and the ability to live authentically. While many people viewed home as a refuge during lockdowns, participants in this study described it as a site of constraint and misrecognition. For queer individuals who rely on chosen families, community spaces, or urban networks for affirmation, the forced retreat into familial homes often resulted in return to the closet and a profound sense of isolation.

Sedgwick's (1990) concept of the "epistemology of the closet" resonates strongly here: the closet is not a singular event of concealment or disclosure, but an ongoing negotiation of visibility and secrecy. The pandemic intensified this negotiation by collapsing physical boundaries—work, family, and personal life all converged into a single domestic setting. For many LGBTQ+ participants, this convergence erased the safe spaces where they could previously express themselves freely.

Yu, a transgender man in his early twenties, described the emotional toll of living with his unsupportive parents: "I had to erase who I am every day, like performing a role. It's exhausting to hear my parents call me by my old name, but I can't correct them. I don't have the energy to fight during a pandemic."

Aoi (JJ, 18–24), a lesbian in her twenties, echoed this sentiment: "I used to feel free, but here I can't even mention my partner. I feel like I'm losing myself." Similarly, Hitomi (JJ, 25–34), a transgender woman, explained: "I had just started to come out to a few friends before COVID hit. Going back to my family home felt like undoing all that progress. They don't see me as who I really am."

3.2.1 Re-Closeting and Forced Cohabitation

Several participants in their late teens and twenties described returning to unsupportive family environments after losing jobs or leaving school dormitories. This sudden cohabitation led to intense emotional strain, as individuals had to conceal their relationships, pronouns, or gender expression.

Daichi (JJ, 18–24), a gay university student, reflected: "I was just starting to be open about being gay with my friends at university. But when I moved back home, I couldn't talk about it. I felt like I was hiding again, and it was depressing."

Misaki, a 29-year-old lesbian, described the anxiety of constant surveillance: "Even sending messages to my girlfriend feels risky. I delete them in case my parents see my phone. It's like I have to erase part of myself just to live here."

The psychological burden of this "double life" was described as a form of "psychological violence"—an erasure of self that, while not overtly abusive, left participants feeling fragmented. Kumiko summarized: "I stayed quiet because I didn't want to cause fights, but it felt like my identity was disappearing day by day."

3.2.2 Emotional Distress and Mental Health Struggles

Lockdowns and social distancing measures compounded these domestic tensions, leading to widespread feelings of anxiety, depression, and loneliness. Many participants reported that the closure of LGBTQ+-friendly spaces removed critical outlets for emotional support.

Hiroshi (JJ, 55–64), a 58-year-old gay man living alone, explained: "I've been through loneliness before, but this time it felt heavier. I considered seeing a therapist but worried they wouldn't understand my life as a gay man."

Emily (FJ, 25–34), an asexual (ACE) teacher in Tokyo, described the emotional toll of isolation: "Most people in the LGBTQ+ community meet through events or mutual friends. With everything canceled, I felt completely cut off from the world. It's hard to find anyone who understands what it means to be ACE here."

For some, attempts to seek professional mental health support were met with subtle but harmful prejudice. Fenhua (FJ, 18–24), a Chinese gay graduate student, recalled: "When I told the doctor I'm gay, his tone changed. I felt judged and left feeling worse than when I arrived."

Mirai (JJ, 18–24), a pansexual university student, described a decline in motivation and self-esteem: "I started skipping online classes. Without my queer friends around, I felt invisible and unmotivated. It was like nothing I did mattered."

3.2.3 Loss of Queer Social Networks

One of the most commonly cited difficulties was the disruption of queer social life. LGBTQ+ community spaces, such as Shinjuku Ni-chōme in Tokyo, are not only places of leisure but also vital for building identity and solidarity. Their closure due to state of emergency measures left participants feeling disconnected.

Daichi described: "I met most of my friends through Ni-chōme. With bars closed, it felt like my community vanished overnight."

Skyler (FJ, 25–34), a queer woman with ADHD, expressed how the absence of in-person spaces affected her mental health: "I've tried dating apps and online meetups, but nothing feels the same as being with people who understand you."

For older LGBTQ+ individuals, the closure of bars and cafés severed longstanding support networks. Hiroshi, who had frequented the same gay bar for decades, said: "That bar was like my second home. Without it, I felt completely adrift."

3.2.4 Coping Strategies and Small Acts of Defiance

Despite these hardships, participants described inventive ways of preserving their sense of self. These coping mechanisms ranged from online support groups to personal rituals.

Misaki began journaling as a form of self-affirmation: "I write letters to my girlfriend and to my younger self. It helps me remember who I am."

Kentaro (JJ, 35–44), a pansexual man, formed a small LINE group that functioned as a digital "chosen family": "We talk every night—sometimes serious, sometimes just joking. It's like a lifeline."

Mirai turned to artistic expression: "I began creating queer-themed comics and putting them online. Hearing from strangers that my work made them feel represented reminded me that my voice still mattered."

These actions, though modest, resonate with Berlant's (2011) concept of "affective infrastructures"—the small, sustaining networks and practices that allow individuals to endure systemic neglect.

3.2.5 Theorizing Isolation and Resilience

The pandemic did not merely produce physical isolation but layered forms of emotional and social invisibility. Participants were often forced to navigate multiple "closets"—at home, in digital workplaces, and even within some online communities. This resonates with Halberstam's (2005) notion of "queer time," where non-normative life paths are disrupted or delayed by crises.

Yet, the resilience displayed by participants suggests that these hardships also fostered creative survival strategies. Whether through digital counterpublics (Warner, 2002), personal art projects, or quiet affirmations of love and identity, participants demonstrated a capacity to "world-build" in small but meaningful ways.

Yu summarized this spirit: "I can't be myself at home, but talking to other trans guys online reminds me that I'm not alone. We share tips, laugh, and plan for when this is over. It gives me hope."

3.2.6 Generational Perspectives on Isolation

The experiences of isolation during the pandemic were shaped not only by sexual or gender identity but also by generational positioning. Older LGBTQ+ individuals often described a deep sense of temporal dislocation, having lived through decades when queer life in Japan was largely hidden or confined to urban enclaves like Shinjuku Ni-chōme. The sudden closure of these familiar community spaces felt, for some, like a return to earlier eras of invisibility.

Hiroshi, a 58-year-old gay man, reflected on this feeling of regression: "The bar I go to has been like my second home for 20 years. When it closed, I felt like I was going back to a time when I had no one to talk to. It was like starting from zero again."

For Hiroshi and other older participants, the loss of physical spaces was especially painful because these venues were hard-won safe havens, cultivated over decades in a culture that often marginalized queer lives. The absence of these spaces intensified loneliness and eroded the informal networks of care that older LGBTQ+ individuals had built outside traditional family structures.

In contrast, younger participants often turned more quickly to digital platforms for connection. Daichi, a 20-year-old gay university student, explained: "I was already using apps and online groups, so when everything shut down, I just spent more time online. It's not the same as seeing friends, but at least I can still talk to people who understand me."

Mirai, a 23-year-old pansexual student, described online creativity as her lifeline: "During COVID, I drew comics about queer life and posted them. The comments and shares gave me a sense of connection I couldn't find offline."

These generational contrasts illustrate how different age groups mobilize distinct "affective infrastructures" (Berlant, 2011). While older participants lamented the loss of embodied spaces of intimacy, younger ones often leveraged online spaces to create alternative forms of community. This suggests that queer resilience is not uniform but shaped by historical experiences of visibility, technology, and community-building.

While the previous section explored the emotional toll of isolation, the following section turns to family dynamics, examining how forced cohabitation and cultural expectations intensified tensions for many LGBTQ+ individuals.

3.3 Family Dynamics and Domestic Conflicts

While isolation shaped participants' psychological well-being, it also profoundly altered family dynamics, as explored in the following section.

While the pandemic amplified isolation and mental health challenges, it also reconfigured domestic life, often exacerbating pre-existing family tensions for LGBTQ+ individuals. In Japan, cultural ideals of the family are closely linked to heteronormative expectations of marriage and reproduction. Even in contemporary society, these expectations persist, supported by legal frameworks such as the *koseki* (family registry) system, which recognizes only heterosexual marriages and reinforces binary gender categories. During the pandemic, these normative structures were not suspended but rather intensified by calls for family cohesion and shared responsibility.

For many participants, the home—long regarded as the center of care and belonging—became a site of scrutiny, misrecognition, and microaggressions. While some families remained neutral or indifferent, the absence of open acceptance often felt like erasure. This section explores how familial dynamics during lockdown produced both emotional strain and small acts of resistance.

3.3.1 Hostile or Non-Accepting Home Environments

Participants frequently described the burden of living with family members who ignored, misunderstood, or rejected their identities. For transgender participants, misgendering and invasive questions were common sources of stress. Yu, a young trans man, recalled: "It felt like I was trapped in someone else's body. They kept using my old name, and it wore me down. I just didn't have the strength to push back."

Hinata (JJ, 18–24), an 18-year-old trans man, described the constant fear of being exposed: "I hid my binder every day and avoided talking about anything personal. My parents think I'm just shy, but really, I'm scared they'll find out who I am."

For queer women, the challenge was often silence or invisibility. Kumiko, a 42-year-old lesbian, shared: "I couldn't talk about my partner or my life. My mother would ask when I was going to 'settle down' and marry a man. I had to smile and change the subject, but inside I was screaming."

Yuka (JJ, 18–24), a bisexual woman in her early twenties, echoed this sentiment: "Every conversation with my mother turns to boyfriends and marriage. I want to say, 'What if I like girls?' but I stay quiet. It's easier than fighting."

For some, even families that claimed to be supportive failed to fully respect identities. Shu (JO, 35–44), a 41-year-old transgender man, explained: "My parents say they love me, but they can't call me by my chosen name. Every time they use my birth name, it feels like I'm being erased."

These narratives underscore what Sedgwick (1990) calls the "performative labor of the closet." Concealment is not simply about withholding information but about the exhausting daily performance of heteronormativity to maintain peace at home.

Vignette: Yuka's Digital Escape

Yuka described developing coping strategies during lockdown: "I started listening to queer podcasts while cooking or cleaning, just to hear voices that reflect who I am. It's my private time, even if it's only through headphones." This small ritual, though seemingly minor, provided her with a sense of self-affirmation in an otherwise heteronormative environment.

3.3.2 Intergenerational and Cultural Tensions

The pandemic intensified generational divides, especially in households where older relatives expected younger family members to conform to traditional life stages: heterosexual marriage, childbearing, and filial caregiving. These expectations were frequently cited as sources of conflict and emotional pressure.

Hiroto (JJ, 35–44), a 39-year-old gay man living with his parents, explained: "I'm expected to take care of the family and continue the family name. They don't see my life with my partner as real. When I mention him, they just ignore it."

Yusuke (JJ, 45–54), who lives with his partner and his partner's elderly parents, described a similar dynamic: "We can't show affection at home. Even sitting close is seen as strange. With COVID, we were around them all the time, and it was suffocating."

Women participants reported facing gendered expectations of caregiving. Kumiko noted: "Because I'm single, my parents assume I'll take care of them. They think my life is on hold until I marry a man. They don't understand that I already have a family with my partner."

Cross-cultural tensions added another layer for foreign participants. Aanan (FJ, 45–54), a South Asian gay man, described video calls with his family: "As the eldest son of a conservative Muslim family, I'm supposed to marry a woman and carry the family line. Every call reminded me that I was failing their expectations."

Vignette: Hiroto's Dinner Table Silence

Hiroto recounted:

> "Over dinner, my parents often talk about cousins getting married or having children. When they turn to me, I smile and steer the conversation elsewhere. I wish I could share that I have a partner, but I stay silent. Afterward, I retreat to my room and cry where they can't hear me."

This vignette illustrates how everyday family interactions can become emotionally draining for LGBTQ+ individuals, especially when heteronormative expectations are constantly reinforced.

3.3.3 Long-Distance Strain and Relationship Challenges

Travel restrictions and border closures separated many queer couples. Shufen (FJ, 35–44), a Taiwanese lesbian working in Osaka, shared: "I can't go back to Taiwan to see my girlfriend. It's been more than a year. Our lives feel like they're drifting apart."

For couples living together, lockdowns magnified domestic tensions. Harry (FJ, 25–34), a gay British man, observed: "Being together all the time is both a blessing and a curse. We've had more arguments, probably because we can't see friends or get space from each other."

Kumiko described similar challenges with her partner: "We love each other, but being home all the time with no break was hard. It felt like every little issue became bigger."

Vignette: Shufen's Digital Love

Shufen explained how she and her girlfriend maintained intimacy despite the distance: "We have video calls almost every night. We cook dinner together while the camera is on. It helps, but it also makes me miss her more. I cry after the call ends because I can't hug her." This illustrates how digital tools functioned as both lifelines and painful reminders of separation.

3.3.4 Cultural Lens: Oya Kōkō *and Heteronormative Expectations*

The concept of *oya kōkō*—fulfilling one's duty to parents—remains a powerful cultural expectation in Japan. It is often intertwined with the assumption that children will marry and produce heirs, thereby "continuing the family line." For LGBTQ+ participants, this expectation created constant friction with their own life trajectories.

Kumiko reflected: "My mother still hopes I'll get married to a man and give her grandchildren. She doesn't see my life with my partner as real."

Similarly, Yusuke remarked: "Even if I live with my partner for 20 years, to my family it doesn't count. They think I'm just wasting time."

This cultural pressure has no equivalent outlet for recognition in legal frameworks, as Japan's laws do not validate same-sex partnerships, thereby reinforcing familial and societal erasure.

3.3.5 Family as a Site of Conflict and Resistance

Despite these tensions, participants demonstrated small acts of defiance to assert their identities. Yusuke described his nightly rituals with his partner: "At night, after everyone was asleep, we shared tea and whispered. Those moments reminded me that we are still us."

Yuka used social media and queer podcasts to create a sense of personal affirmation: "Listening to stories of other bisexual women helped me remember that my life is valid, even if my family doesn't see it that way."

These quiet acts of self-affirmation exemplify Ahmed's (2006) argument that queer lives often require creating alternative orientations—subtle realignments of attention and care that resist normative expectations.

3.3.6 Cultural and Legal Context

The conflicts described in this chapter cannot be fully understood without examining the cultural and legal frameworks that structure family life in Japan. Central to this is the koseki, or family registry system, which not only organizes citizenship and inheritance but also embeds a heteronormative family model as the foundation of social recognition. Only heterosexual marriages are recognized within the koseki, meaning same-sex couples cannot legally marry or register as a family unit. This legal exclusion not only denies queer couples rights related to inheritance, housing, and spousal benefits but also reinforces the notion that LGBTQ+ relationships are "less legitimate" in the eyes of both the state and society.

For participants like Kumiko and Yusuke, this legal invisibility compounded the familial pressures they experienced. Kumiko noted: "My partner and I have been together for over ten years, but to my parents, that doesn't matter. They still ask when I will marry a man. It's like my real family doesn't exist because the law doesn't see it."

The persistence of marriage as a social milestone also shaped parental expectations. In Japan, marriage is often viewed not just as a personal choice but as a duty to one's family and lineage. During the pandemic, when participants spent more time with parents or relatives, these expectations became more pronounced. Hiroto, who lives with his parents, explained: "Whenever they mention my cousins' weddings, it feels like I've fallen short of their expectations. They don't recognize that my partner is already my family."

Moreover, the absence of comprehensive anti-discrimination laws—especially in housing, employment, and healthcare—leaves LGBTQ+ individuals dependent on family for social and economic security, even when those families are unsupportive. This dynamic was especially visible during the pandemic when economic precarity forced some participants to return home, regardless of how unwelcoming those environments were.

Comparatively, participants were keenly aware that queer individuals in countries with legal recognition of same-sex marriage or partnerships often had more social legitimacy and institutional protections. Aanan, a South Asian gay man, observed: "In my partner's home country, his family could see our marriage certificate if we were married there. Here, we are invisible both legally and socially."

This combination of cultural conservatism and legal exclusion exacerbated the emotional challenges participants faced during the pandemic, turning family dynamics into arenas where structural inequality played out in intimate, everyday ways.

3.3.7 International Comparison

While similar dynamics of family conflict were reported in other countries during COVID-19, participants noted that the lack of institutional and cultural recognition for LGBTQ+ identities in Japan made their struggles distinct. Unlike some Western countries where same-sex marriage and broader LGBTQ+ rights are legally protected, Japanese queer individuals had few formal supports to counterbalance family pressures. Aanan summarized: "In Japan, if your family doesn't support you, there are almost no other systems to protect you. It's like you're on your own."

3.3.8 Theoretical Reflection

Ahmed's (2006) idea of the family as a "straightening device" is especially relevant here. Lockdowns intensified the family's disciplinary function, forcing queer individuals to navigate a space designed to align them with heterosexual norms. Sedgwick's (1990) closet also takes on a renewed resonance—not as a static structure but as a living condition under constant negotiation.

3.3.9 Stories of Reconciliation or Partial Acceptance

Although many participants experienced family conflict or erasure, a smaller but significant group shared moments of unexpected support or partial acceptance during the pandemic. These narratives reveal that family dynamics are not static; under conditions of crisis, some relatives became more open or tolerant, even if only in subtle ways.

Kumiko, who temporarily returned home to care for her ill father, recalled a moment of connection with her mother: "One night, I showed my mother photos of a trip my partner and I took before COVID. I didn't say 'partner,' I just said 'friend,' but she smiled and said, 'She looks like someone who makes you happy.' It wasn't full acceptance, but it felt like she understood."

Similarly, Hiroto described a gradual softening of his parents' attitude toward his partner: "They never say 'your boyfriend,' but they started thanking him for helping around the house. When my mother offered him tea without me asking, I felt like maybe she sees him as part of the family, even if she doesn't say it."

For younger participants, the pandemic sometimes created opportunities for conversation that had not existed before. Daichi, a university student, said: "My sister asked why I don't have a girlfriend. I hesitated, but I told her I like guys. She just said, 'I thought so,' and smiled. It wasn't a big talk, but it made me feel less alone at home."

Yuka shared how a tense relationship with her parents slightly improved over time: "I think they sensed I was unhappy. My mother started asking about my friends more, without mentioning marriage. Maybe she's realizing I have my own life."

While these stories do not necessarily indicate full acceptance, they demonstrate small shifts toward empathy and recognition. The pandemic, by forcing families to spend more time together, sometimes created moments where unspoken truths could surface, or where gestures of care replaced silence.

These accounts also complicate the narrative of the family as purely oppressive. As Ahmed (2006) suggests, while families can act as "straightening devices," they are also spaces of negotiation and reorientation. Participants like Kumiko and Hiroto found that even minor acknowledgments—a shared smile, an unspoken acceptance—carried profound emotional weight. Such moments remind us that resilience is not only forged through defiance but also through fragile, tentative connections that emerge in unexpected ways.

3.3.9.1 Conclusion: Homes as Emotional Battlegrounds

The family narratives in this chapter reveal how the pandemic intensified the tension between filial duty and queer identity, turning domestic spaces into both emotional battlegrounds and sites of subtle negotiation. For many participants, the home was not a place of unconditional support but a structure where heteronormative expectations—often shaped by cultural ideals of marriage and reproduction—overshadowed personal authenticity. Stories like those of Yu, Hinata, and Kumiko illustrate how misgendering, parental questioning, and the pressure to conform created an atmosphere of psychological strain. Ahmed's (2006) idea of the family as a "straightening device" is evident here: participants were repeatedly nudged back toward normative life trajectories, regardless of their own desires.

Yet, these accounts also demonstrate that the family is not solely a site of repression. As seen in Sect. 2.9, some participants described moments of reconciliation, empathy, or quiet acceptance. For instance, Hiroto found that his parents' simple gestures—like thanking his partner for helping around the house—signaled a shift toward tacit acknowledgment, even if the word "partner" was never spoken. Kumiko experienced a similar moment when her mother commented warmly on photos of her girlfriend, recognizing the joy the relationship brought her without naming it directly.

These subtle but powerful moments highlight that family dynamics are not static. Even in households where heteronormativity dominated, small openings for care and understanding emerged, especially under the shared stress of a global crisis. For younger participants like Daichi, these openings sometimes came through conversations with siblings or cousins, while others, like Yuka, sensed that their parents were slowly shifting from disapproval to tolerance—not through direct confrontation but through softened silences or changes in conversational tone.

The coexistence of conflict and care within these households suggests that queer resilience is often built on fragile but meaningful gestures of recognition. As Ahmed notes, orientation is not fixed; families can be "reoriented" through small acts of care that do not erase difference but begin to accommodate it. For participants like Shu, even partial recognition—a moment when a family member paused before using his old name—felt like a victory, an acknowledgment of his ongoing selfhood.

These layered dynamics reveal that domestic life for LGBTQ+ individuals during the pandemic cannot be reduced to a single narrative of hardship or exclusion. Rather, it was a complex interplay of suppression, adaptation, and incremental change. On one hand, the persistence of marriage expectations and the structural invisibility of queer relationships within the koseki system amplified feelings of alienation. On the other, moments of connection—a shared meal, a kind remark, or a respectful silence—acted as quiet affirmations of identity and belonging.

Ultimately, the family stories in this section remind us that resilience often takes shape in the margins, in small acts of defiance as well as in gestures of care that defy social norms. These narratives form a crucial backdrop for the next chapter, which examines how similar tensions between recognition and invisibility played out in workplaces, digital platforms, and public life during the pandemic.

Building on the themes of social isolation and family conflict, the conclusion synthesizes these narratives to highlight both the structural roots of these challenges and the resilience strategies participants employed.

3.4 Conclusion: Homes as Sites of Struggle and Defiance

The narratives in this chapter reveal how the pandemic transformed domestic life into a space of precarious visibility for LGBTQ+ individuals in Japan. National discourse framed the home as a refuge, yet for many participants, home was a site where visibility was both demanded and denied—where being seen could mean recognition but also surveillance, misgendering, and erasure. Yu described the exhaustion of "performing a role" for his parents, while Aoi noted how even mentioning her partner felt impossible, underscoring the psychological toll of negotiating identity under constant scrutiny.

The closure of queer social networks, from Shinjuku Ni-chōme to local LGBTQ+ cafés, further amplified this precariousness. These spaces, often serving as affective lifelines, were replaced by digital interactions that, while helpful, could not fully replicate the sense of safety and solidarity found in physical community spaces. As Misaki lamented, "With everything canceled, it felt like I didn't exist anymore." The collapse of these "affective infrastructures" (Berlant, 2011) left many feeling adrift, especially those who already experienced family rejection or isolation.

Yet, as this chapter demonstrates, participants responded with remarkable resilience. Quiet acts of defiance—like Kentaro's nightly LINE chats with queer friends, Misaki's journaling, or Mirai's online art—became small but powerful gestures of self-preservation. These actions align with Muñoz's (2009) idea of "queer futurity," suggesting that even in moments of crisis, LGBTQ+ individuals carve out alternative worlds of connection and meaning.

Family dynamics, while often tense, were not universally hostile. As noted in Sect. 2.9, moments of partial recognition emerged: Kumiko's mother's warm comment on photos of her girlfriend, or Hiroto's (JJ, 35–44) parents quietly acknowledging his partner's presence. These gestures—however understated—illustrate that visibility is not a simple binary of being "in" or "out," but a shifting negotiation that can open space for subtle forms of care.

The chapter also highlights generational contrasts in navigating isolation. Older participants like Hiroshi felt the loss of physical queer spaces as a return to an era of invisibility, while younger participants, such as Daichi and Mirai, adapted more readily to digital communities. This reflects how precarious visibility is mediated not only by family and culture but also by age, technology, and historical experience.

Looking ahead, the challenges described here underscore the need for stronger institutional support—legal recognition of same-sex partnerships, anti-discrimination protections, and mental health services attuned to LGBTQ+ needs. As the next chapter turns to workplaces and digital platforms, we will see how precarious visibility extends beyond the domestic sphere, shaping the public and professional lives of LGBTQ+ individuals during the pandemic.

3.4.1 Queer Theoretical Perspectives on Social Isolation and Family

The experiences explored in this chapter can be understood through the lens of queer theory, which interrogates how normative structures—such as family, marriage, and domesticity—shape and constrain LGBTQ+ lives. Sedgwick's (1990) concept of the closet illuminates how participants like Yu and Hitomi performed constant acts of concealment under the surveillance of unsupportive families. Here, "home" becomes what Ahmed (2006) calls a "straightening device," orienting bodies and desires along heteronormative trajectories that invalidate alternative forms of kinship. The pandemic intensified these dynamics, as domestic confinement blurred the boundaries between public and private identity, leaving queer individuals with fewer spaces of affirmation.

Butler's (1990) notion of performativity is also key to understanding the psychological toll described by participants. Identity, as Butler argues, is enacted through repeated acts rather than being an innate essence. The lockdown forced participants to repeat heteronormative roles, often against their will, in order to maintain family peace—acts of "performance" that both concealed and strained their authentic selves.

Meanwhile, Berlant's (2011) idea of "affective infrastructures" helps explain why the loss of queer bars, cafés, and events left participants feeling adrift: these spaces were not just sites of leisure but critical structures of emotional survival.

Finally, Muñoz's (2009) concept of queer futurity highlights how participants' small acts of defiance—online art, LINE chats, secret rituals with partners—were not merely coping strategies but also glimpses of alternative, more livable futures. Even under conditions of repression, these micro-acts created what Muñoz calls "utopian fragments," moments where queer worlds were reimagined despite the constraints of pandemic life.

3.4.2 Mental Health and the Collapse of Queer Networks

The experience of precarious visibility—being seen in ways that can simultaneously affirm and harm—was not confined to family settings. It also extended to the sudden disappearance of queer social infrastructures that had once offered safety and recognition. The pandemic's lockdown measures forced the closure of LGBTQ+ bars, cafés, and community centers, disrupting what Berlant (2011) calls "affective infrastructures." For many participants, these closures severed lifelines of belonging and left them feeling both isolated and invisible.

Isolation during the pandemic was not limited to family homes. The closure of LGBTQ+ bars, cafés, and community centers—especially urban hubs like Shinjuku Ni-chōme—severed vital "affective infrastructures" (Berlant, 2011) that sustained participants' sense of belonging. These venues are not merely social spaces but also function as queer counterpublics (Warner, 2002), where individuals find affirmation and mutual recognition that may be absent in their family or workplace environments.

Participants like Hiroshi and Misaki emphasized that the loss of these spaces left them feeling adrift and invisible. While online platforms such as LINE groups and Discord servers provided a partial substitute, the absence of in-person interaction heightened feelings of loneliness and detachment. Skyler captured this tension succinctly: "Online chats help, but they can't replace the feeling of being with people who understand you."

The psychological toll of isolation was compounded by the lack of LGBTQ+-affirming mental health resources in Japan. Fenhua, a gay graduate student from China, recounted feeling judged by a psychiatrist after disclosing his sexuality. Others, like Emily, spoke of the challenges of finding anyone who understood their asexual identity. These stories reveal how the mental health infrastructure in Japan often fails to accommodate queer experiences, pushing individuals to seek support through peer-led digital networks or chosen families.

3.4.3 Family as Both Barrier and Bridge

Section 3.2 illustrated how families became both sources of conflict and, occasionally, sites of reconciliation. Cultural expectations around marriage, reproduction, and filial duty (*oya kōkō*) often heightened tensions during the pandemic. For participants like Kumiko and Hiroto, family conversations about "settling down" or continuing the family name served as constant reminders of their deviation from normative life paths. These interactions reflect Ahmed's (2006) notion of the family as a "straightening device," orienting individuals toward heterosexuality and pressuring them to fulfill roles defined by the *koseki* (family registry) system.

However, some participants reported small but significant shifts in familial attitudes. Hiroto observed that his parents began to treat his partner with quiet respect, even if they avoided naming the relationship. Kumiko described her mother's warm comment about her girlfriend, noting that this brief acknowledgment felt like a breakthrough. For younger participants like Daichi, conversations with siblings became opportunities for soft disclosure and acceptance. These moments, though modest, suggest that family dynamics are not static but can be reoriented through subtle gestures of care and recognition.

3.4.4 Generational Contrasts

The narratives also highlight generational differences in coping with isolation. Older participants like Hiroshi often relied on physical community hubs—bars, cafés, and Pride events—that have historically provided safe spaces for queer people in Japan. The closure of these spaces felt like a return to a time when queer lives were less visible and more stigmatized. In contrast, younger participants such as Daichi and Mirai turned more readily to digital platforms, using online forums, social media, and creative projects to sustain connections. This generational contrast underscores how queer resilience evolves over time, shaped by access to technology, historical experiences of marginalization, and the availability of chosen families.

3.4.5 Intersections of Vulnerability

The stories in this chapter also reveal how intersecting identities magnify vulnerability. Transgender participants faced the dual challenge of family rejection and interrupted access to hormone therapy or gender-affirming healthcare. Immigrant participants like Aanan navigated both xenophobia and homophobia, while rural residents such as Misaki struggled with the near-total absence of local LGBTQ+

networks. These experiences reflect Crenshaw's (1991) framework of intersectionality, demonstrating how multiple forms of oppression converge to produce unique hardships during crises.

3.4.6 Resilience Through Micro-Acts and Digital Worlds

Despite these overlapping challenges, participants demonstrated remarkable resilience. Small acts of defiance—a rainbow bracelet, a secret note to a partner, or a late-night chat with queer friends—served as lifelines. As Berlant (2011) suggests, survival is often sustained by "small, sustaining acts" that may seem trivial but are deeply meaningful in the context of systemic neglect.

Digital spaces also became new arenas of queer worldmaking. LINE groups, online book clubs, and virtual Pride events allowed participants to maintain social ties and advocate for LGBTQ+ rights. Misaki's online book club for queer women, for example, became a form of grassroots community-building that transcended geographical boundaries. These online spaces align with Muñoz's (2009) concept of "queer futurity," offering glimpses of alternative worlds where queer lives are celebrated and connected, even when physical spaces are inaccessible.

3.4.7 Rethinking the "Good Life"

The pandemic compelled participants to reconsider what a "good life" means outside the frameworks of marriage, reproduction, and conventional success. Many expressed a renewed appreciation for small, everyday moments of connection—whether through cooking with a partner, writing in a journal, or sharing memes in a group chat. These seemingly minor gestures reflect a form of queer ethics of care, centered not on achieving societal validation but on nurturing intimate and chosen forms of family.

As Berlant (2011) argues, crises open a "space for rethinking the good life," challenging dominant notions of happiness and success. For the participants in this study, the pandemic did not diminish their pursuit of authenticity; rather, it highlighted the importance of alternative relational structures—networks of friends, partners, and online communities—that sustain queer lives in times of adversity.

3.4.8 Looking Forward

The domestic struggles explored here are deeply connected to broader structural issues, from the lack of legal recognition for same-sex partnerships to the absence of LGBTQ-inclusive mental health and social services. These systemic gaps forced participants to rely heavily on informal networks of care, which, while vital, cannot replace the need for institutional reforms.

These narratives highlight how precarious visibility was not limited to public spaces but was acutely felt in the domestic sphere, where recognition and erasure coexisted.

The next chapter will shift focus to the public and economic spheres, examining how workplaces, digital platforms, and intersectional identities shaped LGBTQ+ experiences during the pandemic. Just as the home was both a space of constraint and resilience, these broader arenas also reflect a dual dynamic of marginalization and empowerment. Workplace discrimination, economic precarity, and visa insecurity were compounded by digital innovations, grassroots activism, and new forms of community solidarity.

By tracing this continuum—from the private tensions of home life to the public struggles of employment and digital activism—we see how the pandemic not only exposed deep-seated inequalities but also catalyzed new forms of queer resistance and imagination. These stories remind us that even under conditions of crisis, LGBTQ+ individuals and communities in Japan continue to adapt, create, and envision futures where care and authenticity are prioritized over conformity.

The themes explored throughout this chapter underscore how precarious visibility shaped pandemic-era queer life in Japan. Domestic spaces, which were expected to provide safety, often became battlegrounds for identity recognition, while public and community spaces that once offered refuge and affirmation were suddenly inaccessible. These conditions compelled participants to rely on digital networks, personal acts of resilience, and chosen families to maintain a sense of self-worth and belonging.

Looking ahead, the tensions between visibility and safety that emerged during the pandemic point to broader structural issues that persist beyond this crisis—ranging from legal invisibility to insufficient mental health support. The next chapter builds on these insights by examining how similar dynamics of recognition and erasure unfolded in workplaces, online platforms, and broader public life.

References

Ahmed, S. (2006). *Queer phenomenology: Orientations, objects, others*. Duke University Press.

Berlant, L. (2011). *Cruel optimism*. Duke University Press.

Butler, J. (1990). *Gender trouble: Feminism and the subversion of identity*. Routledge.

Crenshaw, K. (1991). Mapping the margins: Intersectionality, identity politics, and violence against women of color. *Stanford Law Review*, 43(6), 1241–1299.

Halberstam, J. (2005). *In a queer time and place: Transgender bodies, subcultural lives*. New York University Press.

Muñoz, J. E. (2009). *Cruising utopia: The then and there of queer futurity*. New York University Press.

Sedgwick, E. K. (1990). *Epistemology of the closet*. University of California Press.

Warner, M. (2002). *Publics and counterpublics*. Zone Books.

Chapter 4
Work, Digital Communities, and Intersectional Challenges

Masami Tamagawa

Abstract This chapter examines how the COVID-19 pandemic reshaped the work, digital, and social lives of LGBTQ+ individuals in Japan, exposing structural inequalities while catalyzing new forms of resilience. The economic fallout disproportionately affected queer workers employed in precarious sectors such as nightlife, freelance, and service industries. Transgender participants, in particular, faced compounded challenges, including workplace discrimination, bureaucratic barriers, and interruptions in gender-affirming care. These dynamics align with Butler's (2009) concept of "instability" and Standing's (2011) "precariat," underscoring how queer labor remains vulnerable within Japan's segmented labor market. The chapter also highlights the migration of queer communities to online spaces during lockdowns, where digital platforms served as critical "counterpublics" (Warner, 2002) for activism, creativity, and emotional support. Online book clubs, virtual Pride events, and social media campaigns emerged as affective infrastructures (Berlant, 2011) sustaining community when physical venues were inaccessible. Yet, these digital spaces revealed intersectional divides, with immigrants, racial minorities, and rural participants navigating additional barriers. By combining first-person narratives with theoretical insights, the chapter demonstrates how pandemic conditions both magnified structural exclusions and inspired innovative hybrid forms of queer community-building, offering a glimpse into future possibilities for solidarity and advocacy in Japan.

4.1 Introduction: Work, Digital Communities, and Intersectional Challenges

The preceding chapter explored how domestic spaces became sites of tension, concealment, and occasional reconciliation for LGBTQ+ individuals during the pandemic. Yet these private struggles cannot be fully understood without examining how they intersected with public and economic arenas. The COVID-19 pandemic brought not only emotional strain but also financial instability, workplace discrimination, and the abrupt loss of public queer spaces. These overlapping pressures

M. Tamagawa, *Japanese LGBTQ+ Lives, Diasporic Voices, and Resilience*,
https://doi.org/10.1007/978-981-95-3105-9_4

highlight a key theme of this book: precarious visibility—the ways LGBTQ+ individuals in Japan navigated being seen in professional and digital spaces, often at the cost of safety, stability, or recognition.

Workplaces emerged as crucial arenas where inequalities were both exposed and exacerbated. Japan's segmented labor market, with its divide between permanent employees (*seishain*) and non-regular workers (*hiseikishain*), has long disadvantaged marginalized groups. LGBTQ+ individuals—particularly those employed in nightlife, service industries, or freelance work—were among the first to face layoffs or reduced income. For some, remaining visible at work risked discrimination or lost opportunities; for others, invisibility was a necessary strategy for survival. Ryo (JJ, 35–44), a transgender man working on temporary contracts, captured this sense of instability: "I worried every day that my shifts would be canceled. As a trans man, I already feel invisible at work, but during COVID, I felt like I could disappear completely — no job, no income, nothing."

The shift to digital life compounded these dynamics. With bars, Pride events, and community gatherings suspended, queer communities migrated to online platforms that served as critical lifelines for advocacy, creativity, and solidarity. These digital spaces—book clubs, virtual Pride celebrations, and social media campaigns—were sites of both empowerment and constraint. As Misaki (JJ, 25–34) noted, "I joined an online book club for queer women. It was my only chance to be myself during lockdown." Yet, digital platforms also introduced new layers of precarious visibility, where participants negotiated how much of their identities could be safely expressed online, especially for those with intersecting vulnerabilities such as immigrants, racial minorities, or rural residents.

Despite these challenges, participants demonstrated remarkable resilience, blending digital creativity with grassroots activism to forge new communities and sustain visibility. This chapter examines these dynamics across three sections: 4.1explores workplace discrimination and economic precarity, 4.2 highlights the rise of online queer communities, and 4.3 addresses the intersectional challenges that compounded vulnerabilities during the pandemic. The concluding section, 4.4, reflects on how these experiences—marked by both erasure and defiance—offer insights into future forms of queer labor, care, and solidarity.

4.2 Work, Employment, and Economic Precarity

Building on these broader social disruptions, Sect. 4.1 examines the pandemic's economic toll, highlighting how LGBTQ+ workers faced not only job losses but also increased pressures to conceal their identities or invisible within heteronormative workplace cultures.

The COVID-19 pandemic intensified the financial instability that LGBTQ+ individuals in Japan already faced due to the absence of comprehensive anti-discrimination laws, rigid labor hierarchies, and heteronormative workplace cultures. While many people across Japan experienced job insecurity during the pandemic, LGBTQ+ workers were disproportionately impacted, particularly those employed in non-regular or informal sectors such as service work, freelance positions, or nightlife industries. The narratives in this section illustrate how structural inequalities intersected with individual vulnerabilities, creating a complex web of financial strain, identity suppression, and psychological stress.

4.2.1 Precarity as a Structural Condition

Butler's (2009) concept of instability—the condition of heightened vulnerability shaped by social and political frameworks—is crucial to understanding the economic hardships faced by participants. Precarity is not just about financial instability but about the unequal distribution of insecurity across populations. LGBTQ+ individuals in Japan, who often occupy marginal labor positions due to workplace discrimination or lack of career advancement opportunities, were among those hardest hit by the pandemic. Standing's (2011) notion of the "precariat"—a class defined by unstable employment and minimal labor rights—resonates strongly with the experiences recounted by participants.

Ryo, a 29-year-old transgender man, described how the pandemic deepened the insecurity of his dispatched work (*haken*):

> I worried every morning about getting a text saying my shift was canceled. I had no savings, and being trans made it harder to find other jobs. People think you can just 'go home' during a pandemic, but for me, home isn't safe or supportive.

Similarly, Tetsuya (JJ, 45–54), a gay man who runs a small consulting business, recounted losing half his clients when restaurants and small retailers—his primary clientele—closed: "It felt like watching my life shrink. I kept working, but every day I wondered if I should hide who I am even more, because being gay sometimes makes people hesitate to hire me."

4.2.2 Workplace Discrimination and Invisibility

Even for those who maintained employment, the pandemic amplified the need to conceal their identities or partially invisible in professional settings. Many participants noted that Japanese workplaces are often dominated by heteronormative assumptions, such as colleagues asking about opposite-sex partners or marriage plans. Alejandro (FJ, 25–34), a gay man from Peru working at a corporate office in Tokyo, explained: "At work, people assume I have a girlfriend. I don't correct them because I've seen what happens to colleagues who are different — they get ignored or treated as jokes. During COVID, when everything was tense, I stayed even quieter."

For transgender participants, workplace challenges were compounded by bureaucratic barriers, such as the mismatch between their gender identity and official documents. Ryo shared: "My ID still shows my old name and gender. Every time I have to show it at work, I get stares or questions. It makes me feel like I don't belong, and during the pandemic, I didn't want any extra trouble."

In sectors like hospitality and service industries, where appearance and gender presentation are closely policed, participants often felt pressure to conform. Hitomi (JJ, 25–34), a transgender woman who had worked in nightlife, noted: "Before COVID, I felt free at the bar because everyone knew I was trans. But when bars closed, I had to take part-time work in a convenience store. There, I hide who I am. It's exhausting."

4.2.3 Nightlife and Informal Economies

The closure of nightlife districts such as Shinjuku Ni-chōme had a dual impact on LGBTQ+ individuals: it eliminated both income sources and community spaces. For workers like Tomo (JJ, 25–34), who was employed at a Ni-chōme bar, the sudden loss of income was devastating: "When the bar shut down, I lost my job overnight. It wasn't just work — it was the place where I could be myself. I felt like I lost my family."

Tomo attempted to apply for government relief but found the process inaccessible: "They asked for documents I didn't have — like proof of business registration. In nightlife, so much is informal. I felt like the government didn't see me as a worker."

Others, like Chihiro (JJ, 35–44), a transgender woman formerly employed in the entertainment sector, faced discrimination when attempting to pivot to other jobs: "I applied for retail jobs, but once they realized I was trans, they stopped responding. People talk about finding new work like it's easy, but it's not for someone like me."

4.2.4 Remote Work: Relief and Alienation

While some participants transitioned to remote work, this shift brought its own challenges. For a few, remote work provided temporary relief from hostile office environments, but it also created new forms of isolation. Harry (FJ, 25–34), a gay British translator, observed: "I'm glad I can spend more time with my partner, but online meetings are full of assumptions — colleagues ask about girlfriends, not boyfriends. It's easier to stay quiet, which makes me feel like I'm back in the closet."

Skyler (FJ, 25–34), a queer woman with ADHD, found remote work both helpful and alienating: "Working from home is good for my mental health, but I feel invisible. No one knows who I really am, and every Zoom meeting reminds me of that distance."

Others noted that remote work blurred boundaries between professional and personal life. Ayano (JJ, 25–34), an asexual part-time worker, explained: "Before COVID, I could leave work and be myself. Now I work from my bedroom, and it feels like I'm always half-pretending, even when I'm alone."

4.2.5 *Visa Insecurity and Immigrant Workers*

For non-Japanese participants, the intersection of employment and immigration status created additional anxieties. Job loss often meant losing visa eligibility, forcing some to endure exploitative work conditions just to remain in Japan. Amelie (FJ, 25–34), a bisexual English teacher in the Chubu region, reflected: "A colleague of mine got fired after catching COVID. Without a job, you can't renew your visa. It's terrifying to think that getting sick could mean being forced to leave Japan."

Aanan (FJ, 45–54), a South Asian gay man involved in corporate redevelopment, described the tightrope of hiding his sexuality to maintain professional standing: "I can't afford to be open. A negative reaction could affect my project, my visa, and my life here with my partner."

These experiences highlight how legal instability compounds workplace vulnerability, particularly for LGBTQ+ immigrants who lack both domestic family support and institutional protections.

4.2.6 *Coping, Reinvention, and Mutual Aid*

Despite these challenges, participants demonstrated remarkable resourcefulness. Tomo turned to freelance design work, using online platforms to secure small jobs: "It's not stable, but at least I don't have to hide who I am when I work for myself."

Ryo described a small mutual aid LINE group of transgender men who shared job leads, advice, and emotional support: "We help each other find work and talk about our struggles. It's not much, but it reminds me I'm not alone."

Ayano used her downtime to participate in online seminars on queer labor rights: "Learning about activism gave me hope. I realized our struggles are connected, and we have to fight for better protections."

These acts of collective resilience reflect the formation of alternative support networks in the absence of state or corporate recognition.

4.2.7 Theoretical Reflection

The experiences of participants highlight how the pandemic intensified the precarious status of LGBTQ+ labor. Butler's (2009) idea of instability is particularly relevant here, as participants were often excluded from social safety nets and formal protections. The closure of nightlife spaces—which, for many, were both workplaces and community hubs—exemplifies how queer economies are treated as peripheral and expendable.

Standing's (2011) "precariat" framework further illuminates these dynamics. Many participants described a perpetual state of instability, where employment was not only insecure but also contingent on self-erasure. As Tetsuya noted, "It's not just about keeping your job. It's about keeping your dignity." The labor of "being invisible"—staying closeted, masking gender identity, or avoiding conversations about partners—was an unspoken requirement in many workplaces, creating a dual burden of financial and emotional strain.

4.2.8 Looking Ahead

The economic challenges detailed in this section illustrate that workplaces are not neutral spaces but arenas where heteronormativity and structural inequality are enforced. For LGBTQ+ individuals, the pandemic made visible the fragility of labor rights and social protections. These narratives also point to the need for comprehensive policy reforms, including workplace anti-discrimination measures and legal recognition of queer partnerships that would grant access to benefits and spousal rights.

As the following sections will show, the loss of physical queer spaces was partially mitigated by the rise of online communities and activism. Online platforms became crucial not only for maintaining personal connections but also for reimagining what queer labor and community can look like in times of crisis.

As workplaces grew increasingly hostile or unstable, many participants sought alternative sources of support. For some, online platforms became not only a substitute for lost income opportunities but also an emotional refuge.

4.3 Digital Communities and Resilience

Section 4.2 turns to the rise of online communities, which emerged as lifelines for LGBTQ+ individuals. These virtual spaces offered connection, mental health support, and activism at a time when physical gatherings were inaccessible.

As the pandemic disrupted physical LGBTQ+ spaces—from Shinjuku Ni-chōme bars to Pride parades and community centers—many participants turned to online platforms as vital lifelines. Online spaces became arenas of connection, affirmation, and activism, filling the void left by the closure of physical venues. These online communities did more than replicate in-person interactions; they often created new modes of queer intimacy and political engagement that transcended geographical boundaries.

The rise of digital queer spaces during the pandemic illustrates what Warner (2002) calls "counterpublics"—alternative spaces where marginalized voices articulate their identities, challenge mainstream narratives, and build solidarity. For participants, digital tools like LINE, Discord, Zoom, Twitter, and Instagram were not just communication platforms but critical infrastructures of care and creativity.

4.3.1 Virtual LGBTQ+ Spaces as Lifelines

Participants frequently described online spaces as emotional anchors during the long months of isolation. Emily (FJ, 25–34), an asexual teacher in Tokyo, explained: "I couldn't meet anyone in person, but online groups became my support system. We shared stories, checked in on each other, and even had virtual Pride celebrations. It was the only place where I felt seen."

For some, online platforms were their first exposure to a supportive queer community. Daichi (JJ, 18–24), a gay university student, shared: "Before COVID, I was too shy to go to Ni-chōme. During the lockdown, I joined a Discord group for LGBTQ+ students, and it changed my life. I could talk openly for the first time."

Yu (JJ, 18–24), a transgender man, joined a private LINE chat with other trans men: "We talked about everything — family, clothes, even hormones. Those conversations kept me sane when I felt invisible at home."

While online interactions could not fully replace the warmth of face-to-face meetings, participants agreed that online spaces offered critical affirmation during a time of profound isolation.

Vignette: Misaki's Online Book Club

Misaki, a 29-year-old lesbian living in a mid-sized city, started an online book club for queer women:

> I posted on Twitter asking if anyone wanted to read queer novels together. Within a week, 15 people joined. We meet every two weeks on Zoom, reading books like Ekuni Kaori's Kirakira Hikaru. We laugh, cry, and share our own stories.

For Misaki, these virtual meetings were more than literary discussions: "Even though I can't be open at home, for two hours on Zoom, I'm surrounded by people who understand me. It reminds me that I'm not alone."

4.3.2 Online Mental Health and Peer Support

The lack of LGBTQ+-affirming mental health resources in Japan was a recurring theme among participants. Many turned to peer-led online groups for emotional support and advice. Fenhua (FJ, 18–24), a gay graduate student from China, found comfort in international WeChat groups: "We share everything — our fears, how to deal with stress, even recipes. Talking with people who get it helped me stay grounded."

Amelie, a bisexual English teacher, used Reddit forums to discuss personal struggles she couldn't share at work: "I could talk about my anxiety and my relationship without feeling judged. Sometimes just writing it out and getting a kind response made a huge difference."

For Japanese participants, small LINE groups or Twitter circles became virtual chosen families. Kentaro (JJ, 35–44) described a nightly routine of chatting with a group of LGBTQ+ friends: "We share our day — even small things like what we cooked. It's like group therapy. Those conversations kept me from feeling totally alone."

Vignette: Tsubasa's Healing Group

Tsubasa (JJ, 35–44), a 38-year-old transgender woman, joined a private Facebook group for trans women: "We do online mindfulness sessions and talk about our struggles. Even through a screen, I felt less alone. It gave me hope that I could keep going."

These peer-led initiatives highlight how queer networks of care often emerge in the absence of institutional support, aligning with Berlant's (2011) idea of "affective infrastructures"—informal systems of care and solidarity that sustain individuals during crises.

4.3.3 Digital Activism and Community-Building

Beyond personal support, online spaces became powerful tools of activism and advocacy. Grassroots organizations and individual activists adapted quickly, using online platforms to host webinars, petitions, and virtual Pride events. Harry, a gay British man, explained: "Online petitions and events kept the momentum going. Even though we were physically apart, I felt part of something bigger — something that was fighting for us."

Tokyo Rainbow Pride (TRP), the largest LGBTQ+ event in Japan, held fully virtual events in 2020 and 2021, featuring live-streamed speeches, drag performances, and panel discussions. Hiroshi (JJ, 55–64), a 58-year-old gay man, shared: "I never went to Pride before because it felt too loud or young for me. Watching it online was perfect — I could listen, learn, and feel part of the community."

Smaller initiatives also thrived. Mirai (JJ, 18–24), a pansexual student, created and shared queer-themed illustrations online: "People messaged me saying my art helped them feel seen. It made me realize that activism isn't just protests — it can be creative and personal."

Vignette: Misaki's Twitter Activism

In addition to running her book club, Misaki used Twitter to amplify calls for marriage equality: "I shared my story about being a lesbian during COVID, and people sent me messages saying they felt less alone. I realized that even small online voices can make a difference."

These digital efforts illustrate how counterpublics (Warner, 2002) can thrive online, creating spaces of representation and dialogue that bypass mainstream media or political indifference.

4.3.4 Cross-Generational Digital Connections

One of the unexpected outcomes of the digital shift was increased interaction between older and younger LGBTQ+ individuals. While some older participants initially found online platforms intimidating, many adapted and discovered new communities. Hiroshi reflected: "Before COVID, I never used Zoom or LINE groups. But now I join weekly online chats. I've met young people who remind me of my younger self. It's healing to talk openly with them."

Younger participants, such as Mirai, appreciated these exchanges: "Listening to older LGBTQ+ people talk about the past made me realize our struggles are connected. We're part of a bigger story."

Tsubasa emphasized the intergenerational solidarity fostered online: "An older trans woman shared her story of transitioning decades ago. It gave me courage to keep going."

4.3.5 Challenges and Limitations of Digital Spaces

While online platforms provided vital support, participants also noted their limitations. Skyler described "Zoom fatigue": "After months of online events, I started feeling drained. I miss the energy of being in the same room with people."

Privacy was another concern, particularly for those living with unsupportive family members. Emily explained: "I worry about being outed online. Even just using my real name on Zoom makes me nervous."

Moreover, not all participants had equal access to technology or stable internet, creating new forms of exclusion. Rural participants like Ryu (JJ, 25–34) described unreliable connections that made attending online events difficult.

4.3.6 Digital Creativity and Queer Futurities

Despite these challenges, online platforms offered new avenues for queer creativity and imagination. Participants like Mirai and Misaki used art, writing, and storytelling to envision alternative futures where LGBTQ+ lives are recognized and celebrated. These creative acts align with Muñoz's (2009) concept of "queer futurity," which emphasizes the power of imagination to challenge oppressive structures and cultivate hope.

Mirai summarized this feeling: "Posting my art online felt like planting seeds. I may not see the change now, but I know these small acts will grow into something bigger."

4.3.7 Theoretical Reflection

The rise of digital queer communities during the pandemic highlights the resilience of LGBTQ+ networks in the face of structural exclusion. These online spaces not only provided personal affirmation but also acted as counterpublics and affective infrastructures (Warner, Berlant), sustaining both individual well-being and collective activism. They show how queer relationality (Ahmed, 2006) thrives through the creation of alternative orientations—not despite crisis, but because of it.

4.3.8 Looking Ahead

While online spaces provided crucial support, they also revealed how intersectional vulnerabilities—shaped by gender, race, and geography—persisted during the pandemic.

Online communities were not just temporary substitutes for physical spaces; they are likely to remain integral to LGBTQ+ life in Japan. Participants expressed hope that hybrid models—blending online and offline gatherings—will persist post-pandemic, making queer communities more accessible to those in rural areas or those who cannot be publicly out.

Section 4.3 turns to intersectional challenges, exploring how factors such as gender identity, race, immigration status, and geography compounded the difficulties faced by LGBTQ+ individuals during the pandemic.

While online platforms offered new avenues for visibility and solidarity, not all participants could access or benefit equally from these online spaces.

4.4 Intersectional Challenges

Section 4.3 explores these uneven experiences, showing how intersecting factors—such as gender identity, race, geography, and immigration status—deepened existing inequalities within both offline and digital contexts.

The pandemic revealed that LGBTQ+ experiences in Japan are far from homogeneous. While all participants encountered heightened instability, the degree and form of these challenges varied significantly depending on gender identity, race, socioeconomic class, geographic location, and immigration status. This section examines how these intersecting identities compounded vulnerabilities and shaped unique survival strategies.

Crenshaw's (1991) framework of intersectionality is particularly useful here. Intersectionality highlights how multiple axes of power and oppression—such as sexism, racism, homophobia, and transphobia—intersect to produce distinct experiences of marginalization. The stories presented here illustrate how these structural forces worked together during the pandemic, amplifying both invisibility and exclusion.

4.4.1 Gender Identity and Trans Experiences

Transgender participants faced some of the most severe challenges during the pandemic, particularly due to interruptions in gender-affirming healthcare, workplace discrimination, and familial hostility. Yu, a transgender man in his twenties, recounted how the temporary closure of medical facilities disrupted his hormone therapy: "When the hospital limited visits, I felt like I was losing control of my transition. At home, I had to pretend I was someone I'm not. It felt like going backwards."

For trans women, the economic fallout was especially harsh, as many were employed in the service and nightlife industries—sectors that were disproportionately affected by closures. Chihiro, who previously worked in a Shinjuku bar, shared: "The bar was not just work; it was where I could live as myself. Losing it meant losing income and losing my safe space."

Tsubasa, a 38-year-old trans woman, described the emotional toll of being forced to live with her parents again: "I had to wear unisex clothes just to avoid arguments. Even simple things like growing my hair long became a battle. Every day felt like erasing myself."

These experiences demonstrate how the pandemic not only interrupted personal progress—such as medical transition—but also intensified feelings of alienation within family structures.

4.4.2 Race, Ethnicity, and Foreignness

For foreign residents and racial minorities, the pandemic introduced another layer of marginalization. Fenhua, a gay graduate student from China, reported encountering subtle forms of xenophobia: "I felt people avoiding me in public, like I was bringing the virus. I was already isolated, but this made me feel even more like an outsider."

Similarly, Aanan, a South Asian gay man, described how racial prejudice and queer invisibility intersected in both his personal and professional life: "Being both foreign and gay puts me on the fringes of society here. I have to hide my sexuality at work because I'm already treated differently due to my race."

These accounts highlight the double marginalization faced by non-Japanese LGBTQ+ individuals, who often lack both legal protections and the social networks available to their Japanese counterparts.

Vignette: Fenhua's Double Isolation

Fenhua's story illustrates how xenophobia compounded queer isolation: "When I walked into a store, I felt people staring. At home, I couldn't talk openly about being gay, and outside, I felt blamed for the virus. It was like I didn't belong anywhere."

4.4.3 Urban–Rural Divide

Geographic location had a marked impact on participants' experiences. Those living in rural or semi-rural areas reported a profound sense of isolation, as LGBTQ+ community spaces are concentrated in metropolitan centers like Tokyo and Osaka. Pandemic travel restrictions further cut off access to these hubs.

Misaki, a lesbian living in a mid-sized city, said: "There are no LGBTQ-friendly spaces here. During the pandemic, I felt like I didn't exist. I wanted to go to Pride in Tokyo, but it was canceled two years in a row."

Ryu, a 30-year-old gay man in rural Kyushu, described feeling like an "invisible minority": "There's no community here, no events, nothing. Online is the only place I can talk to other gay men. But even then, the time difference with big cities makes it hard to join live events."

Vignette: Ryu's Rural Disconnect

Ryu's experience shows how rural environments magnify feelings of invisibility: "When I talk about LGBTQ+ issues here, people say, 'That's a Tokyo thing.' They don't see that we exist everywhere. COVID made me feel even more disconnected because I couldn't travel to meet people who understand."

4.4.4 Immigration Status and Legal Precarity

For non-Japanese LGBTQ+ individuals, job loss carried not only financial consequences but also the risk of losing visa eligibility. Amelie, a bisexual English teacher, described this fear: "If I lost my job, I would have to leave Japan. There's no safety net for people like me, and with the pandemic, the stakes were even higher."

Aanan highlighted how this legal instability influenced every aspect of his life: "I can't afford to come out to everyone at work. A negative reaction could affect my project, my visa, and my life here with my partner."

Binational couples faced particular hardships, as Japan does not recognize same-sex partnerships for spousal visas or other legal protections. Harry recalled: "We had to rent our apartment under my name alone. There's no legal recognition of us as a couple. The pandemic made me realize how fragile our life here really is."

4.4.5 Gender, Class, and Queer Precarity

The pandemic also exposed the intersection of gender identity and socioeconomic class. Transgender women and non-binary participants, who were overrepresented in informal labor sectors like nightlife or part-time retail, faced disproportionate job loss and financial hardship. Hitomi shared: "When the bar closed, I had no backup plan. Other places don't want to hire trans women. It's like being pushed out of the workforce entirely."

For queer women, the economic burden was often compounded by unpaid caregiving responsibilities. Kumiko (JJ, 35–44) observed: "Because I'm single, my parents expect me to take care of them. My partner and I feel like we don't count as a real family, but I still have to fulfill these duties."

4.4.6 Coping and Intersectional Resilience

Despite these overlapping challenges, participants found ways to cope and resist. Ryu joined an online support group for rural LGBTQ+ individuals, while Fenhua found solidarity in transnational WeChat groups. Kentaro, who identifies as both biracial and pansexual, emphasized the importance of finding intersectional communities: "For years, I felt like I didn't fit anywhere — not fully Japanese, not fully accepted as queer. Online, I found people like me, and that changed everything."

These stories highlight how intersectional resilience is built through collective recognition and the creation of spaces—often digital—that honor complex identities.

4.4.7 *Theoretical Reflection*

Crenshaw's (1991) notion of intersectionality underscores that queer individuals are never marginalized along a single axis. The experiences of participants like Yu, Tsubasa, Aanan, and Fenhua demonstrate how multiple forms of instability converge—from transphobia to xenophobia, from economic instability to legal invisibility.

Ahmed's (2006) concept of "orientation" is also instructive. LGBTQ+ individuals often feel "out of line" with dominant social norms; during the pandemic, these misalignments were magnified, particularly for those who lacked family support, legal recognition, or access to safe spaces. To navigate these challenges, participants created alternative "lines of care"—online communities, peer networks, and micro-acts of affirmation.

4.4.8 *Looking Ahead*

Intersectional vulnerabilities are not peripheral to understanding the LGBTQ+ experience during the pandemic—they are central. These narratives demonstrate that structural reforms (such as anti-discrimination laws, recognition of same-sex partnerships, and inclusive healthcare policies) must consider the complex realities of marginalized groups.

Section 4.4, Conclusion: Digital Futures and Intersectional Resilience, will synthesize these themes, showing how online platforms and grassroots activism have both mitigated and illuminated these inequalities, offering pathways toward more inclusive futures.

The stories of transgender individuals, immigrants, and rural LGBTQ+ participants reveal how multiple layers of marginalization coalesced during the pandemic. Yet, these same narratives point to innovative strategies of resilience, from grassroots digital networks to hybrid community-building.

4.5 Conclusion: Digital Futures, Queer Labor, and Precarious Visibility

The narratives presented in this chapter reveal how precarious visibility shaped LGBTQ+ experiences in both professional and digital spaces during the pandemic. Workplaces, often governed by heteronormative assumptions and rigid hierarchies, became spaces where queer individuals were either forced into silence or penalized for being authentic. The pandemic heightened this tension by destabilizing sectors where LGBTQ+ individuals are overrepresented—nightlife, service industries, and freelance work—while offering few institutional safeguards. As Tetsuya observed,

"I lost half my clients when small businesses closed. I've learned to stay quiet about my sexuality because I can't risk losing more work."

Sedgwick's (1990) concept of the closet offers an important lens here: many participants performed constant acts of concealment at work, navigating what Sedgwick calls the tension between being known and remaining silent. For immigrants and non-regular workers, the cost of being "out" was particularly high, making invisibility a form of strategic survival. Likewise, Ahmed's (2006) notion of orientation illuminates how queer workers and digital participants had to "reorient" themselves within spaces not designed for them, finding alternative pathways for recognition and support.

Digital platforms emerged as vital counterpublics (Warner, 2002), providing alternative infrastructures of care (Berlant, 2011) and collective resilience. Online initiatives—from Misaki's book club to Mirai's queer-themed art—allowed participants to maintain connection, share experiences, and advocate for social change. Yet these platforms also underscored new vulnerabilities, particularly for immigrants like Aanan who worried that online visibility could impact both employment and visa status: "Being foreign and gay means I have to be careful at work and online. One wrong step and I could lose my visa or my job."

Intersectional inequalities were at the heart of these challenges. Transgender participants faced bureaucratic barriers that made both employment and healthcare precarious, while racial minorities and rural residents often lacked supportive networks altogether. These narratives underscore the need to view pandemic-era hardships not as isolated events but as reflections of broader structural exclusions—legal, cultural, and economic—that shape queer lives in Japan.

At the same time, the chapter highlights how queer resilience thrives under constraint. Participants built mutual aid networks, organized virtual Pride events, and imagined hybrid futures where online and offline spaces complement each other. These acts of digital worldmaking align with Muñoz's (2009) concept of "queer futurity," offering glimpses of inclusive and interconnected futures even in the face of systemic neglect.

Moving forward, the insights from this chapter point to urgent policy needs—workplace anti-discrimination protections, legal recognition of same-sex partnerships, and accessible LGBTQ-inclusive mental health care. As the next chapter examines media representations and political activism, the theme of precarious visibility continues to illuminate how queer communities navigate the complex terrain between recognition and risk.

4.5.1 Economic Precarity as Queer Reality

The pandemic intensified the condition of precarious visibility in workplaces, where LGBTQ+ individuals were often forced to choose between authenticity and financial stability. For many participants, staying visible risked discrimination, while invisibility required constant self-erasure. The economic toll, especially on those working in informal or nightlife sectors, revealed how queer labor is both structurally marginalized and socially undervalued.

Section 4.1 highlighted how the pandemic deepened the structural instability of LGBTQ+ labor. Workers in non-regular employment, freelance roles, and nightlife industries were among the first to lose income, while transgender individuals faced additional barriers due to discriminatory hiring practices and the mismatch between their identities and official documents. Ryo described the fear of losing his dispatched work, while Tomo recounted the double blow of losing both income and community when Ni-chōme bars shut down.

This dual loss—economic and emotional—illustrates what Butler (2009) calls "instability," a condition of vulnerability that is unevenly distributed across society. LGBTQ+ individuals often bear the brunt of such instability because their livelihoods are intertwined with informal economies that lack institutional safeguards. The testimonies of Tetsuya and Hitomi demonstrate how queer labor is often rendered invisible, both in state policy and public discourse, further reinforcing social exclusion.

However, as participants like Ayano and Kentaro showed, queer communities responded to these challenges by building mutual aid networks, sharing job leads, and offering emotional support online. These initiatives resonate with Berlant's (2011) concept of "affective infrastructures," which emphasize how informal systems of care sustain individuals when formal institutions fail them.

4.5.2 *Digital Counterpublics and Creative Resistance*

The migration of queer communities to online platforms, explored in Sect. 4.2, reveals how technology can function as both a lifeline and a platform for activism. Participants like Misaki and Emily described how online book clubs, Twitter campaigns, and virtual Pride events offered spaces of recognition when physical gatherings were impossible. These digital initiatives exemplify Michael Warner's (2002) notion of "counterpublics," wherein marginalized groups create alternative spheres of discourse that challenge mainstream narratives.

Digital creativity also emerged as a powerful tool for resilience. Mirai shared queer-themed art online, using illustration to spark conversations about identity and belonging. These creative acts, though personal, had a broader political dimension, challenging the silence imposed by both family and workplace contexts. As Muñoz (2009) argues, such moments of "queer futurity" provide glimpses of worlds that are "not yet here"—worlds where queer lives are valued and celebrated.

However, participants also acknowledged the limitations of online spaces. Skyler described Zoom fatigue, while others, like Ryu, faced technological barriers due to poor internet infrastructure in rural areas. Moreover, the online world does not shield individuals from discrimination; some participants expressed concerns about privacy and the risk of being outed.

4.5.3 Intersectional Vulnerabilities

Section 4.3 illustrated how pandemic experiences were shaped by intersectional factors. For transgender participants like Yu and Tsubasa, the pandemic interrupted medical care and intensified familial rejection. Non-Japanese participants such as Aanan and Fenhua encountered both xenophobia and homophobia, while rural participants like Ryu struggled with a lack of local queer spaces.

Crenshaw's (1991) concept of intersectionality helps us see that these challenges are not isolated but mutually reinforcing. Legal exclusion (e.g., the absence of same-sex marriage or anti-discrimination laws) intersected with cultural norms like oya kōkō, leaving LGBTQ+ individuals doubly vulnerable—first to family-based pressures, and second to the systemic neglect of queer rights.

Yet, intersectional identities were also a source of community-building. Participants sought out hybrid networks—such as online groups for queer immigrants, biracial LGBTQ+ individuals, or trans workers—that validated their multifaceted experiences. Kentaro, for instance, found solidarity in online spaces that recognized both his biracial background and pansexuality:

> For years, I felt like I didn't fit anywhere — not fully Japanese, not fully accepted as queer. Online, I found people like me, and that changed everything.

4.5.4 Resilience Through Digital and Hybrid Futures

The pandemic forced LGBTQ+ communities to rethink what connection means. While physical spaces like Ni-chōme will always remain central to queer life, participants expressed optimism about the continuing role of online platforms. Many envisioned hybrid futures where online and offline gatherings complement one another, making queer spaces more accessible to those in rural areas, those who are closeted, or those unable to attend events in person.

Harry captured this sense of digital resilience: "Online petitions and events kept the momentum going. Even though we were physically apart, I felt like we were still fighting for something bigger."

This shift toward hybrid forms of connection reflects not just a technological adaptation but a broader queer strategy of survival and worldmaking. By leveraging digital tools, participants were able to circumvent structural exclusions and build networks of care that extended beyond geographic and cultural boundaries.

4.5.5 Rethinking Work, Care, and Community

The pandemic also prompted participants to reimagine work and community on their own terms. Freed from the constraints of traditional offices, some found creative ways to integrate authenticity into their professional lives. Tomo pivoted to freelance design work, while Mirai turned to online art commissions as both a livelihood and a form of self-expression.

These adaptive strategies underscore a shift in values among LGBTQ+ individuals during the pandemic. Rather than seeking validation solely through corporate success or legal recognition, many emphasized personal fulfillment, chosen families, and collective care. As Berlant (2011) notes, crises have the potential to "open a space for rethinking the good life," challenging dominant scripts of happiness and achievement.

4.5.6 Toward Structural Change

While the resilience of LGBTQ+ communities during the pandemic is remarkable, these narratives also underscore the urgent need for structural reforms. Legal recognition of same-sex partnerships, workplace anti-discrimination measures, and accessible, LGBTQ-inclusive mental health services are essential for creating an equitable post-pandemic society.

The digital innovations and mutual aid networks described here cannot substitute for systemic protections. Instead, they highlight both the creativity of queer communities and the failures of the state to address their needs. Without structural change, the burden of survival will continue to fall disproportionately on marginalized individuals and grassroots networks.

4.5.7 Looking Forward

As the world transitions into a post-pandemic era, the lessons learned from this period of digital adaptation and intersectional solidarity are invaluable. The pandemic has shown that queer resilience is not merely about survival but about reimagining community, work, and care in ways that defy normative expectations.

Digital platforms will likely remain a cornerstone of this reimagining, enabling hybrid forms of activism that combine the power of in-person gatherings with the reach of online communities. At the same time, the fight for legal and social recognition continues, with many participants expressing hope that the heightened visibility of LGBTQ+ struggles during COVID-19 will accelerate policy reforms.

This chapter has traced how LGBTQ+ individuals in Japan navigated financial instability, digital transformation, and intersectional challenges during the pandemic. The next chapter will build on these insights, exploring how media representations, political activism, and cultural narratives shaped public perceptions of LGBTQ+ lives during this unprecedented crisis.

The themes of digital resilience, economic vulnerability, and intersectional inequality explored in this chapter are all underpinned by the tension of precarious visibility. Whether in workplaces, online platforms, or informal networks of care, being seen could open possibilities for connection and advocacy but also risk exposure, misunderstanding, or exclusion. These narratives point toward the need for hybrid strategies of visibility—balancing authenticity with safety—while continuing to fight for legal and institutional reforms that reduce the costs of being visible.

The next chapter builds on these insights by exploring how pandemic conditions intensified healthcare and mental health disparities, particularly for transgender individuals.

References

Ahmed, S. (2006). *Queer phenomenology: Orientations, objects, others*. Duke University Press.
Berlant, L. (2011). *Cruel optimism*. Duke University Press.
Butler, J. (2009). *Frames of war: When is life grievable?* Verso.
Crenshaw, K. (1991). Mapping the margins: Intersectionality, identity politics, and violence against women of color. *Stanford Law Review*, 43(6), 1241–1299.
Muñoz, J. E. (2009). *Cruising utopia: The then and there of queer futurity*. New York University Press.
Standing, G. (2011). *The precariat: The new dangerous class*. Bloomsbury Academic.
Warner, M. (2002). *Publics and counterpublics*. Zone Books.

Chapter 5
Healthcare and Mental Health—Barriers to Care

Masami Tamagawa

Abstract This chapter examines how the COVID-19 pandemic deepened healthcare and mental health disparities for LGBTQ+ individuals in Japan, particularly transgender people requiring gender-affirming care. While Japan's universal health system is praised for its accessibility, it remains largely heteronormative and ill-prepared to meet the needs of sexual and gender minorities. The pandemic amplified these structural inequalities: gender-affirming treatments such as hormone therapy and surgeries were delayed or canceled as hospitals prioritized "emergency" procedures, while public health measures failed to address privacy concerns or the realities of non-heteronormative families. Drawing on narratives from participants such as Chihiro (JJ, 35–44), Yu (JJ, 18–24), and Amelie (FJ, 25–34) the chapter highlights how medical discrimination, systemic neglect, and social stigma discouraged individuals from seeking testing, vaccination, or routine healthcare. The mental health crisis—marked by rising anxiety, depression, and re-closeting—was compounded by isolation, economic precarity, and the lack of inclusive mental health resources. Yet, the chapter also underscores community resilience: grassroots initiatives, online counseling, virtual Pride events, and mutual aid networks emerged as vital lifelines. These findings reveal both the vulnerabilities and strengths of Japan's LGBTQ+ communities and call for structural reforms that prioritize inclusive healthcare and mental health support.

5.1 Opening Vignette: Chihiro's Story

When Chihiro (JJ, 35–44), a transgender woman in her thirties, received her COVID-19 vaccination voucher, she hesitated. It was not the vaccine itself she feared, but the moment her name would be called in a crowded community hall. Her identification documents still bore her old name and gender marker, and she imagined the stares of strangers, the quiet judgment, and the possibility of being outed in a place meant for health and safety. "I postponed my vaccine until I could find a small clinic," she explained. "I wanted to stay safe, but I couldn't face being humiliated."

M. Tamagawa, *Japanese LGBTQ+ Lives, Diasporic Voices, and Resilience*,
https://doi.org/10.1007/978-981-95-3105-9_5

Chihiro's hesitation captures the compounded challenges faced by LGBTQ+ individuals in Japan during the pandemic: the need to protect one's health while navigating systems that often disregard or invalidate queer and transgender identities. For Chihiro, as for many others, the pandemic magnified the inequities embedded in the healthcare system, revealing both the vulnerabilities and the quiet resilience of those forced to navigate it.

5.2 Introduction: Healthcare Inequalities and LGBTQ+ Vulnerabilities

The COVID-19 pandemic exposed the fragility of Japan's healthcare and mental health systems, particularly for LGBTQ+ individuals whose needs have long been marginalized or misunderstood. While Japan's universal healthcare is often praised for its accessibility and efficiency, it remains structured around heteronormative and cisnormative assumptions that render queer and trans lives either invisible or problematically visible. For LGBTQ+ individuals, the healthcare setting often functions as a space of precarious visibility—where being recognized can mean both affirmation and risk of humiliation, misgendering, or discrimination.

This dynamic was particularly acute for transgender participants. Chihiro, a transgender woman, described how even something as routine as getting vaccinated became an ordeal. She delayed her appointment until she could locate a small clinic where she felt less likely to face humiliation, underscoring how fear of mistreatment shapes access to care. Her experience highlights how public health measures, though designed to protect, can inadvertently amplify the structural and cultural biases embedded in medical systems.

Healthcare access in Japan, while grounded in universal coverage, has long been shaped by cultural norms prioritizing conformity, discretion, and collective well-being. While this system generally meets the needs of the majority, it often fails to account for the lived realities of marginalized populations. For queer and transgender people, healthcare settings can feel less like spaces of healing and more like sites of misrecognition or erasure. Even routine visits can involve experiences of being called by legal names rather than chosen names, facing moral judgment, or enduring dismissive treatment. Transgender patients, for instance, reported feeling invalidated when administrative staff or doctors addressed them using outdated names or gender markers. Similarly, same-sex couples often encountered skepticism or heteronormative assumptions when seeking reproductive or sexual health services.

Prior to the pandemic, advocacy organizations and scholars had already documented the absence of LGBTQ+-affirming medical protocols in Japan. Surveys conducted by NGOs such as Nijiiro Diversity and ReBit revealed that healthcare professionals rarely receive training on sexual orientation or gender identity, resulting in pervasive insensitivity toward LGBTQ+ patients. This knowledge gap often manifests as intrusive questions, pathologizing attitudes, or breaches of confidentiality when a patient's sexual orientation or gender status is revealed without consent. These experiences produce what minority stress theorists describe as chronic anticipatory stress—a persistent expectation of stigma that discourages individuals from seeking care until their conditions become critical.

The onset of COVID-19 only deepened these inequalities. As hospitals and clinics shifted resources to emergency care, non-emergency services—including gender-affirming treatments like hormone therapy and surgeries—were delayed or suspended altogether. For transgender participants, these interruptions were devastating. Hormone therapy, for example, is not an elective procedure but a cornerstone of well-being. Being forced to discontinue or ration hormone treatments due to clinic closures or supply disruptions led to heightened dysphoria and mental distress. Ayumi (JJ, 25–34) described the experience: "When my surgery was postponed indefinitely, I felt like my future was on pause. It was as if my needs didn't matter."

Public discourse around COVID-19 reinforced these exclusions by centering heteronormative family structures. Government campaigns emphasized "households" and family units as the locus of safety and care, implicitly excluding LGBTQ+ individuals who live alone or whose families are unsupportive. For Aoi (JJ, 18–24), a 19-year-old lesbian forced to move back in with her parents, the experience felt like a regression: "I felt like I was back in high school, hiding everything again. I couldn't talk to anyone about who I really am, and the isolation was unbearable."

Economic precarity intensified these challenges. LGBTQ+ individuals, overrepresented in sectors like hospitality, retail, and the arts, were disproportionately affected by job losses and reduced income. The cost of uncovered services, such as mental health counseling, became prohibitive for many, while immigrants like Niran (FJ, 25–34) faced language barriers and visa insecurity that further limited their healthcare access.

Minority stress theory provides a critical lens for understanding these dynamics. Structural stigma, interpersonal discrimination, and internalized prejudice create a constant backdrop of psychological strain for LGBTQ+ individuals. During the pandemic, this stress was compounded by the loss of affirming community spaces—Pride events, cafés, and LGBTQ+ centers—that normally function as protective networks. Emily (FJ, 25–34), a 29-year-old asexual participant, explained: "Digital spaces became our community, but it's not the same. It's hard to find comfort in a Zoom meeting when you're craving real human connection."

The intersection of healthcare, public discourse, and social stigma reveals how precarious visibility became a defining condition for LGBTQ+ people+ during COVID-19. Seeking care often meant risking misgendering or judgment, while avoiding care meant sacrificing health and well-being. Against this backdrop, this chapter asks: How did the pandemic reshape healthcare access for LGBTQindividuals in Japan, especially transgender people needing gender-affirming care? How did systemic neglect and policy gaps deepen these inequalities? And what forms of grassroots and digital resilience emerged in response?

In answering these questions, the chapter highlights not only the vulnerabilities but also the collective strength of LGBTQ+ communities. It calls for systemic reforms—such as LGBTQ+ training for healthcare providers, legal protections against discrimination, and crisis-ready protocols for gender-affirming care—to ensure that marginalized groups are not left behind in future public health emergencies.

5.3 Medical Discrimination and Avoidance of Care

The narratives in this section highlight how precarious visibility permeated medical encounters during the pandemic. For LGBTQ+ individuals, especially transgender participants, simply seeking care often meant navigating the tension between being seen—and potentially outed or misgendered—and remaining invisible at the cost of delayed or inadequate treatment. These dynamics illuminate how healthcare settings, which should provide safety and healing, frequently became spaces of anxiety and erasure.

Healthcare interactions in Japan have historically been structured around heteronormative and cisnormative assumptions that render LGBTQ+ patients invisible or illegible. While the Japanese healthcare system prides itself on efficiency and cost-effectiveness, it operates within a cultural framework that values conformity and discretion. In practice, this means that non-normative identities—such as those of transgender, non-binary, or queer individuals—are often met with silence or discomfort rather than acceptance. Prior to the COVID-19 pandemic, transgender individuals frequently reported being misgendered by doctors, nurses, and administrative staff, with little recourse or acknowledgment of their preferred names and pronouns. This lack of recognition was compounded by the absence of gender-neutral medical forms and the rigid adherence to legal sex markers on insurance cards and health records, which forced patients into repeated acts of "outing" themselves in clinical settings.

These structural shortcomings were more than mere oversights—they reflected a deeper institutional failure to recognize LGBTQ+ patients as legitimate stakeholders in the healthcare system. As a result, many participants in this study noted that they had learned to approach hospitals with caution, often preparing scripts or rehearsing explanations in advance. Yu (JJ, 18–24), a transgender man in his early twenties, described this anticipatory anxiety:

> Even before COVID, I felt I had to prepare myself mentally before going to a hospital. I would write down what I wanted to say because I knew the staff would call me by my old name. During COVID, I stopped going altogether unless it was an emergency. I just didn't want to deal with that stress when everything else was already so heavy.

Yu's experience highlights a broader pattern: LGBTQ+ patients are not only responsible for managing their own health conditions but also for navigating the ignorance or discomfort of healthcare professionals. This extra burden can have severe consequences, as delays in care can worsen medical conditions and increase psychological distress.

5.3.1 Pandemic-Era Barriers and Exacerbated Stigma

The onset of the COVID-19 pandemic intensified these pre-existing challenges. As hospitals shifted their focus to emergency care, the already limited availability of LGBTQ+-affirming services diminished even further. Clinics reduced non-urgent consultations, and overburdened staff often displayed less patience or sensitivity in interactions with patients. For transgender individuals, the pandemic's new rules—such as bans on visitors accompanying patients—meant that supportive friends or partners, who could help advocate for them, were no longer allowed inside healthcare facilities. Without allies present, many participants reported feeling more vulnerable to misgendering or intrusive questioning.

Hitomi (JJ, 25–34), a transgender woman in her late twenties, recalled a particularly humiliating experience:

> The receptionist called out my legal name and gender loudly, in front of everyone. I felt all eyes on me. It's like my privacy didn't matter. I felt humiliated and wanted to leave, but I needed the medication. After that, I delayed appointments as much as I could.

Ryo (JJ, 35–44), a transgender man, faced similar issues. He described how a nurse refused to acknowledge his chosen name, insisting that "it's not the name on your insurance card." This type of rigid, rule-based response underscores how bureaucratic systems and staff training—or lack thereof—can collide to create a hostile environment for trans patients.

5.3.2 Fear of COVID-19 Testing and Vaccination

The lack of LGBTQ+-inclusive policies also discouraged participants from seeking COVID-19 testing or vaccination, despite their willingness to follow public health measures. Chihiro, a transgender woman in her thirties, delayed her vaccination out of fear that her gender identity would be questioned: "I wanted the vaccine, but I waited until I found a clinic that was less crowded and where I could talk to the staff quietly. I just couldn't face the possibility of being outed at a big vaccination center."

This was not an isolated incident. Several participants described anxiety about how their identity documents—bearing legal names and genders that no longer matched their appearances—would be handled during registration at public health facilities. Such fears highlight how systemic neglect directly affects public health outcomes, as marginalized groups may avoid lifesaving services due to anticipated discrimination.

The pandemic significantly magnified these structural constraints. As hospitals and clinics shifted resources to manage COVID-19 cases, procedures deemed "non-emergency" were deprioritized or indefinitely postponed. Gender-affirming treatments, including HRT consultations, were swept into this category, reflecting a persistent misunderstanding of trans healthcare needs as optional or cosmetic. For many participants, this categorization was deeply painful, as it denied the essential role such care plays in affirming their identity and preserving their mental health.

5.5.1 Disruptions in Hormone Therapy

HRT, which requires regular monitoring and prescription renewals, was one of the most frequently disrupted forms of care during the pandemic. Several participants reported difficulties in obtaining their usual medications due to clinic closures, supply chain disruptions, or reduced office hours. Tsubasa (JJ, 35–44), a transgender woman in her late thirties, shared her experience: "I went from every day to every other day. It was not enough, and I could feel my body changing, my skin roughening, and my emotions becoming unstable. The doctor apologized, but they said they had to prioritize emergency cases."

Aki (JJ, 18–24), a young transgender woman in rural Japan, described her frustration at the unpredictability of hormone supplies: "The pharmacy told me they could not get the hormone injection I usually take because shipments were delayed. It felt like I was slipping backwards every day. My body was betraying me again, and I had no control."

Participants emphasized that interruptions in HRT were not minor inconveniences but destabilizing events with immediate psychological consequences. Many reported experiencing acute anxiety, mood swings, and a resurgence of gender dysphoria as their bodies began to change in ways inconsistent with their gender identity. One participant, Ryo, who had been on testosterone therapy for years, recalled: "It's hard to explain how much a small delay affects you. I felt like my progress, my sense of self, was unraveling. It's not just medical—it's about who I am."

The lack of telemedicine alternatives further compounded these problems. While some countries, such as Canada and Australia, quickly implemented online consultations and extended prescriptions for HRT, Japan's medical system remained rigid, requiring in-person visits for renewals. This meant that individuals living in rural areas or under strict movement restrictions were left with few, if any, options.

5.5.2 Postponements and Cancellations of Surgeries

The pandemic's impact was particularly acute for those awaiting gender-affirming surgeries, which are already limited to a small number of facilities in Japan. The waiting lists for procedures such as chest reconstruction, vaginoplasty, or breast augmentation are notoriously long—often stretching over a year. For participants who had finally secured a date, the sudden wave of postponements felt like a devastating setback.

Ayumi, a transgender woman in her twenties, shared her disappointment and emotional exhaustion: "They said all non-urgent surgeries were postponed indefinitely. I had waited almost two years for this appointment. I cried for days. It was like being told, 'Your identity is not important enough.'"

Aki echoed these sentiments, describing the psychological toll of repeated cancellations: "I saved money, I mentally prepared, and then it was all canceled. I felt like my future was taken from me. Each time I heard the surgery was postponed again, I sank into depression."

For some, these delays extended beyond a year, as hospitals struggled to recover from consecutive waves of COVID-19 infections. The emotional toll was compounded by the financial strain of having to repeatedly save for procedures, as deposits were sometimes forfeited or administrative fees applied for rescheduling.

5.5.3 Psychological Impact of Interrupted Care

The psychological repercussions of interrupted gender-affirming care were severe. Participants reported increased rates of depression, panic attacks, and a sense of being "suspended in limbo." The loss of bodily autonomy—being unable to continue HRT or move forward with surgeries—was described as a form of erasure, as if the pandemic had erased years of personal effort to assert and affirm one's gender identity. Haru (JJ, 18–24), a 22-year-old trans man, explained: "I had finally reached a point where I was comfortable with my body because of hormones. But when I had to stop, it felt like I was being forced back into the old me. It was terrifying."

The link between continuous gender-affirming care and mental well-being is well-documented, yet Japanese health authorities failed to issue any guidance ensuring continuity during the pandemic. This neglect, participants argued, communicated that their needs were considered secondary or even frivolous compared to other forms of healthcare.

5.5.4 Policy Gaps and Institutional Neglect

The absence of official guidelines for maintaining gender-affirming care during health crises reflects a broader policy gap. Clinics were left to make decisions independently, leading to uneven access depending on location and institutional attitudes. While some urban clinics attempted to maintain HRT services through limited appointments, rural areas were particularly underserved. Tsubasa noted that a friend living in a rural prefecture had to travel over three hours to Tokyo for an appointment, despite the risks associated with travel during the pandemic.

In contrast, Western countries implemented emergency measures to preserve continuity of trans healthcare. For example, the UK's National Health Service (NHS) prioritized hormone therapy renewals and offered remote consultations to avoid unnecessary interruptions. The disparity between Japan and these international practices underscores a lack of institutional recognition of transgender healthcare as essential.

From a minority stress perspective, the classification of gender-affirming care as "non-essential" exacerbated existing vulnerabilities. By deprioritizing trans healthcare, the system reinforced harmful narratives that trans lives and identities are peripheral to mainstream society. This systemic erasure, combined with the isolation of the pandemic, left many participants feeling abandoned by both medical institutions and public policy.

5.5.5 Collective Coping and Community Workarounds

In the absence of institutional support, transgender individuals and LGBTQ+ organizations sought alternative solutions. Online peer-support groups circulated information on how to safely ration hormone supplies or access care through sympathetic providers. Some participants reported relying on informal networks to obtain medication or advice, though this often came with risks related to unregulated supplies. These workarounds, while not ideal, demonstrate the resilience of trans communities in the face of systemic neglect.

5.6 Summary

The COVID-19 pandemic did not create barriers to gender-affirming care in Japan, but it revealed and intensified them. Trans participants like Tsubasa, Aki, and Ayumi faced not only logistical delays but also emotional and psychological challenges that stemmed from being told—explicitly or implicitly—that their healthcare needs were secondary. These narratives highlight the urgent need for systemic reform, including telemedicine options for HRT, the expansion of surgical facilities, and the integration of LGBTQ+-affirming protocols within emergency healthcare planning.

5.7 Access to COVID-19 Testing and Vaccination

Access to COVID-19 testing and vaccination in Japan was complicated by logistical hurdles, inconsistent information dissemination, and bureaucratic procedures. These challenges were especially acute for LGBTQ+ individuals, whose needs were rarely considered in the planning and implementation of public health measures.

While the Japanese government emphasized universal access, the reality was far from inclusive. Transgender participants, in particular, expressed anxiety about presenting identification documents that did not match their gender presentation, fearing public misgendering, invasive questioning, or outright refusal of services. Such concerns led some to postpone or avoid seeking testing and vaccination despite understanding their importance for personal and community health. For foreign LGBTQ+ residents, language barriers and the lack of culturally sensitive information compounded these challenges, often forcing individuals to rely on informal networks for guidance.

5.7.1 Privacy Concerns and Stigma

Privacy concerns emerged as one of the most significant barriers. Public testing and vaccination centers—often located in large, open venues like gymnasiums or community halls—did not provide the anonymity or sensitivity that LGBTQ+ patients needed. Chihiro, a transgender woman in her thirties, vividly described her apprehension:

> I imagined standing in a line of strangers and hearing my old name shouted by staff. It felt humiliating even in my mind. I postponed my vaccine until I could find a smaller clinic that would let me explain things quietly.

Chihiro's fear was not unfounded. Other participants reported being publicly called by their legal name or asked invasive questions about their gender identity in front of strangers. Ryo, a transgender man, shared his discomfort during a PCR test: "It felt like I was on display, as if my identity was an oddity they needed to clarify. All I wanted was to know if I had COVID. I left feeling more anxious than before."

For many transgender individuals, the prospect of being misgendered in a public setting carried not just emotional harm but also the risk of involuntary outing. This is particularly dangerous in a society where trans and queer identities are often stigmatized and misunderstood. The fear of being outed led some participants to delay testing even when they experienced symptoms, which had potential implications for public health and disease transmission.

The issue of privacy also intersected with broader structural stigma. Staff at many vaccination and testing centers lacked training on LGBTQ+ issues, leading to situations where individuals were either misgendered or treated as curiosities. This not only discouraged queer and trans individuals from seeking care but also reinforced the perception that healthcare spaces were unsafe or unwelcoming.

5.7.2 Language and Information Gaps

Foreign LGBTQ+ residents faced an additional set of challenges due to language barriers and the lack of multilingual public health information. While local municipalities mailed vaccination vouchers and information pamphlets to residents, these materials were almost exclusively in Japanese, with little consideration for non-Japanese speakers.

Skyler (FJ, 25–34), a queer non-binary participant from the United States, described the confusion: "We got these vaccination vouchers in the mail, but everything was in Japanese. There wasn't even a QR code for translation. For foreigners who don't read Japanese, it was like guessing how to protect ourselves." Skyler also criticized the invisibility of minority groups in public health discourse: "The government talked about 'families' and 'households,' but what about people like me, living alone, or queer couples who aren't legally recognized? It was as if we didn't exist."

Language gaps were particularly pronounced for immigrant LGBTQ+ individuals from Southeast Asia and other regions, who often lacked access to both translation resources and LGBTQ+-affirming healthcare information. For example, Niran, a gay man from Thailand, relied on online forums and social media groups for accurate information about testing and vaccination, stating: "If it weren't for my LGBTQ+ friends online, I wouldn't have known what to do. The city hall hotline didn't have anyone who spoke Thai, and they didn't seem to care about my concerns."

5.7.3 Structural Inequalities in Public Health Infrastructure

These challenges were not isolated incidents but symptoms of a larger structural issue: Japan's public health response relied on a one-size-fits-all model that largely ignored marginalized populations. Vaccination protocols assumed that all patients had supportive families to assist with scheduling and transportation, an assumption that excluded LGBTQ+ individuals estranged from their families or living alone. Moreover, there were no explicit guidelines to ensure privacy for transgender individuals, nor any effort to collaborate with LGBTQ+ organizations to identify community needs.

In contrast, other countries implemented more inclusive approaches. For example, Canada and parts of the United States introduced gender-neutral intake forms, while some vaccination centers in Europe created private booths to respect confidentiality. These measures recognized that public health must account for diversity, particularly when marginalized groups are disproportionately affected by both the pandemic and the stigma surrounding healthcare access. Japan's failure to adopt similar measures highlights its institutional reluctance to acknowledge LGBTQ+ needs as part of its broader public health mandate.

5.7.4 Emotional and Social Consequences

The lack of inclusive testing and vaccination measures had not only logistical but also emotional repercussions. Participants described feeling invisible, neglected, and alienated. The public health messaging during the pandemic, which focused on "traditional" households and caregiving roles, left many queer and trans individuals feeling excluded from the national narrative of collective solidarity. This symbolic exclusion further eroded trust in public institutions.

Chihiro reflected on this sense of alienation: "When the government talked about protecting families, they weren't talking about families like mine. It was like being told that our health and lives don't matter as much."

Skyler also emphasized that this invisibility was not just a matter of oversight but a reflection of deeper societal biases: "The way they communicated during COVID made it clear who they consider part of society. Queer people were never mentioned, not even once. It hurt."

5.7.5 Community Workarounds and Advocacy

In response to these systemic failures, LGBTQ+ organizations and informal networks stepped in to provide accurate information, translation services, and guidance on safe vaccination and testing practices. Groups like Nijiiro Diversity and local Pride centers organized online webinars and posted multilingual resources, including step-by-step guides on how to navigate municipal vaccination procedures. These grassroots efforts filled critical gaps left by public institutions, but they also highlighted the uneven burden placed on community organizations to compensate for government inaction.

5.7.6 Critical Perspective on Public Health Policy

From a critical perspective, Japan's exclusion of LGBTQ+ concerns from its public health response reflects a larger biopolitical framework that privileges normative family structures and marginalizes those who do not conform. By failing to integrate LGBTQ+ perspectives into testing and vaccination protocols, authorities perpetuated both practical and symbolic forms of exclusion. This not only compromised the physical safety of LGBTQ+ individuals but also reinforced feelings of erasure and secondary citizenship. Minority stress theory helps explain how such systemic neglect compounds mental health risks, as individuals internalize the message that their lives are of lesser value.

5.8 Mental Health Crisis During the Pandemic

The COVID-19 pandemic triggered a mental health crisis that disproportionately affected LGBTQ+ individuals in Japan, many of whom were already navigating social isolation, familial rejection, and the absence of institutional support. For queer and trans people, the pandemic not only brought fears of infection but also dismantled the fragile networks of care, friendship, and solidarity that often serve as lifelines in a heteronormative society. Lockdowns, travel restrictions, and prolonged states of emergency intensified feelings of alienation and uncertainty, leaving participants with a heightened sense of vulnerability.

This sense of precarity was magnified by the fact that mental health services in Japan are not only stigmatized but also difficult to access, particularly for LGBTQ+ individuals who fear discrimination from counselors or therapists unfamiliar with queer issues. Participants in this study reported increased levels of anxiety, depression, and suicidal ideation, frequently linking these struggles to both pandemic-related disruptions and pre-existing societal stigma. The findings resonate strongly with minority stress theory, which posits that structural stigma, internalized prejudice, and interpersonal discrimination generate a chronic state of social stress that undermines the mental and physical well-being of sexual and gender minorities. The pandemic exacerbated these stressors by curtailing access to affirming spaces and support networks, amplifying psychological vulnerabilities.

5.8.1 Rising Anxiety, Depression, and Suicidal Ideation

Participants described the pandemic as a period marked by both visible and invisible losses—loss of social connection, freedom of movement, and the ability to live openly without fear of judgment. For many, this translated into heightened anxiety and depressive episodes. Emily, a White asexual woman in her late twenties, vividly described how her isolation spiraled into panic: "Digital spaces became our community, but even then, the loneliness was overwhelming. Without in-person events or gatherings, it felt like I didn't exist outside my apartment walls. Some days I had panic attacks just thinking about going outside."

Emily's words highlight how the virtual world, while a temporary substitute, could not fully replace the affirming energy of physical queer spaces. A sense of being "invisible" pervaded her account—a recurring theme across multiple interviews.

Niran, a Thai gay man studying in Sendai, spoke candidly about experiencing suicidal ideation:

> I am an extrovert, but with the pandemic, I was alone most of the time. My Japanese wasn't good enough to make new friends, and I missed my boyfriend in Thailand. I talked to a university counselor, who told me I have an adjustment disorder. I was scared of how often I thought about hurting myself.

His narrative underscores how intersecting factors—such as language barriers and physical separation from loved ones—created compounding layers of stress. Others reported struggling with sleep disturbances, weight changes, and chronic fatigue, all symptoms linked to both anxiety and depressive states.

For younger participants, the abrupt disruption of school life and peer networks was particularly destabilizing. Mai (JJ, 18–24), a 21-year-old pansexual student, explained: "University was the only place where I could be open about who I am. When classes went online, I lost that safe space. At home, I couldn't even mention my girlfriend."

5.8.2 *Isolation, Re-Closeting, and Family Rejection*

The pandemic's lockdown measures forced many LGBTQ+ individuals to return to or remain in unsupportive home environments, leading to re-closeting and strained family relationships. Aoi, a 19-year-old lesbian, described how this eroded her sense of self: "I was stuck at home with my parents for months. I couldn't talk to anyone about being lesbian, and I felt like I was back in the closet. I cried a lot during that time, but I had no one to tell."

Similarly, Ryo, a transgender man in his forties, found family cohabitation particularly difficult: "My parents don't know I'm trans, and being home with them meant hiding my identity every day. I felt suffocated, but I had nowhere else to go."

For individuals who were out to their families, the stress took other forms. Some participants noted that pandemic-related financial or caregiving pressures exacerbated familial tensions, with queer identities sometimes blamed for bringing "shame" or "complication" during an already stressful time. Such dynamics highlight how heteronormative family structures can intensify the mental health burdens of LGBTQ+ individuals when they are unable to retreat into affirming spaces outside the home.

5.8.3 *Intersectional Challenges: Migrant and Multicultural LGBTQ+ Lives*

Immigrant and multicultural LGBTQ+ participants faced unique challenges that were both structural and cultural. Niran's story illustrates how language barriers and cultural dissonance heightened his isolation. Without a robust social circle or language proficiency, he struggled to access reliable mental health support, often relying on online resources and informal peer groups. Skyler, a queer non-binary individual from the United States, echoed these sentiments: "Working from home meant I didn't meet anyone. I already felt like an outsider because of being foreign and queer. The pandemic just intensified that feeling—I felt invisible and disposable."

Other foreign participants, like Chia-hao (FO, 25–34), a gay man from Southeast Asia, noted that the lack of culturally competent counseling services in Japan left them feeling "doubly excluded—once as a foreigner, and again as someone who is queer." The intersection of race, nationality, and sexual orientation created a layered sense of alienation, as these participants faced not only pandemic-related isolation but also systemic barriers tied to immigration status and cultural stereotypes.

5.8.4 *Youth vs. Older Generations: Contrasting Coping Mechanisms*

Generational differences in coping strategies were also apparent in participants' accounts. Younger LGBTQ+ individuals, like Aoi and Mirai (JJ, 18–24), expressed frustration and grief over the loss of formative experiences—university life, romantic exploration, and participation in Pride events. While digital platforms such as LINE, Discord, and Zoom provided some sense of connection, they were also sources of alienation due to online harassment or the limitations of virtual intimacy. As Aoi noted: "Text messages can't replace a hug from a friend who understands you. It felt like I was talking to avatars, not real people."

In contrast, older LGBTQ+ participants tended to describe a more stoic form of isolation, shaped by years of societal invisibility and self-reliance. Hiroshi (JJ, 55–64), a gay man in his sixties, reflected: "I have lived alone for years, so staying inside wasn't new for me. But the pandemic made me think about mortality more. If I died of COVID, who would even know?".

For older participants, the pandemic amplified feelings of loneliness and existential reflection, particularly around aging without legal recognition of same-sex partnerships, which could complicate hospital visitation or inheritance rights.

5.8.5 *Minority Stress and Pandemic-Specific Precarity*

The collective experiences of participants underscore how minority stress interacts with pandemic-specific conditions to intensify mental health risks. The isolation mandated by public health measures curtailed opportunities for collective affirmation—the sense of belonging and validation derived from being among other LGBTQ+ individuals. Without community events, support groups, or even informal gatherings, many participants reported a resurgence of internalized stigma and self-doubt.

Intersectionality is critical in understanding these dynamics. The overlapping pressures of gender identity, sexuality, race, class, and migration status created unique patterns of vulnerability. For example, a young Japanese trans man living with unsupportive parents faced different challenges than a foreign gay student isolated by language barriers and cultural distance. Both, however, were caught in the crossfire of a pandemic response that failed to recognize marginalized communities as priority populations.

As Emily and Niran emphasized, the pandemic did not create these inequalities—it magnified the structural cracks already present in Japanese society and its healthcare system. In this sense, the mental health crisis experienced by LGBTQ+ individuals during COVID-19 is not just a product of the pandemic but also a reflection of deeper societal patterns of exclusion and neglect.

5.9 Community Responses and Alternative Mental Health Resources

The healthcare and mental health barriers faced by LGBTQ+ individuals during the COVID-19 pandemic were partially mitigated by grassroots initiatives, online counseling, and community-driven support systems. As formal healthcare institutions failed to account for the specific needs of queer and transgender populations, LGBTQ+ organizations and informal peer networks stepped in to fill critical gaps. These community efforts were not merely reactive; they reflected longstanding traditions of self-reliance and collective care within queer communities, which have historically had to create alternative support systems in response to state neglect and social marginalization.

Virtual platforms became lifelines, offering both practical resources—such as crisis hotlines, mental health webinars, and bilingual counseling—and spaces for social connection and affirmation. These digital spaces fostered what might be described as "community resilience"—a collective capacity to adapt and support one another in the face of systemic neglect. For participants, these networks often represented the only sources of comfort, validation, and practical help during prolonged lockdowns.

5.9.1 Online Counseling and Crisis Hotlines

Several NGOs and advocacy groups rapidly expanded their online mental health services to address the psychological toll of the pandemic. Organizations such as Nijiiro Diversity, Peer Friends, ReBit, and regional LGBTQ+ centers (e.g., Kansai Queer Network) began hosting virtual counseling sessions, peer-to-peer discussion groups, and mental health webinars tailored to queer audiences. These online platforms provided safe, judgment-free spaces where individuals could openly discuss issues like anxiety, depression, family rejection, and re-closeting. Importantly, many of these services were run by LGBTQ+ counselors or allies trained in queer-affirmative approaches—an essential factor in building trust among participants.

Emma (FJ, 25–34), a queer woman living in rural Hokuriku, described how online counseling became her "emotional lifeline" when in-person interactions were no longer possible:

> I couldn't travel to cities like Osaka or Tokyo, where I used to meet other queer women. Joining online peer groups and counseling sessions was the only way I felt connected and understood. It wasn't perfect, but it was better than feeling like I was alone on an island.

Similarly, Amelie (FJ, 25–34), a bisexual woman originally from France, found solace in bilingual mental health resources offered through LGBTQ+ immigrant support groups: "I discovered a support group for LGBTQ+ immigrants in Japan that held online meetings. Hearing others' experiences helped me feel less isolated, and they even shared practical advice about accessing mental health services in English."

The narratives of Emma and Amelie highlight how digital platforms bridged both geographical and linguistic divides, reaching individuals who might otherwise have been excluded due to rural location, immigration status, or language barriers. Other participants mentioned the importance of 24/7 LGBTQ+ crisis hotlines, where trained volunteers provided emotional support, particularly for those struggling with suicidal thoughts or relationship breakdowns during the pandemic.

5.9.2 Virtual Pride and Digital Community Spaces

The cancellation of major LGBTQ+ events, such as Tokyo Rainbow Pride, was a significant loss for many participants, as these gatherings provided rare opportunities for visibility and community affirmation. However, digital alternatives soon emerged. Virtual Pride celebrations, streamed panel discussions, and online queer film festivals offered accessible spaces for connection and education. These events were particularly valuable for young or closeted LGBTQ+ individuals, as online formats allowed them to participate anonymously or without the logistical challenges of traveling to urban centers.

Emily, an asexual participant in her late twenties, reflected on her experience of attending virtual Pride events:

> I joined a virtual Pride party hosted on Zoom. It wasn't the same as being there in person, but I loved seeing so many people on my screen—people like me. It gave me hope that our community can adapt and thrive, no matter what.

In addition to Pride events, participants attended online workshops on topics such as mental health, gender identity, and LGBTQ+ history. These events were described as both educational and therapeutic, creating spaces where participants could learn, share, and feel part of a larger movement despite the physical isolation imposed by the pandemic.

5.9.3 Peer-Support and Mutual Aid Initiatives

Mutual aid networks, often coordinated via social media platforms like Twitter, LINE, and Facebook, became essential community infrastructures. These initiatives provided tangible support, ranging from crowdfunding campaigns to cover medical costs, to meal deliveries and rent assistance for LGBTQ+ individuals facing job losses. Others focused on sharing healthcare information—translated into multiple languages—or providing guidance on navigating bureaucratic systems to access COVID-19 relief.

Amelie emphasized the emotional power of these networks: "When someone in the group needed help—like groceries or rent support—everyone chipped in, even if we didn't know each other personally. It reminded me that we, as queer people, have always had to look out for one another."

Similarly, Yu, a transgender man in his early twenties, described participating in a LINE group where members shared tips on safely obtaining HRT supplies during clinic closures: "It felt like we were all in the same boat. We shared what worked, which doctors were willing to help, and even pooled resources for people who couldn't get their meds."

These stories underscore what José Esteban Muñoz refers to as "queer utopianism"—the creation of alternative worlds and support systems that resist dominant structures. Through acts of mutual care, LGBTQ+ individuals cultivated resilience and solidarity that went beyond the limitations of state or institutional frameworks.

5.9.4 Filling Institutional Gaps

Community-led responses did more than provide immediate relief; they exposed the profound shortcomings of state and healthcare systems. While the Japanese government emphasized generic mental health hotlines during the pandemic, these services often lacked staff trained in LGBTQ+ issues and were perceived as unsafe by queer participants. In contrast, grassroots organizations tailored their resources to address the intersectional realities of their constituents, recognizing that the mental health needs of a young trans student differ from those of an older gay man or an immigrant lesbian couple.

These initiatives challenge the assumption that institutional healthcare alone can provide holistic well-being. By centering lived experience and community knowledge, LGBTQ+ groups offered a model of "care from below"—a bottom-up approach that prioritizes empathy, inclusivity, and flexibility. Moreover, the success of these initiatives highlights the importance of digital infrastructure as a tool for community-building, particularly in rural areas or contexts where physical queer spaces are scarce.

5.9.5 Lessons and Future Directions

The pandemic underscored the adaptability of LGBTQ+ communities in Japan. Participants noted that the experience of building digital networks, online events, and mutual aid efforts during COVID-19 has lasting potential for the future. Even as in-person events resume, many participants expressed a desire to continue online support groups, recognizing that such platforms can reach marginalized individuals who may never feel comfortable attending physical events. These lessons speak to the durability of queer resilience and the need for sustained investment in both digital and physical spaces for LGBTQ+ well-being.

5.10 Policy Gaps and Advocacy

The COVID-19 pandemic exposed the deep structural shortcomings of Japan's healthcare policies, particularly their failure to adequately address the needs of LGBTQ+ individuals. While Japan's universal health insurance is often lauded for its affordability and comprehensive coverage, it is structured around heteronormative and cisnormative assumptions. These assumptions are reflected in the lack of standardized protocols for addressing misgendering, respecting chosen names, ensuring confidentiality regarding sexual orientation or gender identity, and providing access to gender-affirming care. Such omissions effectively render LGBTQ+ patients invisible within the healthcare framework, leaving them vulnerable to discriminatory practices and systemic neglect.

The voices of transgender participants in this study were particularly revealing. As Tsubasa remarked: "I felt like I had to justify every request, even for basic things like renewing my hormones. It was as if my healthcare needs were optional, not necessary."

This invisibility within healthcare policy is closely tied to the Japanese government's broader reluctance to recognize LGBTQ+ rights. While municipalities like Tokyo and Sapporo have implemented symbolic partnership certificates for same-sex couples, there is no comprehensive national anti-discrimination law or formal recognition of LGBTQ+ rights in healthcare. This absence became especially problematic during the pandemic, when timely and inclusive public health measures were urgently needed.

5.10.1 Policy Gaps During the Pandemic

During the pandemic, these policy gaps became increasingly evident. Gender-affirming treatments—already subject to burdensome psychiatric evaluations and approval processes—were often categorized as "non-essential" and suspended by hospitals. Participants like Aki described the uncertainty and distress caused by the lack of clear policies: "When I called the clinic, they just said they didn't know when things would return to normal. I was left to figure it out on my own, with no support."

No official guidance was issued by the Ministry of Health, Labour, and Welfare (Kōsei Rōdōshō, MHLW) to ensure continuity of gender-affirming care, such as hormone therapy or surgical consultations. This left patients to rely on ad hoc solutions, which sometimes meant rationing medication or turning to informal, unregulated sources—both of which posed serious risks to their health.

Similarly, Japan's public health campaigns around COVID-19 testing and vaccination failed to address the privacy and safety concerns of LGBTQ+ individuals. For example, the registration process at mass vaccination sites required legal name verification, which for transgender individuals often meant involuntary outing or misgendering. In Western countries, some vaccination centers implemented gender-neutral intake forms and allowed the use of preferred names. In Japan, no such adjustments were made, signaling an implicit prioritization of heteronormative family structures in pandemic health policy.

5.10.2 Advocacy Efforts

Despite these challenges, LGBTQ+ advocacy groups mobilized to fill the gaps left by government inaction. Organizations such as Nijiiro Diversity, J-ALL (Japan Alliance for LGBT Legislation), and ReBit began lobbying hospitals and clinics to adopt inclusive practices. They distributed educational materials for medical professionals, emphasizing the importance of using correct pronouns, maintaining confidentiality, and recognizing gender-affirming treatments as essential healthcare.

Some groups launched online workshops and training sessions aimed at improving healthcare worker awareness. In metropolitan areas like Tokyo, Osaka, and Fukuoka—where LGBTQ+ communities are more visible—local Pride collectives partnered with healthcare providers to host webinars on inclusive care during emergencies. For instance, one online session hosted by Tokyo Rainbow Pride in early 2021 drew over 500 healthcare professionals and community members to discuss strategies for respecting LGBTQ+ patients during pandemic conditions.

Legal advocacy also intensified during the pandemic. The long-delayed "LGBT Understanding Promotion Bill" was thrust back into public debate, as activists highlighted how the absence of anti-discrimination protections left LGBTQ+ people vulnerable during health emergencies. While the bill remains limited in scope—focused primarily on promoting understanding rather than mandating legal protections—it nonetheless became a rallying point for activists pushing for systemic reform.

One major campaign, #EqualityActJapan, gained traction in this period, urging lawmakers to adopt enforceable anti-discrimination legislation in line with international human rights standards. Online platforms were also used to share personal accounts of healthcare discrimination, often under informal hashtags or community-specific initiatives. While not always part of coordinated national campaigns, these social media testimonies helped draw attention to the intersection of pandemic policy and LGBTQ+ exclusion, even in the face of resistance from conservative politicians.

5.10.3 International Comparisons

A comparison with international practices reveals how far Japan lags behind in implementing LGBTQ+-inclusive healthcare policies. In Canada and the UK, for example, transgender patients were explicitly prioritized to ensure continuity of hormone therapy, with pharmacies offering extended prescriptions and telemedicine consultations. The UK's National Health Service (NHS) issued temporary guidelines to prevent interruptions in gender-affirming care, recognizing the link between treatment disruptions and mental health crises.

In the United States, several states partnered with advocacy organizations to train vaccination site staff on respectful interactions with LGBTQ+ patients, including the use of chosen names and pronouns. Public health campaigns also included messaging targeted at LGBTQ+ communities, acknowledging the specific challenges they faced.

By contrast, Japan's pandemic response maintained a one-size-fits-all approach, failing to consider the unique vulnerabilities of LGBTQ+ populations. Even in countries like Taiwan and South Korea, which share some cultural similarities with Japan, public health policies during COVID-19 were more proactive in addressing the needs of marginalized communities. Japan's lack of such measures reflects not only institutional inertia but also a persistent belief that LGBTQ+ issues are "private matters" rather than public health priorities.

5.10.4 Critique of Government Inaction

The Japanese government's limited response during the pandemic reflects a broader pattern of institutional inertia regarding minority rights. Policymakers consistently framed public safety through the lens of the nuclear family, reinforcing the idea that care and responsibility rest within heteronormative households. This framing left LGBTQ+ individuals—especially those estranged from their families or living alone—excluded from the narrative of collective protection.

Participants expressed frustration with this exclusion. Emma, a queer woman in her thirties, remarked: "The government talks about protecting families during the pandemic, but what they mean is heterosexual families. People like me don't even cross their minds."

Such sentiments were echoed by others who described feeling invisible in national public health campaigns. This lack of recognition deepens distrust in healthcare systems, which are seen as extensions of governmental priorities. For many, the pandemic was not just a health crisis but also a stark reminder of the hierarchies of care embedded within Japanese society. As Skyler noted: “It’s clear who the system is designed for, and it’s not us. If you don’t fit their definition of ‘normal,’ you’re left on your own.”

5.10.5 Toward Inclusive Policy Reform

These policy gaps and advocacy efforts provide a crucial backdrop for understanding how queer theoretical perspectives illuminate both the vulnerabilities and the resilience of LGBTQ+ healthcare experiences during the pandemic.

The experiences documented in this chapter suggest that policy reform must go beyond symbolic gestures, such as the “Understanding Promotion Bill,” to create tangible protections and inclusive healthcare practices. Recommendations include:

- Developing national guidelines for LGBTQ+-inclusive healthcare during emergencies.
- Training healthcare professionals on gender and sexual diversity.
- Establishing anti-discrimination protections within medical institutions.
- Creating public health campaigns that explicitly acknowledge LGBTQ+ families and individuals.

The pandemic highlighted the urgent need for structural change, not just temporary fixes. Grassroots advocacy has laid the groundwork for these reforms, but government action is needed to ensure that LGBTQ+ individuals are not left vulnerable in future crises.

5.11 Queer Theoretical Perspectives on Healthcare and Mental Health

The narratives in this chapter reveal that healthcare systems are not neutral sites of care but contested arenas where survival and exclusion often coexist. In times of crisis, such as the pandemic, these dynamics were amplified for LGBTQ+ individuals—particularly transgender participants—who faced heightened vulnerabilities not only due to the virus but also due to bureaucratic protocols and cultural norms that failed to recognize their existence. Many were compelled to navigate medical environments by performing normative roles or concealing aspects of their identity, a stark reminder of the systemic erasures embedded within institutional practices. Butler’s (2009) notion of precarity captures this dual exposure: to both illness and to the social conditions that determine whose lives are valued.

The emotional toll of medical encounters was often compounded by the risk of being involuntarily outed. Participants recounted moments where outdated legal names, gender markers, or invasive questions forced them into tense negotiations of silence and disclosure. These accounts illustrate how visibility in medical settings can be double-edged—opening doors to treatment while exposing individuals to stigma or harm. Such experiences resonate with Sedgwick's (1990) insight that the closet is not merely a private space but a structure of knowledge and power, shaping how and when queer lives are acknowledged.

Spatial dynamics also played a critical role in shaping participants' sense of safety. Hospitals and clinics are structured along heteronormative and cisnormative "lines," directing care toward normative patients while leaving queer and trans patients feeling "out of line." In response, some, like Chihiro and Yu, actively sought out smaller, queer-affirming clinics, turned to digital counseling, or relied on community-run services to reclaim a sense of belonging and agency. These acts reflect what Ahmed (2006) calls queer orientation—the process of navigating spaces by moving toward what feels livable and away from what threatens harm.

Community responses during the pandemic were equally instructive. Mutual aid networks, virtual Pride events, and grassroots counseling initiatives emerged not as mere stopgaps but as creative interventions that neither fully assimilated into nor rejected mainstream healthcare. Instead, they carved out hybrid systems of care, embodying what Muñoz (1999, 2009) describes as disidentification—a strategy of survival that works both with and against dominant structures. These efforts also gesture toward queer futurity, imagining more inclusive and compassionate healthcare landscapes through collective action and creativity.

5.11.1 Structural Inequities, Precarious Visibility, and Resilience

The COVID-19 pandemic revealed how deeply precarious visibility shapes healthcare and mental health experiences for LGBTQ+ individuals in Japan. Healthcare encounters—already fraught with the risk of misgendering, judgment, and erasure—became even more charged during the pandemic. Being visible could mean gaining access to care, yet it often exposed individuals to invasive questions or humiliation, while invisibility led to delayed treatment, psychological strain, and worsening health outcomes. For transgender participants, interruptions in hormone therapy or postponed gender-affirming surgeries were not mere inconveniences but profound disruptions to selfhood and well-being.

The pandemic's public health messaging, which idealized the nuclear family as the cornerstone of care and safety, further marginalized LGBTQ+ lives by erasing non-heteronormative family structures and chosen families. Participants such as Aoi and Skyler described feeling invisible within national narratives of solidarity, while foreign residents like Niran and Amelie faced additional barriers due to language gaps and xenophobia. These narratives make clear that healthcare inequalities are not isolated to the clinical sphere; they are deeply intertwined with cultural norms, legal structures, and social stigma.

Yet this chapter also demonstrates the resilience of LGBTQ+ communities. Grassroots organizations, mutual aid networks, and online counseling initiatives became vital lifelines when formal healthcare and mental health systems failed to provide adequate support. These alternative infrastructures not only filled immediate gaps but also embodied what Berlant (2011) calls "affective infrastructures"—informal systems of care that sustain marginalized communities in times of crisis.

5.11.2 Intersection of Healthcare, Social Stigma, and Policy Failures

The intersectional nature of these challenges became particularly evident during the pandemic. For example, a young transgender man living with unsupportive parents experienced not only disruptions to his medical care but also a heightened risk of mental health deterioration due to re-closeting and emotional isolation. Similarly, foreign LGBTQ+ residents like Skyler and Niran encountered multiple forms of exclusion—from the lack of multilingual health information to systemic xenophobia—further compounded by their queer or trans identities.

Japan's public health messaging, which largely centered on the nuclear family as the primary unit of care and support, failed to acknowledge the diversity of family structures. This erasure left many LGBTQ+ individuals feeling excluded from national narratives of solidarity and protection. The voices of participants such as Emma and Aoi make clear that the pandemic deepened pre-existing feelings of invisibility, reinforcing the need for structural reforms that recognize the full spectrum of human experiences.

5.11.3 Resilience Through Community Mobilization

Yet, alongside these narratives of vulnerability, this chapter also illuminates a powerful story of resilience. LGBTQ+ organizations, grassroots collectives, and peer-support networks stepped in to fill the gaps left by state institutions. Initiatives such as online counseling, virtual Pride events, bilingual mental health resources, and community-driven mutual aid not only provided immediate relief but also fostered a sense of collective empowerment. For many participants, these grassroots responses were more empathetic and adaptive than formal healthcare or government programs.

Digital platforms, in particular, played a pivotal role in sustaining a sense of belonging. As Amelie reflected: "Even though I was alone in my apartment, I didn't feel alone in the world. Online spaces reminded me that there were people who cared and understood."

These acts of solidarity represent what scholars like Muñoz (1999) and Ahmed (2006) describe as "queer worldmaking"—the construction of alternative forms of care and kinship that challenge dominant norms. The pandemic, while devastating, catalyzed the growth of these networks, illustrating the resourcefulness of LGBTQ+ communities in the face of systemic neglect.

5.11.4 Lessons and Opportunities for Structural Reform

The pandemic offers both a stark reminder of systemic neglect and an opportunity for transformation. The experiences detailed in this chapter underscore the urgent need for reforms that prioritize inclusivity, gender diversity, and the protection of LGBTQ+ rights within Japan's healthcare and mental health systems. Several key recommendations emerge:

Comprehensive LGBTQ+ Training for Healthcare Professionals:

Medical practitioners must receive training on queer and trans health issues, including the importance of using correct pronouns, understanding gender-affirming treatments, and maintaining confidentiality regarding sexual orientation and gender identity.

Uninterrupted Access to Gender-Affirming Care:

Policies should ensure that gender-affirming treatments, such as hormone therapy and related surgeries, are not classified as "non-essential" during emergencies. Telemedicine consultations and extended prescription periods, as implemented in other countries, should be adopted.

Anti-Discrimination Measures:

Legal protections against discrimination in healthcare settings must go beyond symbolic "understanding" bills and ensure enforceable rights. This includes revising intake forms, insurance documents, and hospital procedures to reflect diverse gender identities.

Inclusive Public Health Messaging:

Future public health campaigns should explicitly recognize LGBTQ+ individuals and families, moving beyond the narrow representation of the heterosexual nuclear family as the sole model of care and solidarity.

Support for Community-Based Organizations:

Grassroots LGBTQ+ organizations, which played a critical role during the pandemic, should receive financial and institutional support to continue their work. Their insights and lived experience are invaluable in shaping policies that meet the needs of marginalized populations.

5.11.5 Vulnerability and Strength: A Dual Narrative

The pandemic highlighted both the vulnerabilities and the strengths of LGBTQ+ communities in Japan. While systemic failures intensified the hardships faced by marginalized groups, the resilience demonstrated through community mobilization and digital networks signals a pathway forward. These stories of self-organized care and mutual aid challenge the notion that LGBTQ+ people are mere "recipients" of policy or charity; instead, they are active agents shaping their own futures.

As Hiroshi, a gay man in his sixties, observed: "We learned how to survive without relying on systems that don't see us. But we shouldn't have to do this alone."

This statement encapsulates the central argument of this chapter: while resilience is vital, it should not be used to justify systemic neglect. True equity requires both community strength and institutional accountability.

The resilience displayed by LGBTQ+ communities throughout the pandemic must be understood against the backdrop of precarious visibility. While participants created alternative networks of care and solidarity, their survival strategies were shaped by the risks of being misrecognized or dismissed by mainstream healthcare systems. This dual narrative of vulnerability and strength underscores that meaningful equity requires both community ingenuity and structural change.

5.11.6 Looking Forward

The lessons of COVID-19 extend beyond the immediate crisis. Building on the resilience demonstrated during the pandemic, policymakers and healthcare providers must create systems that not only acknowledge but actively support the diverse needs of LGBTQ+ populations. This includes integrating community voices into policymaking, funding LGBTQ+-inclusive mental health programs, and fostering collaborations between grassroots organizations and public health institutions.

Ultimately, the pandemic provides a moment of reckoning—a chance to address the structural inequities that have long undermined LGBTQ+ well-being. By embracing inclusivity, affirming diversity, and supporting community-driven innovations, Japan can move toward a healthcare system that is not only efficient but also equitable, ensuring that LGBTQ+ individuals are no longer left behind in future public health emergencies.

The lessons of the pandemic underscore that visibility alone is not enough—LGBTQ+ individuals must be recognized not only as patients but as full citizens entitled to safe, affirming, and accessible care. Policies must address both structural and cultural barriers, ensuring that being visible in healthcare settings is not synonymous with risk. As the next chapter explores media representations and political discourse, the concept of precarious visibility will continue to frame how queer voices were amplified, contested, and transformed during the COVID-19 crisis.

The next chapter explores how transnational dynamics—migration, border closures, and legal challenges—further complicated the lives of LGBTQ+ individuals during the pandemic.

References

Ahmed, S. (2006). *Queer phenomenology: Orientations, objects, others*. Duke University Press.
Berlant, L. (2011). *Cruel optimism*. Duke University Press.
Butler, J. (2009). *Frames of war: When is life grievable?* Verso.
Muñoz, J. E. (1999). *Disidentifications: Queers of color and the performance of politics*. University of Minnesota Press.
Muñoz, J. E. (2009). *Cruising utopia: The then and there of queer futurity*. New York University Press.
Sedgwick, E. K. (1990). *Epistemology of the closet*. University of California Press.

Chapter 6
Transnational Experiences: Migration, Travel Bans, and Legal Challenges

Masami Tamagawa

Abstract This chapter, Transnational Experiences: Migration, Travel Bans, and Legal Challenges, explores the compounded vulnerabilities faced by Japanese LGBTQ+ migrants abroad and non-Japanese LGBTQ+ residents in Japan during the COVID-19 pandemic. Through participant narratives, the chapter examines how border restrictions, visa insecurities, and the absence of legal recognition for same-sex partnerships fractured intimate relationships and exacerbated systemic inequalities. For Japanese LGBTQ+ individuals overseas, the lack of spousal visa eligibility and limited state support created a precarious environment, while non-Japanese queer residents in Japan experienced racial discrimination, job-related visa threats, and restricted access to culturally competent healthcare.

Binational same-sex couples were among the most severely impacted, as Japan's immigration policies excluded them from the humanitarian entry exemptions granted to heterosexual spouses. The loss of LGBTQ+ community spaces, such as Ni-chōme nightlife and Pride events, further eroded social connections, with digital alternatives providing only partial relief.

By situating these narratives within queer diaspora studies and global human rights frameworks, the chapter underscores the urgency of legal reforms to recognize diverse family structures, protect foreign workers, and ensure equitable healthcare. It calls for transnational advocacy and solidarity to challenge heteronormative state policies and create conditions of genuine equality and belonging.

6.1 Chapter Overview

The COVID-19 pandemic revealed how queer lives are shaped by the interplay of national borders, legal recognition, and global inequality. This chapter shifts focus to transnational experiences, examining the compounded vulnerabilities faced by Japanese LGBTQ+ migrants living abroad and non-Japanese queer residents in Japan. By analyzing participant narratives of border closures, visa insecurity, and racialized exclusion, this chapter highlights how pandemic-era policies intensified existing inequities while severing intimate and communal ties. It also situates these

M. Tamagawa, *Japanese LGBTQ+ Lives, Diasporic Voices, and Resilience*,
https://doi.org/10.1007/978-981-95-3105-9_6

personal accounts within broader debates on queer diaspora, state recognition, and global human rights frameworks.

6.2 Introduction: Queer Lives Across Borders

The COVID-19 pandemic disrupted global mobility, producing an unprecedented regime of border closures and travel bans that reshaped the lives of transnational communities. For Japanese LGBTQ+ migrants and non-Japanese LGBTQ+ individuals living in Japan, these restrictions intersected with pre-existing legal exclusions, cultural barriers, and social stigmas, resulting in a condition of precarious visibility. LGBTQ+ individuals were often "seen" by immigration authorities or public health systems only when their relationships or identities failed to meet normative expectations, while remaining invisible when protections and benefits were allocated to heterosexual couples and families.

This chapter explores how these dynamics unfolded across transnational contexts, particularly for binational couples and migrants navigating legal invisibility, racialization, and healthcare access during the pandemic. Participants, such as Shufen (FJ, 35–44), separated from her partner in Taiwan, and Emma (FJ, 25–34), a bisexual American teacher, describe how state policies not only fractured intimate relationships but also exposed the heteronormative assumptions embedded in immigration and public health measures. For Japanese LGBTQ+ migrants abroad, the lack of spousal visa eligibility or family recognition under Japanese law compounded insecurities around residency, healthcare, and financial stability. For foreign queer residents in Japan, the challenges were amplified by racial discrimination, job-related visa precarity, and a lack of culturally competent healthcare.

The legal framework in Japan, which does not recognize same-sex partnerships, created acute hardships during COVID-19. While heterosexual spouses were routinely granted humanitarian entry exemptions, same-sex partners were excluded, treated as legal strangers. Shufen's experience illustrates the deep personal cost of Japan's pandemic-era border closures. Unable to return to Taiwan to marry her partner—or even see her in person—she described feeling that the future they had envisioned together was slipping further out of reach.

For Japanese LGBTQ+ migrants living abroad, similar issues emerged in reverse. Without official recognition of same-sex partnerships at home, these individuals often lacked the documentation needed to secure spousal visas, healthcare benefits, or other rights abroad. Chia-hao (FO, 25–34), a gay Taiwanese data engineer, described how pandemic restrictions deepened his isolation: "COVID-19 prevented me from travelling in Japan or making any new friends while I was here. My life was monotonous. I didn't have many chances to chat with my colleagues, let alone talk about my sexuality."

Non-Japanese LGBTQ+ residents of Japan, meanwhile, encountered unique forms of marginalization shaped by racial bias, employment insecurity, and restrictive immigration policies. Emma voiced her frustration at being both excluded and hypervisible as a foreigner: "I feel the government's response to COVID-19, including its immigration policies, have unfairly targeted foreign residents of Japan. Many international residents have been unable to return home to visit family, even in the case of emergencies."

These accounts reveal how border regimes function not only as logistical systems but as mechanisms of biopolitical control that privilege certain kinship structures while rendering others illegible. As Puar (2007) argues, borders actively reproduce normative definitions of family, citizenship, and belonging. For LGBTQ+ individuals, this means that intimate relationships and personal freedoms can be severed at the whim of the state—a reality made especially visible during the pandemic.

Queer diaspora studies and Muñoz's (1999) notion of disidentification provide a useful framework for understanding these narratives. Participants often navigated structural exclusions through creative, non-traditional means—relying on digital networks, mutual aid, and informal support systems to maintain connection and care. Yet these strategies also underscore the fragility of queer belonging when legal recognition and institutional support are absent.

Healthcare access was another recurring challenge, especially for foreign LGBTQ+ residents who faced language barriers and lacked trust in local medical institutions. Emily (FJ, 25–34), an asexual American teacher, described how these intersecting barriers created a sense of isolation:

> It is difficult to know what clinics I can go to that speak English. Being under pressure, especially in healthcare situations, is embarrassing and overwhelming. Information about costs or procedures is not readily available, and I often feel like I'm on my own.

By weaving together these transnational narratives, this chapter highlights how the pandemic magnified structural inequalities linked to nationality, race, gender, and sexuality. It examines both the vulnerabilities and resilience of Japanese LGBTQ+ migrants abroad and non-Japanese queer residents in Japan, situating their experiences within broader debates on border regimes, citizenship, and global human rights. As the following sections show, these narratives underscore the urgent need for legal reforms, inclusive healthcare, and recognition of diverse family structures to prevent queer lives from being relegated to conditions of precarious visibility.

6.3 Japanese LGBTQ+ Migrants Abroad: Legal Invisibility and Vulnerability

The experiences of Japanese LGBTQ+ migrants abroad further illustrate the dynamics of precarious visibility, where being recognized often exposes individuals to legal or cultural scrutiny while invisibility leads to a denial of rights. Migration, which many imagined as an escape from domestic stigma, instead revealed the transnational reach of legal invisibility and heteronormative policies, particularly when compounded by pandemic-related restrictions.

The COVID-19 pandemic revealed how legal and social structures of inequality transcend national borders, following LGBTQ+ individuals wherever they go. Japanese LGBTQ+ migrants living abroad often imagined migration as an opportunity to escape the social conservatism, family pressure, and legal invisibility they faced at home. However, the pandemic shattered this perception, showing how vulnerabilities rooted in nationality, sexuality, and legal status are compounded in transnational contexts. Travel restrictions and abrupt border closures were not simply logistical hurdles—they served as reminders of the precariousness of queer migrants' lives, where intimate relationships and personal freedoms are often contingent on state recognition.

For many Japanese LGBTQ+ migrants, the absence of legal recognition for same-sex partnerships in Japan became a tangible barrier while abroad. Without state-sanctioned marriage certificates or domestic partnership recognition, queer couples were often excluded from spousal visas, healthcare benefits, and financial relief programs available to heterosexual couples. This structural exclusion was not confined to Japan but was exported through international legal frameworks, where Japanese migrants could not produce the necessary documentation to validate their relationships. In effect, Japanese LGBTQ+ individuals abroad were doubly marginalized: first by Japan's refusal to recognize their relationships, and second by foreign legal systems that required official documentation to extend protections or benefits.

This lack of recognition had a cascading impact on economic and social security. Many Japanese LGBTQ+ migrants found themselves without the financial safety nets that heterosexual couples enjoy, such as access to shared housing contracts, family-based tax benefits, or spousal healthcare coverage. During the pandemic, when job loss and health concerns were widespread, these gaps became particularly acute. Without legal status as "family," queer migrants often faced these hardships alone, lacking both institutional support and the extended family networks they might have relied upon in Japan.

6.3.1 Visa Precarity and Family Recognition

Visa precarity was one of the most frequently cited challenges by Japanese LGBTQ+ migrants during the pandemic. Residency permits for work or study abroad are often tied to employment or enrollment in academic institutions—both of which were severely disrupted by COVID-19. Unlike heterosexual couples, who could often fall back on spousal visas to maintain residency, same-sex couples had no such legal fallback. This exclusion placed many Japanese LGBTQ+ individuals in a position where a single job loss or expired contract could mean losing the right to stay in a foreign country.

Chia-hao, a gay Taiwanese data engineer who had spent over a year working at a Japanese bank, offered a striking example of how such legal and social invisibility manifested during the crisis. Although his position was relatively stable before COVID-19, the company's pandemic-related pay freeze forced him to reconsider his future: "The pay was insufficient. My company stated they wouldn't raise my pay because of the COVID-19 deficit. I decided to leave Japan and pursue a master's degree in my home country."

While Chia-hao did not explicitly link his decision to his sexuality, his account underscores how isolation in the workplace—exacerbated by cultural and linguistic barriers—left him without a social or professional safety net. His reflection on workplace dynamics further illustrates this sense of invisibility:

> Since I worked as a data scientist, it is not necessary for me to mention my private things in the office. Before the pandemic, I could feel that Japanese people are reluctant to speak to foreigners speaking bad Japanese already. After the pandemic, our company forbade gathering during lunchtime. I did not have many chances to chat with my colleagues, let alone [about] my sexuality.

Chia-hao's experience resonates with the broader trend of social isolation faced by many migrants during the pandemic, where work-from-home policies or strict workplace distancing left little room for personal connection.

Niran (FJ, 25–34), a Thai PhD student in Japan, provides a reverse but parallel perspective on cross-border LGBTQ+ struggles. While he is not a Japanese national, his narrative reflects the shared precarity of queer migrants caught between multiple immigration regimes: "I have a boyfriend, he's Thai. He is in Thailand right now, and we are not in an open relationship. We have known each other for eight years... With travel restrictions, I have no way to see him." Niran's inability to reunite with his partner speaks to the emotional toll of pandemic-era border controls, which failed to account for the realities of queer families and relationships.

For Japanese LGBTQ+ migrants living abroad, similar situations often played out when their foreign partners or spouses lacked legal pathways for recognition in Japan. The absence of any reciprocal arrangement for same-sex couples meant that individuals were left with limited legal recourse if they wished to bring a partner to Japan or return as a couple. In many cases, Japanese consulates and embassies offered no advocacy or support, further underscoring the state's reluctance to acknowledge the rights of queer families.

Economic vulnerability compounded these legal insecurities. Temporary or contract workers—often overrepresented among migrants—were among the first to lose jobs during the pandemic. Without a recognized spouse or partner, Japanese LGBTQ+ migrants abroad could not access emergency relief or social safety nets. This left them not only financially unstable but also more susceptible to housing insecurity and forced relocations. These cascading effects reveal how the invisibility of LGBTQ+ individuals in legal systems can translate into tangible, life-altering hardships during crises.

6.3.2 Disruption of Healthcare and Community Access

Healthcare emerged as another major site of struggle for Japanese LGBTQ+ migrants during the pandemic. For transgender individuals, the interruption of global supply chains and medical services meant disruptions to hormone therapy or gender-affirming surgeries. Even for cisgender LGBTQ+ individuals, navigating foreign healthcare systems without a legally recognized partner could prove challenging, as hospital visitation rights and insurance coverage are often contingent upon marital or familial status.

Cultural and linguistic barriers further complicated these challenges. Migrants who did not speak the local language fluently often found themselves excluded from public health information, vaccine registration, or mental health services. For queer migrants, this exclusion was particularly acute given the limited availability of LGBTQ+ -competent care, which is rarely prioritized in mainstream medical systems.

Chia-hao's narrative highlights how his limited Japanese proficiency intersected with pandemic restrictions to heighten isolation: "Before the pandemic, I could feel that Japanese people are reluctant to speak to foreigners... After the pandemic, I had no chances to chat with my colleagues, let alone [discuss] my sexuality." This lack of interpersonal connection not only affected his workplace life but also cut him off from informal networks of support that are often crucial for queer individuals navigating health and social systems abroad.

The pandemic also disrupted queer community networks, which often serve as informal healthcare and mental health resources. LGBTQ+ bars, organizations, and events—places where migrants could seek information, solidarity, and friendship—were shuttered for long periods. For many, digital alternatives like online meetups or chat groups offered some connection, but they were insufficient. Online spaces lacked the embodied sense of belonging that physical gatherings provide, leaving many feeling adrift.

Niran's experience in Sendai underscores this loss of community:

> I feel like there are very few occasions to meet other LGBTQ+ members in Japan, even fewer in Sendai. My Japanese skill is not at the communicable level. I think it is harder to meet new friends during the pandemic. We usually do the same routine every day, so it is difficult to meet LGBTQ+ friends.

His testimony points to the compounded effects of language barriers, limited local queer infrastructure, and pandemic restrictions—factors that combined to create profound social and emotional isolation.

6.4 Binational Same-Sex Couples: Forced Separation and Legal Exclusion

The COVID-19 pandemic laid bare the deep vulnerabilities faced by binational same-sex couples, particularly in Japan where legal recognition of LGBTQ+ partnerships remains absent at the national level. While many heterosexual families were able to rely on marriage certificates to secure entry permits or special re-entry rights during the state of emergency, same-sex couples were systematically excluded from these humanitarian provisions. The crisis exposed the structural inequality at the heart of Japan's immigration and family policies: that the state continues to define "family" in narrowly heteronormative terms, leaving queer couples outside the framework of protection.

This exclusion was not just an administrative oversight but a reflection of a broader cultural and legal stance. In Japan, where same-sex marriage is not legally recognized, even long-term same-sex partners have no spousal rights, inheritance protections, or official family status. During the pandemic, this legal vacuum transformed an already precarious situation into a humanitarian crisis for binational LGBTQ+ couples, who were often separated for months or even years without any clear timeline for reunion. Their stories underscore the profound emotional and psychological costs of being denied the basic right to live with and care for a partner.

6.4.1 The Impact of Japan's Border Policies

Japan's pandemic-era border policies revealed an implicit hierarchy of whose relationships mattered to the state. As borders closed in 2020, Japanese immigration authorities made provisions for heterosexual spouses of Japanese nationals or permanent residents, allowing them to re-enter the country under the banner of family unity. Same-sex partners, however, were deemed ineligible for such exceptions, as their relationships were not recognized under existing legal frameworks. This policy left queer couples stranded, sometimes on opposite sides of the world, with little recourse.

The emotional toll of this exclusion cannot be overstated. Couples who had built their lives together—sharing financial responsibilities, housing, and caregiving duties—were suddenly treated as strangers under the law. Shufen, a Taiwanese lesbian living in Osaka, described how the border closures intensified the fragility of her relationship and sense of security:

> I cannot see my partner because I can't go back to Taiwan. It affected our relationship quite a bit. Our lives are getting further and further apart because I can't see her. I wanted to go back to Taiwan and get married last year, but I can't even see her, let alone get married. I can't see the future because I can't see her.

For couples like Shufen and her partner, the inability to even travel for personal milestones such as marriage ceremonies symbolized the deep disconnect between their lived reality and the state's conception of family. The pandemic thus magnified the invisibility that same-sex couples already experience in Japan, turning it into a tangible barrier to their emotional and relational well-being.

Legal invisibility also compounded logistical and financial challenges. Many couples found themselves unable to apply for dependent or spousal visas that would have allowed them to remain together in one country. Even when partners shared financial obligations or cohabited for years, the absence of a marriage certificate meant that immigration officers treated their relationships as legally irrelevant. This left some individuals with no option but to extend expensive temporary visas, find separate housing arrangements, or live in prolonged uncertainty.

The strain of separation was not limited to logistics but also impacted mental health. Several participants reported heightened anxiety, insomnia, and depression as they grappled with the unpredictability of border closures and the lack of official acknowledgment for their relationships. The pandemic thus acted as a cruel stress test, revealing how the absence of legal recognition translates into a lack of institutional care during emergencies.

6.4.2 Structural Inequalities and Advocacy Efforts

The hardships endured by binational same-sex couples during COVID-19 cannot be understood in isolation from the structural inequality embedded in Japanese family and immigration law. Although some municipalities have introduced partnership certificates (*pātonāshippu seido*), these are symbolic measures with no binding legal power. They offer neither visa rights nor federal recognition, leaving couples without tangible protections during border closures.

The contrast with other countries was stark. Taiwan, which legalized same-sex marriage in 2019, extended travel exemptions to same-sex spouses during the pandemic, allowing for family reunification even under strict border controls. Similarly, several European Union countries recognized registered partnerships or civil unions as valid grounds for family-related travel exemptions. These policies underscore Japan's status as an outlier among advanced economies, particularly in its refusal to modernize family law to account for diverse kinship structures.

Shufen's (FJ, 35–44) narrative highlights how this gap in legal recognition not only affected her ability to reunite with her partner but also eroded her sense of stability and future planning:

> I miss my family. I miss my partner. I haven't seen my partner in over a year, and I am not sure how long it will last. I am worried about how long it will last. The Japanese quarantine is too bad, and the speed of vaccination is too slow.

Her testimony, marked by both longing and frustration, exemplifies how legal exclusion transcends national borders, creating a state of perpetual liminality for queer couples.

Advocacy efforts emerged during the pandemic, both within Japan and internationally, to highlight these inequities. Organizations such as Marriage For All Japan mobilized public attention around the plight of couples separated by border restrictions, using this moment to emphasize that marriage equality is not only a matter of civil rights but also a basic humanitarian concern. Social media and online platforms were actively used to amplify these voices, with campaigns and petitions circulating to pressure lawmakers to address the issue. Activists also drew comparisons to countries that introduced emergency measures to recognize same-sex couples, urging Japan to follow suit.

Nevertheless, these advocacy efforts faced formidable challenges. The Japanese government's conservative stance on family law, coupled with the slow pace of judicial reforms, meant that immediate relief for affected couples was unlikely. While court cases challenging the constitutionality of Japan's marriage laws gained public attention—such as the Sapporo District Court's 2021 ruling that the ban on same-sex marriage was "unconstitutional"—these legal milestones did not translate into policy changes during the pandemic. For couples like Shufen and her partner, the advocacy offered symbolic hope but little concrete assistance.

The plight of binational same-sex couples during COVID-19 thus highlights the deeply intertwined nature of legal recognition, emotional well-being, and mobility. The inability to secure basic rights such as cohabitation or family reunification during crises underscores the urgent need for reforms that extend beyond symbolic gestures. Legal recognition of same-sex marriage or partnerships would not only affirm LGBTQ+ relationships as valid but also provide practical protections—spousal visas, hospital visitation rights, and the ability to make joint decisions in times of emergency.

6.4.3 Legal Debates and Media Visibility During COVID-19

The pandemic period coincided with a pivotal moment in Japan's ongoing debate over marriage equality. In March 2021, the Sapporo District Court ruled that Japan's refusal to recognize same-sex marriage was unconstitutional under Article 14 of the Japanese Constitution, which guarantees equality under the law. While this landmark decision did not result in immediate legal changes, it significantly shifted public discourse, bringing renewed attention to the legal invisibility of LGBTQ+ couples—a reality that was acutely felt by binational same-sex couples separated by COVID-19 border policies.

Media coverage of the Sapporo ruling frequently highlighted the struggles of couples who could not be together during the pandemic. Stories of partners unable to attend each other's medical emergencies or family events gained traction in national and international news outlets, humanizing the abstract legal debate. In interviews with advocacy groups such as Marriage For All Japan, couples shared their experiences of forced separation, illustrating how the lack of legal recognition had tangible consequences during crises. These narratives resonated widely, reinforcing the argument that marriage equality is not merely a symbolic issue but a matter of everyday rights and security.

For example, many online campaigns featured testimonials from binational couples who were denied entry despite years of cohabitation. These personal accounts, much like Shufen's experience, revealed how long-term commitment was rendered invisible by Japan's lack of legal recognition. Activists and couples used social media to share these stories and advocate for reform, drawing attention to the human cost of exclusion. Campaigns often pointed to Taiwan—where same-sex marriage has been legalized—as a model for ensuring that couples could remain together, even during pandemic-related border closures.

Moreover, the pandemic spurred conversations about what constitutes "family" in Japanese law and society. Critics argued that Japan's immigration policies, which prioritized heterosexual marital ties, reinforced outdated notions of kinship that excluded not only LGBTQ+ couples but also unmarried partners and other non-traditional family structures. This discourse created a moment of reflection and potential change, even if legislative progress remained slow.

For binational couples, the media visibility and legal debates offered both hope and frustration. While court cases like the Sapporo ruling symbolized progress, they did not alleviate the immediate pain of separation. As one activist remarked during an online campaign: "The courts recognize that our love is equal, but the law still treats us as strangers. The pandemic made this painfully clear."

The juxtaposition of legal momentum with lived experiences of exclusion underscores the gap between legal recognition and practical rights. Until Japan implements a national system for same-sex marriage or partnership recognition, binational LGBTQ+ couples will continue to face barriers not only in times of crisis but also in daily life.

6.5 Non-Japanese LGBTQ+ Individuals in Japan: Intersectional Barriers

The pandemic brought to light the precarious status of non-Japanese LGBTQ+ individuals living in Japan, whose experiences were shaped by a combination of visa dependency, racial discrimination, linguistic challenges, and social exclusion. For these individuals, queerness intersected with foreignness, amplifying their vulnerability. While Japan is often viewed as a safe place for LGBTQ+ travelers and expatriates, the COVID-19 crisis revealed the systemic barriers that persist, particularly for racialized and migrant queer populations.

The narratives of participants such as Emma (a queer American teacher), Alejandro (a gay man from Peru), Aanan (a South Asian professional), and Fenhua (a Chinese graduate student) illustrate the layers of discrimination they faced during the pandemic. These included not only workplace precarity and exclusion from government financial aid but also microaggressions and overt racial bias, particularly when foreigners were perceived as "virus carriers." The absence of culturally competent healthcare and the closure of queer social spaces further compounded their isolation. These testimonies demonstrate how pandemic conditions intensified the marginalization of non-Japanese LGBTQ+ individuals, who were often rendered invisible in both mainstream policy responses and LGBTQ+ activism that tends to focus on Japanese nationals.

6.5.1 Visa and Employment Insecurity

Japan's visa system, which ties legal residency to employment or education, left many non-Japanese workers with little protection during pandemic-related economic downturns. LGBTQ+ individuals were disproportionately affected due to the lack of alternative family-based pathways to secure residency. Unlike heterosexual spouses who could rely on marriage certificates for dependent visas, same-sex partners had no legal standing, leaving them without fallback options when work contracts were canceled or not renewed.

Emma, a bisexual American woman working as a JET Programme instructor, described her anxieties regarding employment and visa renewal:

> Immigrants who do not have permanent residency rights are at a risk of getting fired if they are infected with COVID-19. Losing your job means not being able to renew your visa. In this crisis, it would be difficult to find work at home too, and there are many fees involved with the entire process.

Her statement reflects the precarious balance many foreign workers had to maintain—continuing to work under risky conditions, even with health concerns, for fear of jeopardizing their visa status.

Aanan (FJ, 45–54), a Canadian citizen of South Asian descent, echoed these fears. His work in a redevelopment project in Tokyo demanded frequent in-person meetings, even during the state of emergency:

> As foreign workers and racial minorities we are here to perform a service and our visas depend on it. If I were to stop going to meetings, my project would be at risk and thus my life here with my partner would also be at risk. I feel especially vulnerable as a visible minority so I do not reveal my sexuality to the entire client team.

For Aanan, being both a foreigner and gay added multiple layers of risk, from the potential loss of legal status to the fear of discrimination in professional settings.

Alejandro (FJ, 25–34), a gay man from Peru, highlighted the stigma associated with foreignness during the pandemic:

> Many people thought COVID-19 was something people who went overseas were bringing, and immigrants and other people with foreign roots were targeted in a way. Even at work, people would ask me if I had been back home recently out of fear I would be infected with COVID.

Although Alejandro retained his job, the xenophobic undertones of these interactions left him feeling hyper-visible yet unacknowledged as part of the Japanese community.

6.5.2 Racial Discrimination and Social Exclusion

The pandemic fueled racialized perceptions of foreigners as potential disease carriers, adding another layer of social exclusion to the experiences of non-Japanese LGBTQ+

individuals. For many participants, this intersected with queerness in ways that heightened their sense of marginality. While Japan's LGBTQ+ community is often portrayed as relatively welcoming, participants noted that racial biases persisted even within queer spaces, particularly against Southeast Asian and Chinese individuals.

Fenhua (FJ, 18–24), a gay graduate student from China, shared his experiences with both housing discrimination and everyday microaggressions:

> When I tried to pay at a convenience store, the clerk suddenly became cold when I said 'with Alipay.' It happened twice. When I moved to a new house for graduate school, a real estate agent asked me what my nationality was even though there was a tag that said 'foreigners are OK.' When I told him I was Chinese, he refused to rent to me.

While Fenhua found Japan less overtly discriminatory compared to China, these incidents reveal the intersection of race and nationality as a barrier to everyday life, which was intensified by the atmosphere of fear during COVID-19.

Emma similarly noted that while she feels safe as a queer woman in Japan, she feels perpetually "unseen" and excluded due to her status as a foreigner: "I will never, ever fit in, no matter how good my Japanese is or how hard I work. It can be very alienating, and I have never gotten the impression that the Japanese government wants any of that to change." Her experience highlights how racialized assumptions about foreignness shape not only access to services but also the ability to build social and professional relationships.

Even within queer spaces, some participants reported racialized hierarchies. Alejandro observed that foreign LGBTQ+ individuals are sometimes treated with curiosity or tokenized for their appearance, while others—especially those from Latin America or Southeast Asia—felt unwelcome. Such experiences of exclusion within spaces that should be affirming exacerbated feelings of isolation during the pandemic.

6.5.3 *Healthcare Access and Language Barriers*

Healthcare access was another area where non-Japanese LGBTQ+ individuals encountered significant challenges. Although Japan's national healthcare system covers most residents, linguistic barriers and the lack of LGBTQ+ -competent medical care often deterred participants from seeking treatment. The pandemic amplified these difficulties as healthcare systems became strained, public information was released primarily in Japanese, and foreign residents struggled to find trustworthy sources of guidance.

Emily, an asexual teacher from the United States, described her experience of navigating healthcare in Japan:

> It is difficult to know what clinics I can go to that speak English. Being under pressure, especially in healthcare situations, is embarrassing and overwhelming. Information about costs or procedures is not readily available on most clinic websites, which makes it doubly difficult to choose one from the thousands that are within a reasonable distance from my apartment.

Her account underscores how the lack of accessible information and English-speaking staff often left foreign residents hesitant to seek care, even for urgent health concerns.

Aanan similarly noted the challenge of finding a healthcare provider who would not only accommodate linguistic needs but also respect his sexual identity:

> I already experience enough discrimination as a foreigner. I don't want to have any more negative energy directed towards me. I think this probably affects my ability to get proper health care and advice from doctors. I am still looking for a more open and gay-friendly and foreigner-friendly doctor.

For transgender or non-binary migrants, the barriers were even greater. While none of the narratives here specifically address transgender foreign residents, global reports during the pandemic showed that trans individuals often faced disruptions in hormone therapy or gender-affirming treatments due to both supply chain issues and lack of medical expertise. The absence of supportive healthcare infrastructures for LGBTQ+ foreigners in Japan made these challenges even more acute.

6.6 Disrupted Queer Networks: Loss of Community Spaces

The COVID-19 pandemic led to the widespread closure of LGBTQ+ spaces in Japan—ranging from Tokyo's Ni-chōme nightlife district to Pride events, informal support groups, and community centers. These closures removed crucial sites of connection, solidarity, and visibility for queer individuals, both Japanese and foreign. While digital platforms emerged as alternative spaces, they were insufficient substitutes for the affective and social dimensions of in-person gatherings. Participants repeatedly described the resulting loss as one of both community and identity—a silencing of the spaces where they felt most "seen" and affirmed.

For many LGBTQ+ individuals, these community venues were more than sites of leisure; they were essential infrastructures of belonging. Ni-chōme, for instance, has long been recognized as a hub for gay nightlife, activism, and cross-cultural connections in Tokyo. With bars shuttered, Pride parades canceled, and gatherings deemed unsafe, participants reported a deep sense of disconnection and loneliness, intensified by Japan's emphasis on self-restraint (jishuku). For foreigners who relied on these spaces to navigate cultural and linguistic barriers, the closures were particularly isolating.

6.6.1 Closure of LGBTQ+ Venues and Events

Ni-chōme's nightlife scene, which thrives on close social interaction, was among the first to be impacted. Bars and clubs either temporarily closed or restricted operations under government pressure. Pride events, which provide not only visibility but also a rare platform for queer networking outside urban centers, were canceled for two consecutive years. These cancellations removed opportunities for participants to connect with others who shared similar experiences and identities.

Emma (FJ, 25–44), a queer American woman, described the impact of these closures on her sense of community:

> There are no women-friendly LGBTQ+ spaces in my area, and I have been unable to travel to cities with more opportunities for meeting people, events, support, etc. (Osaka, Nagoya, Tokyo) during the pandemic. Without that, every aspect of my life is affected... There are extremely few opportunities to meet other members of the LGBTQ+ community, let alone date anyone, outside of the bigger cities.

For Emma, whose rural placement already limited access to queer spaces, the pandemic meant complete isolation from the broader LGBTQ+ network. The absence of Pride and social events intensified feelings of invisibility and disconnection.

Alejandro, a gay man from Peru, reflected on how gay bars and clubs function as safe spaces for self-expression and community-building:

> I think that gay/lesbian bars and similar establishments in general are a big part of daily life for many people in the LGBTQ+ community as they offer a safe place to talk openly about themselves, meet other LGBTQ+ people, etc. With the COVID-19 related restrictions to bars and such establishments, such interactions are now limited... I feel like I've lost my connection to the LGBTQ+ community staying indoors more often than before.

For Alejandro, whose experience as both a foreigner and a queer man already set him apart from mainstream Japanese society, these closures represented the loss of a vital anchor to his identity.

6.6.2 Digital Platforms: Partial but Insufficient Substitutes

While digital tools such as Zoom meetups, social media groups, and dating apps saw increased usage during the pandemic, they rarely offered the same sense of intimacy, safety, and belonging as physical spaces. Many participants expressed "digital fatigue," noting that online events lacked the energy and spontaneity of in-person gatherings. Virtual Pride events, while symbolically important, could not replicate the collective atmosphere of marching through city streets or celebrating queer visibility in public.

Skyler (FJ, 25–34), a queer professional from the United States, described their ambivalence toward online interactions:

> One connection to the community has been entertainment venues on a very occasional basis, and with those closed, likewise has that line of connection. I have also been using dating/social apps (both LGBTQ+-oriented and not) to meet new people but I've held back from meeting too many people in an effort to maintain (figurative) social distance. I think constantly being at home and not going outside as often in general has likely made me feel more isolated from any community, let alone specifically the LGBTQ+ community.

For Skyler, the inability to casually meet others in safe, affirming spaces led to increased feelings of loneliness, even as digital tools provided surface-level connections.

Emma also noted the limitations of online alternatives:

> Most people in the LGBTQ+ community meet each other through previously established friends. Without events in general, there's no way to meet anyone new. All social services require you to go to a physical location, which usually necessitates public transit. When food or drink is involved in an indoor setting, there is always a chance to spread COVID. I cannot go and meet new LGBTQ+ people because all events are either indoors without proper distancing (because of food/drink, etc.), or because the other events were canceled.

Her testimony highlights the interdependency of physical spaces, social networks, and community-building, as well as how digital alternatives often exclude those who are new to a community or lack pre-existing contacts.

6.6.3 The Emotional Toll of Community Loss

The absence of queer spaces and events carried not just social consequences but also emotional and psychological ones. For many LGBTQ+ individuals—especially those facing family rejection or isolation in workplaces—community spaces serve as affirming environments where they can freely express their identities. Their closure during the pandemic left many participants feeling invisible, as Emma reflected: "As a queer woman, I feel much safer in Japan. I'm not worried about telling someone and getting an extremely negative or violent reaction. What's uncomfortable is feeling unseen, uncelebrated, and unimportant."

Alejandro's comments similarly underscore how the absence of shared spaces limited opportunities for collective resilience: without these venues, informal support networks and friendships that often sustain queer individuals during crises were harder to maintain. Digital spaces, while useful for communication, often lacked the affective energy that arises from physical gatherings—an energy that fosters belonging, activism, and emotional sustenance.

6.7 Analysis: Borders, Citizenship, and Queer Belonging

The narratives presented in this chapter reveal that nation-state borders and immigration policies function as powerful heteronormative apparatuses that define who is considered family and, therefore, who is entitled to rights, mobility, and care. Borders are not simply geographic boundaries but ideological constructs that reinforce normative kinship structures, privileging heterosexual marital bonds while rendering queer relationships illegible. During the COVID-19 pandemic, these dynamics were amplified. For Japanese LGBTQ+ migrants and non-Japanese queer residents, the state's failure to recognize same-sex partnerships transformed what should have been a public health crisis into a personal humanitarian crisis.

The Japanese government's refusal to legally recognize same-sex partnerships starkly illustrates the relationship between citizenship and heteronormativity. During the pandemic, heterosexual spouses of Japanese nationals or permanent residents were routinely granted special entry permits and other humanitarian exemptions. Same-sex couples, however, were excluded, as their relationships lacked the legal status required by immigration authorities. This structural omission reinforced a hierarchy of kinship, in which queer families were treated as if they were nonexistent. Shufen's separation from her partner in Taiwan exemplifies this logic of exclusion: despite their committed relationship and intention to marry, their bond was invisible in the eyes of the Japanese state. Her narrative underscores what Berlant (1998) has called the "cruel optimism" of intimacy under neoliberal governance—the promise of private happiness and security through love, thwarted by state structures that recognize only certain forms of intimacy as legitimate.

Borders, as theorized by Puar (2007), are not neutral mechanisms of regulation but are deeply embedded in the biopolitical production of normativity. The Japanese state, through its immigration and family policies, reproduces an ideal of family rooted in heterosexuality, patrilineal continuity, and the nuclear household. By refusing to recognize same-sex partnerships, Japan effectively externalized its domestic heteronormativity into the transnational realm, forcing queer couples to navigate a system that privileges biological and heterosexual ties over chosen families. The pandemic magnified this existing bias, leaving queer couples in a state of legal and emotional limbo.

This transnational exclusion forms what might be described as a "chain of vulnerability" that spans multiple jurisdictions. Japanese LGBTQ+ migrants abroad faced difficulties in securing spousal visas or family benefits, while non-Japanese queer residents in Japan encountered similar legal invisibility, with no rights to sponsor a same-sex partner or access family-based relief programs. These experiences demonstrate that legal recognition in one country—or its absence—often reverberates across borders, shaping the life chances of queer individuals in profoundly inequitable ways.

6.7.1 Queer Diaspora, Mobility, and Disidentification

From the perspective of queer diaspora studies, these narratives illuminate the tension between mobility and belonging. Migration is often imagined as a form of liberation—an opportunity to escape domestic homophobia or restrictive cultural norms. Yet, as the testimonies of Chia-hao and Niran reveal, queer migrants remain constrained by legal systems, cultural hierarchies, and border regimes that are not designed to accommodate non-normative forms of intimacy. Muñoz's (1999) concept of disidentification—where marginalized subjects navigate and resist dominant cultural logics—resonates here. Many participants employed creative strategies to maintain relationships and build community when institutional pathways were blocked: digital platforms, social apps, and informal online networks became crucial tools for sustaining queer intimacy and solidarity.

However, as both Alejandro and Emma's experiences suggest, these digital spaces were inadequate substitutes for physical gatherings. Online interactions lacked the affective energy, spontaneity, and embodied affirmation that queer community spaces provide. The pandemic thus revealed how fragile queer belonging can be when it relies on infrastructures—nightlife districts, Pride events, or advocacy groups—that were among the first to shut down during lockdowns and among the last to recover.

6.7.2 Citizenship, Race, and Queer Exclusion

Citizenship itself emerged as a central axis of inequality. Non-Japanese LGBTQ+ residents like Emma, Alejandro, and Aanan faced the precarity of temporary visas, often tied to employment contracts that could be terminated without warning. This left them with few options to remain in the country during periods of economic instability. Their status as foreigners intersected with their sexual or gender identity to create what Cohen (1997) would call a "secondary marginalization," where racialized and queer identities compound vulnerability rather than existing as separate categories of oppression.

Racial discrimination added another layer of exclusion. Fenhua's encounters with housing discrimination and microaggressions highlight how racialized perceptions of "foreignness" were heightened during the pandemic, often intersecting with homophobia or queer invisibility. Japanese citizenship—tied to ideas of ethnic homogeneity and cultural conformity—remained a barrier to belonging for many LGBTQ+ foreigners, even those who were fluent in Japanese or deeply embedded in local communities. These experiences underscore that legal membership in the nation-state is intertwined with racialized and heteronormative conceptions of who counts as a legitimate member of society.

6.7.3 Queer Kinship and Intimate Publics

The narratives also challenge conventional definitions of family and kinship, pointing to what Eng (2010) describes as "queer kinship" and Berlant's notion of "intimate publics." Queer couples and chosen families often operate outside the boundaries of legal recognition, yet they form robust networks of care and support. The pandemic disrupted these networks, exposing their fragility in the absence of institutional backing. The exclusion of same-sex partners from border exemptions not only separated couples like Shufen and her partner but also sent a broader message that their love and commitment were less valuable than those of heterosexual couples.

The lack of recognition also had a symbolic effect, eroding the sense of belonging that queer couples had painstakingly built across national borders. As Aanan reflected, his life in Japan—despite being with a Japanese partner—felt tenuous because his relationship lacked any legal protection. This sense of "perpetual foreignness" extended beyond nationality to encompass sexuality, as queer couples were denied the legal markers that signify stability and legitimacy.

6.7.4 *The Need for Rethinking Borders and Belonging*

Ultimately, the narratives in this chapter highlight the urgent need to rethink how borders, citizenship, and family recognition intersect with queer lives. Legal recognition of same-sex partnerships would not only provide symbolic affirmation of LGBTQ+ relationships but also confer tangible protections: spousal visas, access to healthcare, inheritance rights, and the ability to remain together during crises. Without such recognition, queer individuals remain at the mercy of arbitrary state policies that fail to account for the realities of non-heteronormative kinship.

The pandemic thus serves as a wake-up call, revealing the inadequacy of current legal frameworks to protect all families. It also underscores the potential of transnational queer solidarity and activism. As the advocacy efforts of Marriage For All Japan and international networks have shown, the visibility of separated couples during COVID-19 has galvanized broader support for marriage equality. Yet, these efforts will require sustained pressure on policymakers to dismantle the heteronormative assumptions embedded in state structures.

The narratives presented here emphasize that the challenges faced by LGBTQ+ individuals during the pandemic were not solely about border closures or policy failures but about the deeper issue of precarious visibility. Queer migrants and binational couples were seen only when they fell outside normative definitions of "family" or "citizen," yet remained invisible when rights and protections were allocated. This tension underscores the urgency of rethinking legal recognition, border policies, and the meaning of belonging in ways that affirm the diversity of queer lives.

6.7.5 *Queer Theoretical Perspectives on Borders and Belonging*

The following conclusion brings together these insights to highlight pathways toward legal recognition, healthcare reform, and transnational solidarity.

The experiences in this chapter reveal how borders, citizenship, and legal recognition operate as heteronormative apparatuses, reinforcing who is deemed worthy of protection and who is not. Humanitarian entry exemptions during the pandemic, for instance, prioritized heterosexual family units while disregarding the realities of binational same-sex couples. Puar's (2007) concept of homonationalism helps explain this selective recognition, where "acceptable" queer subjects—often white, married, and economically stable—are legitimized, while others are excluded.

This exclusion placed immense strain on intimate relationships. Many participants expressed faith in love and partnership as sources of stability, only to see those bonds legally invalidated at the border. Berlant's (2008) notion of "cruel optimism" captures this tension: the very ideals that sustain hope—such as marriage and family—can become obstacles when filtered through state structures that deny queer legitimacy. For Shufen and her partner, the desire to reunite became entwined with legal frameworks that treated their relationship as nonexistent.

Rather than accepting these exclusions, Japanese LGBTQ+ migrants and foreign residents devised creative ways to endure and resist. Through digital networks, mutual aid, and campaigns like #BringUsTogether, they practiced what Muñoz (1999) calls disidentification—engaging with dominant systems while subtly reworking them to sustain queer kinship across borders. These acts were neither fully oppositional nor fully assimilative, but adaptive strategies that kept connections alive.

The erasure of queer families in immigration policies also mirrors the logic of the closet, where recognition is partial, conditional, and easily revoked. Eng's (2010) idea of queer kinship and Sedgwick's (1990) analysis of the closet highlight how these legal invisibilities produce both structural and emotional harm. Yet, participants' insistence on their right to live with and care for their partners challenges these state-imposed boundaries, carving out what Muñoz would describe as "queer horizons"—alternative visions of belonging that surpass the narrow definitions enforced by law.

6.8 Conclusion: Lessons and Legal Reforms

The narratives presented in this chapter illustrate how precarious visibility shaped the lives of Japanese LGBTQ+ migrants abroad and non-Japanese queer residents in Japan during the COVID-19 pandemic. Border closures, visa insecurities, and the absence of legal recognition for same-sex partnerships rendered queer relationships both hyper-visible—as "exceptions" scrutinized by immigration authorities—and invisible, as they were excluded from protections routinely extended to heterosexual couples. For participants like Shufen, the inability to reunite with her partner in Taiwan was not simply a logistical issue but a painful reminder of how legal systems erase queer kinship. Similarly, foreign residents such as Emma and Alejandro described the dual burden of racialized assumptions and a lack of institutional support, which compounded their sense of alienation.

The pandemic exposed how heteronormative and nationalist logics intersect to define who counts as family, who is entitled to mobility, and who is left behind. Immigration and labor policies reinforced these exclusions, while public health measures offered little consideration for queer or binational couples. Yet, despite these systemic barriers, participants demonstrated resilience, turning to digital platforms, advocacy campaigns like #BringUsTogether, and informal support networks to sustain connection and care.

6.8.1 Legal Recognition of Queer Families

The need for legal recognition of same-sex partnerships is inseparable from the broader condition of precarious visibility described throughout this chapter. Without formal recognition, queer families are rendered both hyper-visible when denied rights—such as spousal visas or re-entry permits—and invisible when state protections and benefits are distributed exclusively to heterosexual couples.

The urgent need for the legal recognition of same-sex partnerships cannot be overstated. Without legal recognition, same-sex couples are denied access to spousal visas, hospital visitation rights, joint property ownership, and critical financial protections—rights automatically granted to heterosexual couples. The inability of binational queer couples to reunite during the pandemic made visible the devastating consequences of such legal invisibility.

Legalizing same-sex marriage or establishing a nationwide partnership recognition system would not only align Japan with global human rights standards but also fulfill obligations outlined in international frameworks, such as the Yogyakarta Principles, which affirm the right to family and freedom from discrimination based on sexual orientation and gender identity. Furthermore, Japan's failure to recognize same-sex partnerships is increasingly at odds with its image as a modern, globally connected democracy. Countries like Taiwan, which legalized same-sex marriage in 2019, have demonstrated how recognition can enhance both domestic equality and international credibility.

6.8.2 Reforming Immigration and Labor Protections

The pandemic highlighted the vulnerability of foreign residents, whose visa status is tightly bound to employment. For LGBTQ+ foreigners, who lack the option of a spousal or family visa, this dependency can become a source of acute instability. Policy reforms are necessary to create alternative pathways to permanent residency, particularly for long-term residents and those who contribute to Japan's economy and culture. Additionally, extending anti-discrimination protections in the workplace—covering both sexual orientation and gender identity—would address the compounded precarity faced by foreign queer workers who may experience both racial and sexual bias.

During COVID-19, government relief measures were largely unavailable to non-citizens or tied to specific employment categories. This exclusion revealed a need for inclusive emergency support policies that recognize the contributions and vulnerabilities of foreign residents, regardless of their marital status or visa type.

6.8.3 Healthcare Access and Cultural Competence

Healthcare accessibility for queer migrants must become a priority. The pandemic exposed significant gaps in public health communication, which was often available only in Japanese and failed to consider the needs of sexual minorities. Participants like Emily described the overwhelming challenge of finding English-speaking or LGBTQ+ -friendly clinics. To address this, Japan should invest in multilingual public health services, train healthcare professionals in culturally sensitive and LGBTQ+ -affirming care, and ensure that foreign residents have equal access to mental health resources.

For transgender and non-binary migrants, the situation is particularly urgent. Interruptions to gender-affirming healthcare during COVID-19 revealed the absence of robust systems to support their unique medical needs. Providing clear guidance, streamlining hormone therapy access, and offering targeted counseling services would mitigate the structural barriers these individuals face.

6.8.4 Global and Transnational Advocacy

The pandemic revealed the power of international queer solidarity. Online campaigns, petitions, and transnational advocacy efforts during COVID-19—such as those led by Marriage For All Japan—helped bring visibility to the struggles of separated binational couples. These movements not only highlighted domestic injustices but also connected Japan's LGBTQ+ issues to a broader global discourse on human rights.

Aligning with frameworks like the United Nations Sustainable Development Goals (SDGs)—specifically SDG 10 (Reduced Inequalities) and SDG 16 (Peace, Justice, and Strong Institutions)—could help Japan advance a more inclusive and equitable policy agenda. The experiences of countries such as Taiwan, Canada, and several EU nations, which extended emergency exemptions or recognized same-sex partnerships during COVID-19, offer models for reform that balance public health priorities with human rights.

6.8.5 Toward Equality and Belonging

The pandemic served as both a magnifier and a mirror: it magnified pre-existing inequalities while reflecting the urgent need for systemic change. For Japanese LGBTQ+ migrants and non-Japanese queer residents, COVID-19 underscored how easily legal invisibility and border regimes can sever relationships, disrupt livelihoods, and erode well-being. The stories shared in this chapter reveal not only personal hardships but also the structural foundations of queer exclusion in Japan's legal and social frameworks.

The path forward requires both domestic reforms and transnational collaboration. Legal recognition of diverse family structures, stronger protections for foreign residents, and inclusive healthcare systems are essential steps toward genuine equality. The resilience demonstrated by queer individuals and communities during the pandemic—through online activism, mutual aid, and advocacy—offers a blueprint for building more inclusive systems of care. These acts of solidarity highlight that community ingenuity cannot substitute for institutional responsibility; structural change must accompany grassroots resilience.

Above all, the pandemic highlights the need to dismantle the conditions of precarious visibility—where queer individuals are hyper-visible when excluded or scrutinized, yet invisible when rights and protections are allocated. Legal recognition of same-sex partnerships, inclusive healthcare and labor protections, and equitable immigration policies are vital to creating a society where queer families are valued and supported, both domestically and across borders.

The next chapter turns to media representations and political discourse, exploring how visibility—while often celebrated—can also expose LGBTQ+ communities to new forms of scrutiny, misrepresentation, and contestation.

References

Berlant, L. (2008). *The female complaint: The unfinished business of sentimentality in American culture*. Duke University Press.

Cohen, C. J. (1997). Punks, bulldaggers, and welfare queens: The radical potential of queer politics? *GLQ: A Journal of Lesbian and Gay Studies*, 3(4), 437–465.

Eng, D. L. (2010). *The feeling of kinship: Queer liberalism and the racialization of intimacy*. Duke University Press.

Muñoz, J. E. (1999). *Disidentifications: Queers of color and the performance of politics*. University of Minnesota Press.

Puar, J. K. (2007). *Terrorist assemblages: Homonationalism in queer times*. Duke University Press.

Sedgwick, E. K. (1990). *Epistemology of the closet*. University of California Press.

Chapter 7
Precarious Visibility and Queer Solitude: Two Lives in and Beyond Japan During the COVID-19 Pandemic

Masami Tamagawa

Abstract This chapter examines the pandemic-era experiences of two Japanese LGBTQ+ individuals through in-depth case studies, highlighting the affective complexities of queer survival during crisis. While previous chapters focus on thematic patterns across survey and interview data, this chapter narrows the lens to explore the nuanced lives of "Himari," a bisexual university student studying in the United States, and "Sento," a gay man navigating work and family expectations in Chiba, Japan. Himari's narrative, marked by diasporic isolation, familial estrangement, and mental health struggles, underscores the emotional toll of invisibility and the absence of care. In contrast, Sento's story emphasizes quiet resilience, aesthetic self-stylization, and the refusal to disappear, revealing how queer life can flourish through subtle acts of presence rather than overt activism.

Through a comparative analysis of their experiences—focusing on visibility, kinship, temporality, and spatial navigation—the chapter challenges Western-centric models of "coming out" and underscores the importance of intersectional and culturally situated understandings of queerness. By combining narrative depth with theoretical reflection, this chapter not only documents the uneven realities of LGBTQ+ life during COVID-19 but also calls attention to the everyday acts of endurance and care that sustain queer individuals beyond moments of crisis.

7.1 The Value of Case Studies

While previous chapters have examined the Japanese LGBTQ+ community's pandemic experiences through thematic analysis and collective narratives, this chapter adopts a different approach. It presents two in-depth case studies, offering a closer look at how individual lives intersect with the structural and cultural forces discussed earlier. By slowing the narrative pace, these case studies highlight the complexity of personal histories, illustrating the interplay of identity, migration, family, and resilience in ways that broader surveys or aggregated accounts cannot fully capture.

M. Tamagawa, *Japanese LGBTQ+ Lives, Diasporic Voices, and Resilience*,
https://doi.org/10.1007/978-981-95-3105-9_7

The two cases featured here—Himari, a young bisexual woman studying abroad in the United States, and Sento, a gay man navigating work and family expectations in Japan—serve as representative yet singular voices. Both highlight the pandemic's disruptions to intimacy, mobility, and mental health, but they also reveal strategies of adaptation and self-assertion that transcend national and cultural boundaries. These stories emphasize how the pandemic amplified existing inequalities and vulnerabilities, while simultaneously fostering moments of reflection, growth, and solidarity.

The case study method allows us to revisit key themes—such as isolation, legal precarity, and community networks—through a personal lens. Rather than generalizing, these accounts underscore the diversity of LGBTQ+ experiences and challenge the assumption that there is a singular "pandemic narrative." Instead, they offer a mosaic of struggles and triumphs, reminding us that behind every data point lies a unique life story shaped by intersecting forms of marginalization and resilience.

7.2 Introduction: Precarious Visibility and Queer Solitude

The COVID-19 pandemic reshaped the world unevenly, magnifying longstanding inequities for some while providing moments of pause for others. For members of Japan's LGBTQ+ community—already navigating a complex terrain of legal ambiguity, cultural invisibility, and familial pressure—the pandemic intensified these challenges. This chapter examines these dynamics through two in-depth case studies: Himari, a bisexual university student studying in the United States, and Sento, a gay man in his early thirties living in Chiba, Japan.

These narratives underscore what I call precarious visibility: moments when LGBTQ+ individuals are seen only in partial or risky ways—visible enough to be marked as "different" but invisible when it comes to care, legal recognition, or social support. Himari's diasporic isolation, familial estrangement, and mental health struggles reveal the emotional toll of living in a state of near-invisibility, while Sento's narrative illustrates a quiet resilience grounded in aesthetic self-styling, balance, and everyday presence rather than overt activism. Their lives invite us to rethink how visibility, safety, and survival are negotiated in Japanese queer contexts during crisis.

The COVID-19 pandemic was not a rupture but an intensification of existing structural inequities. It exposed the cracks in Japan's heteronormative social compact and revealed the affective and infrastructural limits of queer life during sustained crisis. In Japan, marriage equality remains absent, anti-discrimination protections are minimal, and the *koseki* (family registry) system naturalizes heterosexual family structures, excluding same-sex couples from rights such as parental recognition, inheritance, and medical decision-making. Transgender individuals face additional legal hurdles, including intrusive requirements for gender-marker changes that, while partially challenged in recent court rulings, continue to pathologize their identities.

When the pandemic began, Japan's response emphasized communal responsibility through slogans like *jijo* (self-help), *kyōjo* (mutual aid), and *kōjo* (public assistance). Yet relief policies were largely structured around the nuclear family, leaving LGBTQ+ individuals—particularly those estranged from kin or living in non-traditional households—excluded from both economic support and public acknowledgment. Public discourse on vulnerability prioritized the elderly and immunocompromised, with far less attention paid to the specific mental health challenges, social isolation, or housing precarity faced by queer individuals.

In this climate of compounded marginalization, LGBTQ+ people in Japan navigated the pandemic with varying degrees of resilience and despair. Some found temporary reprieve in remote work or online classes, which allowed them to avoid hostile family members or heteronormative workplaces. Others, however, suffered deeply from the loss of physical queer spaces—bars, community centers, and Pride events—that had served as rare sites of connection and affirmation. Transgender participants were particularly affected by disruptions to affirming healthcare, such as hormone therapy or planned surgeries, which were delayed indefinitely. Yet amid these challenges, many also built alternative forms of care through digital platforms, mutual aid initiatives, and introspective practices of self-making.

This chapter builds on these themes by presenting a detailed examination of two pandemic-era narratives. It contributes to a growing body of literature documenting queer life under COVID-19 while emphasizing the specific cultural and institutional conditions of Japanese LGBTQ+ individuals. Existing research, often focused on North America and Western Europe, has documented rising mental health concerns, increases in domestic violence, disruptions to gender-affirming care, and broader social precarity (Fish et al. 2020; Salerno et al. 2020). However, the Japanese context adds distinct challenges: linguistic taboos around coming out, structural barriers to recognition, and a persistent reluctance to openly discuss queerness in public discourse.

It is grounded in a mixed-methods study conducted during the pandemic, combining an online survey with follow-up interviews of LGBTQ+ individuals of Japanese nationality or residence. From 137 survey responses, 16 participants were invited for in-depth semi-structured interviews. Two of these narratives, selected for their depth and contrast, form the basis of this chapter. For anonymity, "Himari" and "Sento" represent two poles of queer experience: diasporic introspection and domestic presence; affective unraveling and aesthetic composure.

Himari, a queer-identifying university student in California, reported heightened anxiety, depression, and a profound sense of dislocation—not only from Japan but from herself. Her narrative, marked by loss of intimacy, kinship, and clarity, illustrates how invisibility can become emotionally suffocating. Yet through journaling, online community fragments, and queer literature, she found ways to piece together a fragile sense of self.

Sento, by contrast, lives and works in Chiba, Japan, cultivating a life of balance and quiet resistance. While he is not "out" in the Western sense, he is not closeted either. His visibility is subtle and deliberate—expressed through personal aesthetics, daily rituals, and an insistence on living life on his own terms. While he acknowledges structural barriers, his pandemic experience reflects continuity rather than rupture.

These two narratives are not intended to be representative of all LGBTQ+ experiences in Japan. Rather, they serve as case studies that illustrate the affective textures of queer survival during a global crisis. They challenge dominant narratives of queer visibility and "coming out," showing that survival often relies on subtle strategies of endurance, self-care, and quiet resistance.

7.3 Himari: Queer Isolation and Transnational Unraveling

Himari's story illustrates the emotional toll of precarious visibility in a transnational context—where being queer is simultaneously invisible within her family and hypervisible in unfamiliar cultural settings. Her narrative, marked by isolation and deferred recognition, captures how queer survival abroad is shaped by the constant negotiation between safety, identity, and belonging.

When the COVID-19 pandemic disrupted universities across the United States in early 2020, Himari—then a young queer student in California—was already struggling. "It's not the virus that broke me," she said, looking down at the corner of her screen during our Zoom interview. "It's everything that the virus made impossible to ignore." At 22 years old, Himari lived alone in a small studio apartment, attending classes online, disconnected from family, and suspended in a state she described as "somewhere between Japan and nothing." Her story, like those of many transnational queer individuals during the pandemic, is not one of heroic resilience or political activism. It is a story of affective implosion: of loneliness, refusal, and the quiet work of staying alive without being seen.

Himari identifies as queer, both in terms of gender and sexuality, though she avoids pinning herself to fixed labels. "In English, I say 'queer.' In Japanese… I don't say anything," she said, laughing quietly. "It's safer that way." Her use of queer, then, is not only a sexual or political marker but a diasporic linguistic practice—something available only in English, only in exile. The category of "transgender" does not fit her self-conception, though her narrative is shaped by gender nonconformity and discomfort with normative femininity. "My parents expected a daughter who was cute and obedient," she said. "I couldn't be that. I didn't want to be a son either. I just wanted to be me." Her disidentification with binary gender expectations reflects what Muñoz (1999) described as a refusal to align with normative scripts—a queer gesture not of assertion but of opting out.

In the survey, Himari selected "queer" for both gender and sexual identity, and marked her comfort level in Japanese society as low. She reported feeling "not at all" comfortable expressing her LGBTQ+ identity in Japan and noted that she had experienced discrimination "within her family" and "in school." While currently living in the United States, she remains emotionally tethered to Japan—especially through the absence of familial recognition. "They don't contact me anymore," she said. "They didn't even ask if I was okay during the pandemic. I could have died, and they wouldn't know."

This estrangement weighed heavily on Himari, especially as she watched other students return to family homes or rely on support networks. Her survey response to the question "Where did you live during the pandemic?" was simple: "Alone." When asked how often she communicated with friends or family during the height of the crisis, she selected "rarely." In the interview, she elaborated: "I had friends here before COVID, but they all moved back. I couldn't go anywhere. I had no one."

Her isolation was not merely social—it was existential. The erasure she felt as a queer person in Japan had followed her abroad, intensified by the enforced solitude of lockdowns and Zoom university. "Even though I was in California, I didn't feel like I had escaped Japan," she said. "The pressure was still inside me. I still heard my mom's voice in my head." This internalization of normative gender expectations—what Eve Sedgwick might call the "epistemology of the closet"—produced a form of psychic suffocation. Himari could not come out, but neither could she disappear.

This state of suspension aligns with Berlant's (2011) notion of "crisis ordinariness"—the idea that crisis does not erupt, but settles into the ongoing conditions of life. Himari's everyday was not marked by dramatic loss but by a slow fading. "I stopped showering. I stopped eating well. I stopped going to class," she said. "I wasn't trying to die. But I also wasn't trying very hard to live." This articulation of ambient despair challenges dominant narratives of pandemic resilience. Himari did not innovate or thrive; she endured, quietly and without witnesses.

Yet her story is not devoid of agency. In the midst of her disintegration, Himari began writing again—first in a notebook, then on a private blog. "I don't show it to anyone," she said. "But I write about myself as someone who might survive. Not someone who is strong. Just someone who exists." This act of writing, of narrating the self in fragments, can be read as a form of lateral agency (Berlant 2011)—a small gesture of self-preservation when institutional care fails. It is also an archive of queer time. Her refusal to narrate a linear recovery arc—no "I was lost but now I'm found"—mirrors queer temporalities of drift, delay, and non-development (Halberstam 2005; Freeman 2010).

Academically, Himari struggled to maintain focus during remote learning. "I failed one class and almost dropped out," she said. "I couldn't keep up with deadlines. It felt like time didn't move the same way anymore." Her description resonates with what some scholars have called the "queer experience of COVID time"—a temporal condition shaped not by productivity but by stillness, rupture, and suspended futures (Quathamer & Joy 2021). For Himari, the breakdown of academic structure did not lead to liberation; it intensified her alienation. "I felt like the world was going on without me," she said. "Like I had fallen out of it."

Her coping strategies were minimal but intentional. She set alarms not to wake up for class, but to remind herself to eat. She watched the same anime over and over for comfort. "I needed something predictable," she said. "Something that didn't ask me to be anything." Her self-care practices were not glamorous or shareable, but deeply embodied. These practices, too, are forms of queer endurance—what scholar Cvetkovich (2012) calls "depression archives": the unglamorous, quiet rituals by which marginalized people hold themselves together.

Himari also reflected on her growing discomfort with national identity. "I used to say I was Japanese," she said. "Now I say I'm from Japan. It feels more honest." This shift in language signals a subtle disidentification with the nation-state, a move common among queer diasporic subjects. As Gopinath (2005) and others have argued, queer diaspora involves not just migration, but a refusal to reproduce heteronormative nationalism. Himari's ambivalence toward "being Japanese" during the pandemic—particularly given the state's silence toward queer people—illustrates how national belonging fractures under pressure.

Her reflections on LGBTQ+ inclusion in Japan were similarly bleak. In the survey, she strongly agreed that Japan should legally recognize same-sex partnerships, offer anti-discrimination protections, and support LGBTQ+ youth. But she expressed little faith in these changes happening soon. "They don't care about us," she said. "We don't even exist in their imagination." This sense of erasure—of being unimaginable to one's own country—compounds the personal pain of isolation with a structural form of disappearance.

Still, Himari finds fragments of solace. She watches YouTube videos by other queer Asians in the United States, reads fiction with non-binary characters, and occasionally joins anonymous online chats. "Sometimes I feel like I'm not the only one," she said. "Even if they don't know me." These moments of remote connection form a kind of affective lifeline—a reminder that queer kinship can extend beyond family and geography.

Toward the end of our interview, I asked Himari what she hoped for in the future. She paused for a long time. "I don't know if I have hope," she said finally. "But I have curiosity. I want to see what happens if I keep going."

That act of "keeping going"—without certainty, without closure—is perhaps the most radical gesture in Himari's story. Her pandemic experience challenges narratives of queer liberation that hinge on outness, affirmation, or familial reconciliation. Instead, she offers a portrait of queer becoming shaped by invisibility, estrangement, and slow survival. She is not trying to change the world. She is trying to stay in it.

7.4 Sento: Stylized Presence and the Ethics of Everyday Visibility

Sento is a soft-spoken gay man in his early thirties living in Chiba Prefecture, a region just east of Tokyo that blends urban infrastructure with suburban anonymity. He holds a master's degree, works full-time in a creative profession, and lives alone in a modest apartment. When asked whether he considers himself "out," Sento pauses. "I don't think of it like that," he eventually says. "I don't tell people. But I don't hide either. I exist in the open, but I don't offer explanations." This calibrated balance—between being visible and being legible—is central to Sento's pandemic experience, and more broadly, to his queer orientation in everyday life.

In his survey responses, Sento identified as gay and male, marked himself as single, and noted that he lived alone throughout the pandemic. When asked how much of a threat COVID-19 posed to himself, his family, and his community, he selected "a moderate amount." But for marginalized groups—including LGBTQ+ individuals, immigrants, and older adults—he selected "a great deal." His comments conveyed not only empathy but a clear-eyed understanding of how structural vulnerability is amplified during moments of social crisis. "I wasn't so worried for myself," he said in our interview, "but I thought a lot about people who couldn't rely on family or who didn't have stable jobs. Japan doesn't really see them."

That insight—"Japan doesn't really see them"—is not abstract for Sento. It shapes his understanding of how he, too, is seen. Though he presents as Japanese, he is often racialized as foreign or read as gender-nonconforming. "It's the way I dress," he said. "The way I walk. The way I carry myself." He smiled softly before adding, "People assume I'm not from here. That I don't belong." While he doesn't describe this treatment as overt discrimination, he is acutely aware of how micro-level perceptions accumulate. "I'm not harassed," he said. "But I'm constantly aware of being watched—not aggressively, but with confusion."

Sento's mode of resistance is not confrontational. He does not seek to disrupt spaces, nor does he ask for validation. Instead, he insists on aesthetic presence—what we might call a stylized form of everyday visibility. "I dress for myself," he explained. "Even during lockdown, when no one saw me, I would wear things that made me feel like myself. I think that's important. I think that's care." His attention to grooming, fashion, and posture is not vanity, but a quiet form of queer assertion. It reflects what Butler (1993) and later Halberstam (2005) have theorized as gender performativity—an active composition of self that resists heteronormative coherence.

During the pandemic, this practice of composed selfhood became even more significant. With social life restricted and offices moving online, many people retreated into casual comfort. Sento, by contrast, became more intentional in his daily routines. "It's not about being seen by others," he clarified. "It's about not disappearing to myself." This subtle but profound distinction signals a form of queer interiority that privileges presence over recognition. While Himari's story centered on a crisis of legibility—being neither seen nor named—Sento's narrative centers on a refusal to let social misreading dictate his self-conception.

His work, conducted remotely during parts of the pandemic, remained steady. He did not lose income or housing. In this sense, he is a figure of relative security. But Sento is quick to note that his position is not without tension. "Even in my job, people don't really know me," he said. "They assume I'm single because I'm 'married to my work,' or because I'm shy. It's easier that way." He does not correct their assumptions, nor does he seek their approval. Instead, he performs a kind of affective labor that keeps the peace while holding his ground. This navigation—of being visible but not explained—is emotionally taxing, but Sento has turned it into a sustainable rhythm.

His queer temporality differs markedly from Himari's. Whereas she experienced time as suspended and fragmented, Sento described his days as "structured, but flexible." He wakes early, prepares his own breakfast, takes long walks in his neighborhood, and reads before bed. During lockdown, these rituals became more pronounced. "I needed a rhythm," he said. "I needed to know that I could still move through the day with intention." His approach echoes what Muñoz (2009) might call a queer utopian habitus: a structuring of the present that gestures toward possibility, even in the absence of recognition or revolution.

Interestingly, Sento avoids politicized language when talking about his identity. He does not speak of LGBTQ+ rights or activism in personal terms, though his survey responses suggest he supports legal reforms. When asked whether Japan should implement anti-discrimination laws protecting sexual minorities, he selected "strongly agree." Yet in the interview, he demurred: "I think change will come slowly. Maybe it's already coming. But I don't wait for it. I just make space for myself." This minimalist ethic—"make space for myself"—encapsulates a distinct mode of queer survival, one grounded not in collective action but in affective sovereignty.

This form of survival, however, is not isolationist. Sento maintains a small circle of close friends, mostly other single professionals in their thirties. "We don't talk about being gay," he said. "But we understand each other." These relationships, while not explicitly queer, offer emotional texture. "Sometimes we just sit in silence," he said. "That's enough." This relational modality—quiet, durable, non-verbal—resonates with the affective style often observed in Japanese queer communities, where explicit disclosure is rare, and intimacy takes subtle forms.

Though Sento rarely speaks of his family, he did mention being out to one sibling, who lives in another prefecture. "She knows. She doesn't say anything. But she's kind." When asked about his parents, he shook his head. "They wouldn't understand. So I don't tell them." Unlike Himari, who described her familial rupture as an open wound, Sento frames his distance as a matter of mutual disinterest. "We were never close," he said. "It's not rejection. It's just… absence."

Spatially, Sento is deeply attuned to the politics of movement. He selects routes through the city based on familiarity and anonymity. "There are shops I won't enter because I know they'll look at me funny," he said. "And there are places I go because I know I can just blend in." He does not seek gay spaces in the commercial sense—bars, clubs, or pride events. Instead, he curates his own geography of comfort, built through repetition and intuition. This practice aligns with what Ahmed (2006) calls "queer orientation"—the way individuals move through the world based on where they feel at ease, even when no space is explicitly for them.

During the height of the pandemic, his spatial world shrank, but not drastically. "I already lived quietly," he said. "The city got quieter, that's all." He found pleasure in empty streets and reduced crowds. "It was easier to walk slowly," he said. "Easier to hear yourself think." Unlike narratives that emphasize isolation or loss, Sento's pandemic story is one of refined presence. He did not seek transformation; he sought continuity.

And yet, his story is not without melancholy. When asked whether he ever feels lonely, he answered without hesitation: "Of course. But not all the time. Not in a way that hurts." His relationship to solitude is one of practiced acceptance. "I think being alone is not the same as being abandoned," he said. "Sometimes it's where I feel most free."

This reframing of solitude—from a lack to a site of self-possibility—distinguishes Sento's orientation to queerness. His aesthetic self-composure, his routine, his spatial choices—all function as quiet affirmations of a life that exists beyond normativity but also beyond the need for explanation. He does not claim pride, but neither does he express shame. His politics are intimate, affective, embodied.

If Himari's story offers insight into the psychic cost of invisibility and diasporic dislocation, Sento's provides a counterpoint: a portrait of domestic queer presence managed through calibration, rhythm, and self-trust. He is not seeking liberation, but balance. Not transformation, but texture. His survival strategy is not dramatic or defiant. It is aesthetic, deliberate, and durable.

In this way, Sento expands our understanding of what queer endurance can look like—especially within the Japanese context, where overt disclosure is often discouraged and assimilation remains the norm. He is not assimilated, but neither is he marginal in the traditional sense. He lives at the edges of legibility, crafting a selfhood that is neither hidden nor explained.

As Japan continues to reckon—slowly and unevenly—with issues of sexual minority rights, Sento's life points to the affective labor being performed in the meantime. Not by activists on podiums, but by ordinary queer people who choose, each day, to exist on their own terms.

7.5 Comparative Analysis: Affective Geographies and Divergent Modes of Queer Survival

Placing Himari and Sento side by side—two queer Japanese individuals living through the COVID-19 pandemic in vastly different contexts—illuminates not only divergent experiences but also contrasting modes of survival, shaped by geographic location, social positioning, gender expression, and affective orientation. What emerges from their narratives is a shared awareness of systemic precarity, but profoundly different ways of engaging with it. While Himari's experience is marked by psychic unraveling, spatial dislocation, and a longing for recognition, Sento's is defined by composure, aesthetic agency, and the quiet refusal to explain himself.

This section offers a comparative analysis of the two participants, attending closely to four interrelated themes: (1) visibility and self-presentation, (2) kinship and relationality, (3) temporal orientation, and (4) spatial navigation. Through these lenses, we explore how each individual crafts a queer life in relation to systemic erasure, familial abandonment, and social misrecognition—and how these responses complicate dominant narratives of LGBTQ+ life in Japan and beyond.

7.5.1 Visibility and Self-Presentation: From Disidentification to Stylized Presence

Himari's relationship to visibility is fraught. Her queer identity, expressed only in English and never to her family, is something she carries internally but does not perform publicly. She inhabits what Muñoz (1999) describes as disidentification—neither fully aligning with dominant cultural scripts nor engaging in direct opposition. Her gender nonconformity is a source of familial rupture rather than social assertion. During the pandemic, alone in California, she withdrew further from social contact, her presentation flattening under the weight of invisibility. As she said during our interview: "I wasn't trying to die, but I wasn't trying to live either."

Sento, by contrast, navigates visibility as a chosen and continuous practice. He is visible not because he is out, but because his aesthetic self-expression—his walk, his fashion, his posture—marks him as different. And while he does not seek confrontation, he refuses erasure. "I dress for myself," he said, even when no one else is watching. Sento embodies a kind of stylized survival, a term we might use to describe how queer individuals assert identity affectively and sensorially, even in contexts of social constraint. His self-presentation does not aim for political legibility but for inner continuity.

In this sense, Himari longs to be seen for who she is, while Sento is constantly managing how he is seen. Himari's pain stems from not being recognized, even by her family. Sento's exhaustion stems from being misrecognized, often by strangers. Their contrasting modes—internal concealment vs. public misreading—both illustrate the limits of binary models of "outness." Neither "closeted" nor "liberated," their narratives point to more complex gradations of queer life, where survival is not defined by confession or concealment but by nuanced relational ethics.

7.5.2 Kinship, Estrangement, and Chosen Intimacy

Kinship emerges as another key axis of difference. Himari's pandemic experience is haunted by familial estrangement. Cut off from her parents and unable to return to Japan, she describes herself as "no longer a daughter," suspended in a liminal space of non-recognition. The loss of familial care during a global health crisis—when many sought refuge in natal homes—accentuated her sense of abandonment. Her grief is affectively thick: she mourns not only what she lost, but what was never offered to begin with. In the absence of family, she turns to journaling, online queer content, and imaginary futures. As Eng (2010) writes in The Feeling of Kinship, queer loss is not only personal but structural, produced through systems that deny certain lives their relational legitimacy.

Sento's family, by contrast, is largely absent from his narrative—not through trauma, but through quiet distance. He is out to a sister, not to his parents, and expresses no desire to bridge that gap. "We were never close," he said. His survival does not depend on reconciliation, nor is it shaped by familial judgment. His relational world is composed of a small circle of close friends with whom he shares time, comfort, and silence. These forms of intimacy—non-verbal, non-declared, non-blood—illustrate what Weston (1991) famously termed "families we choose." But in Sento's case, the chosen family is less utopian and more affectively minimalist. He asks for presence, not disclosure. Understanding, not recognition.

This contrast also marks their affective orientation. Himari remains tethered to the pain of rejection; she narrates her queer becoming through the absence of care. Sento, on the other hand, builds his queer life through intentional absence: a careful editing of his social field to include only those who pose no threat. His form of queer kinship is pared down, almost ascetic. Himari's, by contrast, is gestural, speculative, and tied to imagined futures.

7.5.3 *Temporalities of Suspension and Rhythm*

Queer time—its rhythms, delays, ruptures—features heavily in both narratives, though in profoundly different ways. Himari's experience of the pandemic was one of temporal suspension. Her days blurred into each other, structure disintegrated, and her academic progress faltered. "It felt like time didn't move," she said. Her account aligns with Freeman's (2010) theorization of chrononormativity—the way normative time structures social life around productivity, marriage, and reproduction. Himari, detached from those scripts and suspended in diasporic solitude, experiences queer time as drift: passive, melancholic, unmoored.

Sento's temporal experience is marked not by rupture but by rhythm. He wakes early, walks familiar routes, prepares his own meals, and reads before bed. His time is neither accelerated nor arrested; it is cyclical, composed. During the pandemic, he deepened these rituals, using them as anchors. This rhythm is not nostalgic, nor is it rigid. It is, rather, a form of queer calibration—a way to preserve selfhood in a world that offers neither clarity nor affirmation. His routine sustains not productivity, but presence. He is not trying to catch up to normative time, nor escape it, but to reroute it internally.

Himari's queer temporality is that of survival in a void: waiting, floating, sometimes drowning. Sento's is that of sustainable presence: slow repetition, minor aesthetic adjustments, measured solitude. Both unsettle the heteronormative scripts of progression—graduation, marriage, promotion—but in ways that reflect their divergent conditions. Himari is grasping for a future not yet imaginable. Sento is composing a present that does not betray him.

7.5.4 Spatial Navigation and the Ethics of Movement

Finally, their spatial geographies offer insight into how queer individuals move through and shape their environments under constraint. Himari is geographically dislocated from Japan and affectively dislocated from everywhere. Her small apartment in California becomes both a sanctuary and a site of collapse. She does not describe local spaces of queer community, nor does she seek them out. "Even here," she says, "I don't feel like I belong." Her physical mobility was curtailed by lockdowns, but her sense of stuckness predated COVID. The pandemic simply rendered it inescapable.

Sento, by contrast, is acutely aware of space. He selects routes through the city based on where he feels least watched. He avoids certain stores, frequents certain paths, and maintains a mental map of aesthetic safety. "I walk slower in places I like," he said. "Faster in places I don't." This embodied cartography aligns with Ahmed's (2006) notion of queer orientation—the idea that we move toward or away from spaces based on affective alignment, not just physical accessibility.

Sento's queer life is spatially choreographed; Himari's is spatially suspended. His movements are deliberate; hers are involuntary. He curates a geography of self-comfort; she is adrift in placelessness. And yet, both are responding to a shared reality: the structural unavailability of spaces explicitly designed for queer lives in Japan or elsewhere. Their strategies differ—one carving out space through ritual and presence, the other through withdrawal and imagination—but both underscore the affective labor of queer spatial negotiation.

7.5.5 Intersections and Divergences: What These Voices Reveal

Despite their many differences, Himari and Sento share certain convictions. Both view LGBTQ+ individuals as particularly vulnerable during the pandemic. Both express skepticism about the Japanese government's willingness to protect queer lives. Both see family not as a source of support, but as a site of constraint. And both, crucially, continue to live—not triumphantly, not defiantly, but with quiet determination. Their survival strategies are deeply shaped by context, yet they share a refusal to collapse entirely.

Their voices remind us that queer life in Japan cannot be reduced to categories like "out" or "closeted," "victim," or "activist." Himari does not need to be heroic to be valuable. Sento does not need to be politicized to be legible. Their pandemic-era narratives insist on the importance of affective nuance, non-linear temporality, and situated agency. They challenge scholars and policymakers alike to rethink what counts as queer resistance, what forms of survival deserve recognition, and how we might build structures of care that do not demand coherence.

The contrasts between Himari's diasporic invisibility and Sento's quiet but deliberate self-presence reveal that precarious visibility is not a singular condition but a spectrum of negotiated experiences. Both stories highlight that survival during the pandemic was less about overt activism or "coming out" and more about maintaining a sense of self amid the shifting dynamics of recognition, risk, and care.

7.5.6 Queer Theoretical Perspectives on Solitude and Survival

These theoretical reflections set the stage for a concluding discussion of what Himari and Sento's narratives reveal about queer endurance during the pandemic.

The narratives of Himari and Sento resonate with central insights from queer theory, particularly in how visibility, temporality, and affect are negotiated under conditions of crisis. Sento's stylized self-presentation exemplifies what Butler (1993) calls performativity: identity is constructed through repeated, embodied acts. His quiet aesthetic practices—dressing with care, walking familiar routes—subvert rather than reproduce heteronormative expectations, asserting agency through subtle gestures that refuse easy categorization.

The contrast between Himari's strategic invisibility and Sento's understated visibility recalls Sedgwick's (1990) epistemology of the closet. Neither participant fits into a simple binary of "in" or "out." Himari's decision to use "queer" only in English highlights the cultural and linguistic contingencies of disclosure, while Sento's refusal to explain himself challenges Western-centric notions that equate authenticity with public coming out. Their narratives suggest that visibility is less about declaring identity and more about carefully navigating safety, recognition, and selfhood.

Spatial navigation is another critical dimension of their experiences. Drawing on Ahmed's (2006) concept of queer orientation, both participants reveal how queer lives are shaped by movement toward or away from spaces that can affirm or harm. Himari's dislocation from Japan and Sento's curated geography of comfort show how pandemic restrictions intensified this orientation work, reducing the spaces where queer presence felt possible.

For Himari, the hope for familial recognition and cross-cultural belonging reflects Berlant's (2011) notion of "cruel optimism"—the attachment to structures that consistently fail to provide care, leaving her in a state of "crisis ordinariness," where survival feels stalled and fragmented. Sento's narrative, by contrast, embodies Muñoz's (2009) vision of queer futurity. His daily rituals and self-styling form utopian fragments—small but meaningful gestures that imagine a life beyond normative demands.

Taken together, these perspectives reveal that survival for Himari and Sento is neither linear nor spectacular. It emerges through modest but persistent acts—journaling, dressing, walking—that challenge Western-centric narratives of resilience and illuminate a spectrum of queer endurance shaped by cultural context, affect, and the quiet work of everyday life.

7.6 Conclusion: Staying with the Trouble of Queer Life in Crisis

The narratives of Himari and Sento reveal the affective complexities of queer survival during the COVID-19 pandemic. Both lives exemplify precarious visibility—a state of being seen only partially, or in ways that risk misrecognition, while remaining invisible when care and structural protection are most needed. Himari's narrative is shaped by estrangement, diasporic isolation, and an almost painful absence of recognition, while Sento's story shows how visibility can be quietly self-fashioned through aesthetics, routines, and spatial navigation. Together, their case studies underscore that queer survival during crisis is not about a singular trajectory of resilience but about multiple, sometimes contradictory strategies of endurance.

The two case studies presented in this chapter—Himari's journey as a young bisexual woman studying abroad in the United States and Sento's experience as a gay man negotiating work, family, and identity within Japan—offer intimate portraits of queer life under the strain of a global pandemic. While both narratives are deeply personal, they illuminate broader dynamics of precarity, affect, and resilience that characterize LGBTQ+ lives during times of crisis. The pandemic, though universal in its disruptions, manifested unevenly across lines of class, gender, nationality, and family structure. Himari's navigation of cross-cultural belonging and Sento's quiet strategies for survival both reveal how queer life is shaped not only by structural inequities—such as legal precarity and heteronormative expectations—but also by moments of resistance, introspection, and self-assertion.

By closely examining their lived experiences, we see how the pandemic magnified existing vulnerabilities while also creating new spaces for reflection and growth. Himari's sense of diasporic dislocation, compounded by familial estrangement, resonates with recurring themes in this book: the emotional costs of invisibility, the difficulty of navigating non-affirming spaces, and the labor required simply to exist as queer. Sento, by contrast, inhabits a form of everyday resistance that is subtle yet deliberate—styling his life and body as a quiet act of care. Together, their narratives illustrate that survival is not a uniform process but a constellation of adaptive strategies, each shaped by unique social and affective conditions.

Staying with the "trouble" of queer life, as Haraway (2016) suggests, requires us to resist the urge to simplify or resolve the contradictions that surface in these accounts. Both Himari and Sento highlight how resilience coexists with vulnerability, how personal freedom is negotiated within oppressive systems, and how pandemic disruptions—rather than creating entirely new struggles—intensified longstanding tensions within queer life in Japan and its diaspora. Their stories call for recognition of the invisible and often exhausting labor of queer survival, which involves not only external resistance but also interior forms of care, routine, and emotional recalibration.

7.6.1 Beyond the "Coming Out" Paradigm

One of the central insights emerging from these case studies is the insufficiency of "coming out" as a universal metric of queer authenticity. Himari, although out to herself and partially to friends abroad, remains silent about her identity with family, seeing no safe space for disclosure. Sento, on the other hand, performs a visible yet unspoken form of queerness—his aesthetic choices and everyday presence mark him as different, but he does not articulate his sexuality in explicit terms to family or colleagues. Neither narrative conforms neatly to the binaries of "closeted" or "liberated," which are often presumed in Western frameworks of queer life.

As scholars such as Sedgwick (1990) have argued, visibility is always culturally contingent and relational. In Japan, indirectness, discretion, and social harmony frequently take precedence over public assertion of identity. Himari and Sento's stories illustrate how queer survival can thrive in the interstices—through gestures, silences, and aesthetic practices that resist both erasure and hypervisibility. These nuanced modes of being complicate Western-centric notions of queer progress, reminding us that the politics of recognition cannot be measured solely by acts of disclosure.

7.6.2 Kinship and Affective Labor

Both narratives reveal the emotional weight of familial expectations and estrangement. Himari's experience is structured around the absence of parental recognition; her inability to embody the role of the "cute and obedient daughter" has led to a rupture that is both personal and systemic. This absence is particularly acute during the pandemic, when many found solace in returning to family homes while she endured isolation abroad. Sento, by contrast, frames his familial distance as neither traumatic nor resolvable—it is simply a matter of mutual detachment. His chosen kinship structures, composed of quiet friendships and solitary rituals, reflect what Weston (1991) calls "families we choose," though in his case these are intentionally minimal and unobtrusive.

These divergent orientations toward kinship underscore a broader insight from this study: queer life often involves negotiating relationships that are not anchored in traditional family structures. Himari's grief over lost familial care contrasts with Sento's acceptance of its absence, yet both reveal how the pandemic heightened the emotional labor required to sustain a sense of belonging. Whether through imagined futures, as in Himari's case, or through carefully curated present moments, as with

Sento, queer individuals engage in forms of affective worldmaking that challenge normative definitions of family and intimacy.

7.6.3 Queer Temporality and Space

Himari and Sento also illustrate contrasting relationships to time and space. Himari's narrative unfolds in what Lauren Berlant calls "crisis ordinariness," marked by temporal suspension, emotional drift, and academic disorientation. Her days blur into one another, and her sense of self unravels under the weight of isolation. Sento's time, by contrast, is rhythmic and intentional. His days are structured around aesthetic rituals—cooking, walking, reading—that anchor him in the present and protect against emotional erosion. These divergent temporalities show how queer life often unfolds "out of sync" with heteronormative timelines, yet they also highlight how personal strategies of time management can become critical survival mechanisms during a crisis.

Spatially, both participants navigate environments that are not explicitly designed for queer belonging. Himari's apartment in California is both a sanctuary and a site of isolation, while Sento maps his city through affective cues—choosing streets, shops, and spaces where he can move freely, even if anonymously. Ahmed's (2006) concept of "queer orientation" is instructive here: both individuals orient themselves toward or away from certain spaces based on comfort, recognition, and safety. Their narratives remind us that queer geographies are not only physical but also emotional, shaped by everyday acts of movement and avoidance.

7.6.4 The Value of Narrative-Based Inquiry

These case studies affirm the importance of narrative methods for understanding LGBTQ+ experiences during the pandemic. While earlier chapters have analyzed survey data and thematic trends—such as healthcare access, workplace discrimination, or mental health—Himari and Sento's stories bring these issues into sharp, human focus. Their voices challenge the abstraction of "the LGBTQ+ community" by revealing the singular textures of individual lives: the quiet despair of drifting through online classes, the meditative act of choosing an outfit, the silence of a parent who does not call, the joy of walking alone in a city that neither welcomes nor rejects.

In doing so, this chapter aligns with queer theorists like Cvetkovich and Muñoz, who emphasize the value of affective archives and minor gestures. Himari's journaling and Sento's self-styling are not trivial acts; they are forms of lateral agency and affective resistance. They resist the demand for spectacular resilience or activist visibility, instead offering models of queer survival that are intimate, fragmentary, and deeply situated.

7.6.5 *Looking Forward*

As a contribution to both LGBTQ+ studies and pandemic scholarship, this chapter makes three interrelated claims. First, it underscores the value of situated narratives—not as representative samples, but as vital counterpoints to aggregate data. Second, it highlights the role of affect as a critical analytic lens, revealing how emotions like loneliness, aesthetic pleasure, and quiet pride shape queer survival as much as structural factors do. Third, it calls for a broader understanding of queer temporality, recognizing that survival is often about maintaining presence, even when the future feels uncertain.

In the long arc of Japanese LGBTQ+ history, the pandemic may one day be remembered as a moment of exposure—of inequality, but also of voice. Himari and Sento's narratives form part of this emerging archive. They do not present a triumphant or unified vision of queer life. Rather, they insist on the complexity of existing as LGBTQ+ in a world that is not always prepared to see or sustain them. By staying with their "trouble," we gain not only insight into the pandemic's impact but also a deeper appreciation of the quiet, persistent ways queer individuals continue to live, care, and imagine futures beyond the limits imposed upon them. The next chapter shifts from these two individual narratives to the collective voices of participants, foregrounding demands for rights, recognition, and broader cultural change.

7.6.6 *Researcher's Reflection: Witnessing Queer Intimacies in Uneven Conditions*

Writing about Himari and Sento's stories prompted me to reflect not only on their individual experiences but also on my own position as a queer researcher during the pandemic. Their narratives—one shaped by diasporic solitude, the other by quiet domestic resilience—mirror many of the broader tensions I encountered in my data: the friction between visibility and safety, the emotional costs of family estrangement, and the subtle acts of endurance that rarely make headlines but sustain queer lives. Engaging with these two case studies reminded me that research is never a neutral process. My own lived experience, cultural background, and affective responses inevitably shaped how I listened to, interpreted, and represented these voices.

Himari's narrative, with its emphasis on displacement and fragmented self-hood, resonates with my broader findings about the precarious position of Japanese LGBTQ+ youth—particularly those who seek affirmation outside of heteronormative family structures. Her story compelled me to think about how queerness in Japan is often marked by silence, indirectness, and absence. Sento's account, by contrast, is grounded in aesthetic agency and personal rhythm; it challenges dominant frameworks that equate queer authenticity with "coming out" or political assertion. His way of "being visible without explaining" echoed what many participants expressed—a desire for recognition without the pressure of spectacle or self-disclosure.

These two cases also pushed me to consider the limits of thematic analysis when dealing with complex, embodied narratives. While survey data and coding schemes help to identify common patterns—such as mental health struggles, legal precarity, or loss of queer spaces—case studies reveal the emotional textures that defy neat categorization. Himari's self-care rituals, like private journaling, or Sento's daily walks and curated aesthetic presence, are forms of queer worldmaking that often go unnoticed in conventional analyses. They remind me that small, intimate acts can hold as much theoretical significance as collective activism or policy debates.

Finally, reflecting on these stories sharpened my understanding of intersectionality as lived experience. Himari's challenges are inseparable from her positionality as a bisexual Japanese woman navigating US academic and social spaces, just as Sento's resilience is entwined with his experiences as a Japanese gay man balancing cultural expectations with his personal sense of freedom. Their voices underscore that queerness cannot be analyzed in isolation from race, gender, class, or geography. As a researcher, I see my role not only as an interpreter of these dynamics but as a witness to the quieter, often invisible forms of survival that might otherwise be overlooked.

In bringing Himari and Sento's narratives into dialogue with the broader themes of this book, I hope to demonstrate the value of attending to queer intimacies—the everyday practices of care, refusal, and endurance that emerge in contexts of crisis. These are not simply personal anecdotes but fragments of a collective archive of queer resilience, an archive that continues to evolve long after the pandemic. My task, as I see it, is to document these lives with rigor, humility, and a recognition that each story is not only data but a testament to the possibility of living differently.

These portraits of Himari and Sento underscore how precarious visibility is navigated not only in intimate, everyday contexts but also within broader cultural and legal structures that shape what is possible for queer lives in Japan. While their stories reveal the deeply personal costs and creative resilience of living openly, they also point toward the larger systemic challenges—such as legal exclusion and political indifference—that frame these individual experiences. The following chapter expands this focus, shifting from individual narratives to the collective voices of participants who speak to the urgent need for rights, recognition, and cultural transformation.

References

Ahmed, S. (2006). *Queer phenomenology: Orientations, objects, others*. Duke University Press.

Berlant, L. (2011). *Cruel optimism*. Duke University Press.

Butler, J. (1993). *Bodies that matter: On the discursive limits of sex*. Routledge.

Cvetkovich, A. (2012). *Depression: A public feeling*. Duke University Press.

Eng, D. L. (2010). *The feeling of kinship: Queer liberalism and the racialization of intimacy*. Duke University Press.

Fish, J. N., McInroy, L. B., Paceley, M. S., Williams, N. D., Henderson, S., Levine, D. S., & Edsall, R. N. (2020). "I'm kinda stuck at home with unsupportive parents right now": LGBTQ youths'

experiences with COVID-19 and the importance of online support. *Journal of Adolescent Health*, 67(3), 450–452.
Freeman, E. (2010). *Time binds: Queer temporalities, queer histories*. Duke University Press.
Gopinath, G. (2005). *Impossible desires: Queer diasporas and South Asian public cultures*. Duke University Press.
Halberstam, J. (2005). *In a queer time and place: Transgender bodies, subcultural lives*. New York University Press.
Haraway, D. J. (2016). *Staying with the trouble: Making kin in the Chthulucene*. Duke University Press.
Muñoz, J. E. (1999). *Disidentifications: Queers of color and the performance of politics*. University of Minnesota Press.
Muñoz, J. E. (2009). *Cruising utopia: The then and there of queer futurity*. New York University Press.
Quathamer, N. N., & Joy, P. (2021). Being in a queer time: Exploring the influence of the COVID19 pandemic on LGBTQ+ body image. *Nutrition & Dietetics*, 79(3), 400–410.
Salerno, J. P., Williams, N. D., & Gattamorta, K. A. (2020). LGBTQ populations: Psychologically vulnerable communities in the COVID-19 pandemic. *Psychological Trauma: Theory, Research, Practice, and Policy*, 12(S1), S239–S242. https://doi.org/10.1037/tra0000837
Sedgwick, E. K. (1990). *Epistemology of the closet*. University of California Press.
Weston, K. (1991). *Families we choose: Lesbians, gays, kinship*. Columbia University Press.

Chapter 8
Rights and Recognition: Everyday Struggles of the LGBTQ+ Community

Masami Tamagawa

Abstract This chapter examines how legal, political, and cultural structures shape the lived realities of LGBTQ+ individuals in Japan, centering on participants' reflections about rights, recognition, and systemic exclusion. Building on the personal narratives in earlier chapters, this chapter foregrounds voices that confront structural inequalities—ranging from the absence of same-sex marriage and adoption rights to workplace discrimination and the lack of anti-discrimination protections. Participants highlight that legal precarity not only jeopardizes everyday security but also signals a deeper societal indifference, which they describe as a subtler yet equally harmful form of exclusion.

The chapter further explores activism and media representation as contested sites of visibility. While some respondents celebrate Pride events, celebrity coming-out stories, and corporate allyship, others critique these forms of visibility as performative, urban-centric, or neglectful of bisexual, asexual, transgender, and foreign voices. Popular culture, especially Boys' Love and queer-themed entertainment, is seen as simultaneously expanding visibility and perpetuating stereotypes.

Through a combination of personal narratives and theoretical analysis of precarious visibility, this chapter calls for legal reform, intersectional activism, and cultural transformation to achieve meaningful recognition and equality.

8.1 Introduction: Rights and Recognition Through Participant Voices

Building on the personal narratives explored in the previous chapter, Chapter 8 examines the structural dimensions of precarious visibility through the lens of participants' reflections on rights and recognition. While Himari and Sento's stories highlight how visibility is experienced on a personal and emotional level, the voices gathered here shed light on the political, legal, and cultural conditions that shape the broader landscape of LGBTQ+ life in Japan.

M. Tamagawa, *Japanese LGBTQ+ Lives, Diasporic Voices, and Resilience*,
https://doi.org/10.1007/978-981-95-3105-9_8

Legal and political inequalities have long shaped the experiences of LGBTQ+ people in Japan, yet these issues often remain abstract when discussed in isolation from everyday lives. Previous chapters have highlighted how the COVID-19 pandemic amplified social isolation, economic precarity, and familial tensions for LGBTQ+ individuals. While Chapter 1 provided a general overview of Japan's legal landscape—such as the lack of national anti-discrimination laws or marriage equality—this chapter approaches these structural realities from a different angle. By foregrounding participants' reflections on rights, politics, and public attitudes, this chapter reveals how legal precarity intersects with lived experiences, shaping both the possibilities and limits of everyday recognition.

8.1.1 The Voices Gathered Here Come from Two Sets of Responses

- RL (Reflections on Laws and Human Rights): Where participants discussed legal rights, same-sex marriage, and broader questions of equality.
- GI (General Impressions): Where participants reflected on Japanese society, its norms, and their personal experiences of inclusion or exclusion.

Rather than repeating the legal discussion in Chapter 1, this chapter lets participants themselves articulate the challenges they face, while critically engaging with their perspectives. Their testimonies offer a spectrum of views—from frustration with government inaction, to skepticism about the strategies of LGBTQ+ activists, to nuanced insights into how Japanese social norms enforce conformity. While many participants emphasize the urgent need for legal reforms such as marriage equality and adoption rights, others caution that visibility alone does not guarantee social acceptance or personal safety.

8.1.2 Precarious Visibility and Structural Silence

A recurring theme in these narratives is what I call precarious visibility. This condition describes how queer lives in Japan are increasingly visible through popular culture, media, and online activism, but that visibility is often partial, conditional, or commodified. As expressed by one participant (anonymous), "We are visible only when it's convenient for society." Legal recognition has not yet caught up with this cultural visibility, leaving many LGBTQ+ people caught between being "seen" in entertainment or corporate branding and "unseen" in matters of family, healthcare, or inheritance.

Several participants also pointed to the disconnect between political discourse and real-life struggles. For example, while local municipalities have introduced same-sex partnership systems, these remain symbolic and lack the legal force of marriage. As a result, even couples who are "recognized" by their local government face barriers in hospitals, schools, and workplaces. Vicente (FJ, 25–34) explained, "Until Japan recognize same-sex marriage and provide adoption rights to the LGBT + community, there won't be any visible space in society for our community to develop and thrive."

8.1.3 Activism, Resistance, and Critique

Interestingly, participants were not unanimously supportive of current activist approaches. While some expressed gratitude for public advocacy, others felt that activist narratives often highlight only certain voices—typically urban, cisgender, and middle-class gay men—while sidelining others. Ryo (JJ, transgender FtM/X, 35–44) criticized this dynamic:

> If you are a cisgay, able-bodied, high-class person, you are probably the easiest of the sexes to live with. However, it is harmful for gay people who are unaware of their privilege to join the conservative discourse and play the role of an understanding minority.

These critiques reveal that the struggle for rights is not only a matter of challenging the heteronormative mainstream but also of ensuring that diverse queer voices are heard within the LGBTQ+ community itself. As such, this chapter examines not just external oppression but also internal tensions that shape how advocacy and representation are imagined.

8.1.4 Outline of the Chapter

This chapter is divided into six sections. Section 8.2 focuses on legal precarity and how the absence of marriage equality, adoption rights, and anti-discrimination laws affects daily life. Section 8.3 examines participants' views on politics and activism, highlighting both support for and criticism of LGBTQ+ movements in Japan. Section 8.4 addresses the cultural climate of indifference and conformity, which many participants see as a barrier to true social acceptance. Section 8.5 turns inward, exploring issues of inclusion and exclusion within the LGBTQ+ community, particularly for bisexual, asexual, and transgender participants. Section 8.6 considers the role of popular culture and media in shaping public perceptions of queer lives, both positively and negatively. Finally, Sect. 8.7 concludes with participants' calls for legal reform, broader education, and a cultural shift toward genuine recognition and equality.

By weaving participant voices with critical analysis, this chapter highlights that the struggle for LGBTQ+ rights in Japan is not just a legal battle but also a cultural and emotional one. The comments gathered here serve as both testimony and critique, calling attention to the everyday ways in which queer individuals navigate the gap between formal recognition and lived reality.

8.2 Legal Precarity and Everyday Life

Building on these reflections, Sect. 8.1 focuses on the legal foundations of recognition and the everyday implications of systemic exclusion.

Legal recognition—or the lack thereof—remains one of the most pressing issues facing LGBTQ+ people in Japan. Participants repeatedly expressed frustration that their relationships and families are rendered invisible by legal systems that fail to grant them the same protections as heterosexual couples. While some local governments have introduced partnership certificates, these remain symbolic, providing no legal standing for critical matters such as inheritance, hospital visitation, or adoption. For many participants, this lack of recognition is not simply a legal inconvenience; it is experienced as a form of structural erasure that diminishes their dignity and security.

8.2.1 Marriage Equality as a Symbol and a Necessity

Participants frequently identified marriage equality as a key marker of social legitimacy. For example, Nana (JJ, 25–34) lamented the inability to form a family in ways accessible to heterosexual couples: "I want to have a child, but I can't get [a child] in a safe way, including through a hospital. I can't even adopt a child." Vicente echoed this sentiment, arguing that without marriage rights, their lives remain relegated to the margins. One participant summarized this frustration: "Until Japan recognize same-sex marriage and provide adoption rights to the LGBT + community, there won't be any visible space in society for our community to develop and thrive."

Some participants viewed the absence of marriage equality as symbolic of a deeper societal refusal to acknowledge queer relationships as valid. Ayumi (JJ, 25–34) observed, "The opposite of love is indifference. I want people to separate it from politics and think of it as a human rights issue." This framing points to what Butler (2004) describes as the relationship between recognition and livability: to be denied recognition under the law is to be told, implicitly, that one's love and kinship structures are less real, less valuable, or less worthy of protection.

8.2.2 Partnership Systems: Symbolic but Insufficient

While some participants appreciated local partnership systems, others criticized these measures as half-hearted attempts to placate activists without addressing systemic inequalities. Skyler (FJ, 25–34) explained: "The ability to obtain a legal partnership would only be beneficial to my comfort in Japan if it were to fully provide the same benefits as legal marriage."

This observation highlights a recurring theme: while visibility is increasing at the municipal level, such symbolic recognition does little to resolve practical concerns. Partnership certificates, for example, do not grant tax benefits, inheritance rights, or legal decision-making power in medical emergencies. Participants felt that this gap between "symbolic" and "substantive" recognition leaves them vulnerable in moments of crisis.

Some participants linked these legal deficiencies to personal anxieties about long-term stability. For instance, Riku (FJ, 55–64) observed that financial and housing security is precarious for same-sex couples:

> You cannot take out a loan in joint names at a financial institution. You cannot get married. Therefore, the same applies to insurance. Inheritance is also handled differently. Once you step outside of Ni-chōme, there are restrictions on expressions of affection between people of the same sex.

These remarks highlight how legal frameworks intersect with economic realities, reinforcing queer marginality in both public and private spheres.

8.2.3 Parenthood and Family Formation

The issue of adoption was especially charged for participants who wished to raise children. Some pointed to the fact that heterosexual couples—even those in unstable or abusive relationships—can access reproductive and parental rights more easily than stable, loving queer couples. As one anonymous participant put it: "It is strange that same-sex couples can't adopt even if they can provide a safe and loving environment, while heterosexual parents are granted rights without question."

Others expressed anxiety over reproductive technologies. Access to assisted reproduction is not legally extended to same-sex couples in Japan, which means that lesbian couples or transgender individuals who wish to have biological children often face costly, complicated, or legally ambiguous processes. As one respondent lamented: "Even if I want children, I have no legal or safe way to have them here. Adoption is out of reach, and the law tells us that we are not a real family."

These struggles resonate with queer theorist Berlant's (2011) notion of cruel optimism, wherein the desire for normative markers of success (such as marriage and family) collides with structural barriers, leaving individuals caught between aspiration and impossibility.

8.2.4 Legal Silence as Structural Discrimination

Several participants viewed Japan's refusal to legislate against LGBTQ+ discrimination as a deliberate form of structural neglect. In workplaces, for instance, many LGBTQ+ employees remain closeted out of fear that disclosure could harm their careers. While explicit discrimination is not always evident, participants stressed that the absence of legal protections reinforces a culture of silence. One participant observed: "Japan's legal system doesn't hate us openly, but it also doesn't care enough to protect us. That silence is its own form of discrimination."

Participants also commented on the lack of anti-discrimination laws in housing and healthcare. As Chun-chieh (FJ, 35–44) noted: "There are still many landlords who will not rent apartments to foreigners, and I have heard similar stories about people refusing to rent to LGBTQ+ couples. Without legal protection, we have no way to fight back." For queer foreigners in Japan, the combination of legal invisibility and immigration restrictions exacerbates their sense of vulnerability (see Chapter 6 for diasporic perspectives).

8.2.5 *Intersection of Legal Status and Everyday Life*

The COVID-19 pandemic magnified the consequences of legal precarity. For couples separated by border closures, the absence of marriage recognition meant that many could not reunite, even when heterosexual couples with marriage certificates were granted exemptions. Shufen (FJ, 35–44), a lesbian participant, shared her frustration: "I wanted to go back to Taiwan and get married last year, but I can't even see my partner, let alone get married. I can't see the future because I can't meet her."

Others reflected on the compounding effect of visa status, workplace discrimination, and legal invisibility. Harry (FJ, 25–34) described how the absence of marriage rights made his relationship with his Japanese partner precarious:

> The biggest problem I face is with visa issues, and that if I don't have a job that qualifies, I am forced to leave my partner in Japan. Although same-sex partnerships are a step in the right direction, until same-sex marriage is implemented, living in Japan with a Japanese partner comes with many disadvantages.

8.2.6 *Marriage Equality Lawsuits and Participant Perspectives*

Some participants expressed hope that the ongoing marriage equality lawsuits in Japan might lead to legal change, while others were skeptical. A few mentioned the symbolic impact of the 2021 Sapporo District Court ruling, which declared the denial of same-sex marriage unconstitutional, but they also noted that the ruling had not yet translated into policy shifts. One anonymous participant commented: "Court rulings may be a start, but unless politicians act, nothing changes. I am not optimistic because the government still treats this as a minority issue that doesn't matter."

Another participant suggested that the marriage debate, while important, risks overshadowing other urgent issues such as workplace protections and healthcare access: "Everyone talks about marriage, but what about people who are trans and can't even access safe medical care? Or queer youth who are bullied in schools? We need broader change, not just marriage."

This ongoing tension between the symbolic power of marriage equality and the diverse needs of the community reflects larger debates within queer theory, particularly critiques of "homonormativity" (Duggan 2003), which argues that prioritizing marriage can sideline more radical visions of queer liberation.

8.3 Politics and LGBTQ+ Activism

The political landscape for LGBTQ+ rights in Japan is characterized by a combination of slow-moving legal reforms, cautious policymaking, and limited governmental support for minority communities. While the issue of same-sex marriage has received increased media coverage—particularly through ongoing lawsuits—many participants described the political environment as stagnant, even indifferent. They saw politics as a realm where LGBTQ+ people were often instrumentalized for symbolic purposes rather than genuinely supported. In their reflections, participants critiqued not only government inaction but also the strategies of LGBTQ+ activists, revealing tensions between advocacy, visibility, and the diversity of queer experiences.

8.3.1 Frustrations with Government Inaction

Many participants observed that the Japanese government has made few meaningful efforts to address the needs of LGBTQ+ communities, even as international pressure for legal equality grows. Shufen voiced a widely shared sentiment: "The top government officials are not aware of it, and they have no intention of recognizing it."

This sense of deliberate neglect was echoed by others who noted that legislative reforms have often stalled. As one participant noted, "Court rulings may declare discrimination unconstitutional, but politicians do nothing to act on them. They wait until public pressure forces them to move." The LGBT Understanding Promotion Bill, which was proposed by the ruling Liberal Democratic Party (LDP), was criticized by several respondents as symbolic rather than substantive.

Harry, a British gay man living in Japan, captured this frustration:

> The LGBT understanding promotion bill is a start, but it would be nothing without actual structural changes. Considering the current government can't even support straight women, I have very little faith in their ability or interest in working for anyone but themselves.

8.3.2 Marriage Equality as a Political Battleground

While Sect. 8.1 explored marriage equality as a matter of personal rights, participants also viewed it as a political flashpoint. Some felt that political parties, especially the opposition, were leveraging marriage equality as a means of gaining support without a genuine commitment to broader LGBTQ+ rights. One participant bluntly stated: "LGBTQ activists loudly advocate for their rights, and the Constitutional Democratic Party and Social Democratic Party take advantage of them."

For others, the marriage debate symbolized both progress and limitation. It was seen as the one issue that gained public attention, but this narrow focus risked overshadowing other urgent concerns, such as workplace discrimination, trans healthcare, and protections for queer youth. As one respondent observed: "Everyone talks about marriage, but what about young LGBTQ+ kids who are bullied in school or trans people who cannot change their legal gender without surgery? We need wider reforms, not just marriage."

This ongoing tension mirrors critiques within queer theory, particularly Duggan's (2003) notion of homonormativity, which warns that emphasizing marriage and assimilationist goals can depoliticize queer movements, sidelining those whose lives do not conform to heteronormative models of family and respectability.

8.3.3 Activism: Representation and Misrepresentation

Participants' views on LGBTQ+ activism were strikingly diverse. Some expressed gratitude for the increased visibility brought by activists, but others criticized activism for being dominated by a narrow set of voices—often urban, cisgender, and middle-class gay men. This led to a sense that activism did not fully represent the diversity of the community. Shun (JJ, 18–24) pointedly remarked: "Only a few LGBTQ+ people who are convenient for some leftist activists are given the opportunity to appear in public."

Others were concerned that activism sometimes backfired by alienating mainstream society. Kaede (JJ, 25–34) criticized what she saw as confrontational advocacy: "Japan's LGBT activists are getting too carried away. Shame on them." Isamu (JJ, 45–54) similarly noted, "I think that LGBTQ+ is accepted (including letting them pass) to a certain extent, whether you like it or not, but if anything, the radical and selfish activities are making the impression of LGBTQ+ worse."

These critiques highlight an internal tension within LGBTQ+ politics: how to balance the need for visibility and assertive advocacy with the risk of reinforcing stereotypes or provoking backlash. In the Japanese context, where societal norms often prize subtlety and social harmony, activists who push too strongly against the grain can be viewed unfavorably even by other queer people.

8.3.4 *The Question of Privilege Within the Community*

A recurring theme in participants' critiques of activism was the issue of privilege. Ryo emphasized that some activists are unaware of the structural advantages they hold:

> If you are a cisgay, able-bodied, high-class person, you are probably the easiest of the sexes to live with. However, it is harmful for gay people who are unaware of their privilege to join the conservative discourse and play the role of an understanding minority.

This comment suggests that while some activists may push for acceptance, they sometimes do so in ways that prioritize the concerns of a relatively privileged subset of the LGBTQ+ community. As Crenshaw (1989) reminds us through the concept of intersectionality, effective activism must address overlapping systems of oppression—such as those based on gender, class, nationality, or disability—rather than focusing solely on sexual orientation or gender identity.

8.3.5 *Pride, Pinkwashing, and Corporate Activism*

Pride events and corporate-sponsored LGBTQ+ campaigns also drew mixed responses from participants. Some saw these as valuable opportunities to raise awareness, but others criticized them as performative or commodified. Isamu wrote: "Pride events used to be useful for getting the word out, but now they are not useful because they engage in inappropriate activities that lead to misunderstandings."

Similarly, some respondents expressed skepticism about corporate "allyship," which they viewed as motivated by profit rather than genuine support. A participant commented: "Companies put rainbows on their ads for Pride month, but inside their offices, they don't even have proper anti-discrimination policies. It feels fake." This ambivalence reflects what scholars call "pinkwashing," where corporations or political entities adopt superficial gestures of LGBTQ+ support to bolster their public image without enacting meaningful change.

8.3.6 *Media and Political Narratives*

Several participants criticized the way politicians and media outlets portray LGBTQ+ issues. While representation has improved in recent years, some felt that media coverage remains sensationalized or overly focused on "trendy" aspects of queer life. As one participant observed, television often treats being gay as fashionable or comedic, yet off-screen it remains a subject many people avoid altogether.

Another participant highlighted the gap between media visibility and political will: "Seeing celebrities come out didn't make my parents understand me any better. It feels like we are visible only when it's convenient for society."

These remarks underscore the disconnect between symbolic representation and real legal protections. While queer characters or public figures may be celebrated in pop culture, this visibility has not translated into substantive policy change.

8.3.7 Activism and Political Participation

A few participants stressed the need for greater political engagement, both within and beyond the LGBTQ+ community. Emily (FJ, 25–34) commented: "In order to make progress, there needs to be support from outside of the queer community, and people need to actually vote. I haven't seen either yet."

Others felt that activism needs to shift from urban centers like Tokyo to rural and suburban areas, where queer visibility remains limited. As one respondent put it: "It's easy to feel there's progress if you live in Tokyo and go to Ni-chōme. But for those of us outside big cities, there are almost no resources or events. Activism needs to reach all of Japan, not just the capital."

8.3.8 Theoretical Reflections: Queer Politics in Japan

The ambivalence participants expressed toward activism can be read through the lens of queer temporality and visibility (Halberstam, 2005; Sedgwick, 1990). In a society that prizes discretion, many queer individuals prefer strategies of quiet resistance—subtle acts of survival and community-building that do not necessarily seek mainstream recognition. Activism that foregrounds pride parades or marriage equality can therefore feel alien to those who experience queerness as something intimate, relational, and less public.

At the same time, participants' critiques highlight an important tension in Japan's LGBTQ+ movement: how to advocate for legal and social change while respecting cultural norms that value privacy and consensus. The narratives here suggest that activism must not only push against the state but also reflect the diverse realities of queer life, avoiding a one-size-fits-all approach.

8.3.9 Conclusion

Participants' views on politics and activism are far from uniform. While some are hopeful about legal reforms and the efforts of activists, others feel alienated by approaches that they perceive as overly confrontational, exclusive, or performative. What emerges is a call for more inclusive, intersectional, and grassroots forms of advocacy that can address not only marriage equality but also broader issues of workplace discrimination, healthcare, and education.

8.4 Social Attitudes and Indifference

Beyond legal frameworks and activism, participants consistently highlighted a pervasive social indifference toward LGBTQ+ issues in Japan. This indifference—expressed through silence, avoidance, or polite neutrality—was described as both a form of cultural erasure and a source of personal frustration. While outright hostility is less common compared to some Western countries, the absence of genuine recognition or curiosity leaves many LGBTQ+ individuals feeling invisible. As Ayumi put it, "The opposite of love is indifference." This sentiment resonates with Sedgwick's (1990) notion of the "epistemology of the closet," where silence and avoidance are as powerful in enforcing heteronormativity as overt acts of discrimination.

8.4.1 Peer Pressure and Conformity

Many participants pointed to Japan's emphasis on *wa* (harmony) and group conformity as a central barrier to acceptance. The fear of standing out or "causing trouble" often discourages open discussion of sexuality and gender diversity. Kentaro (JJ, 35–44) explained: "We live in a society where peer pressure is so strong that if the government doesn't approve, no one will be happy." Makoto (JO, 45–54) echoed this feeling of constraint: "There is too much peer pressure [in Japanese society] in general, among gay people, and on the internet. I don't want to live in Japan anymore."

This sense of cultural uniformity extends into workplaces and schools, where being different is often equated with being disruptive. A bisexual female participant noted, "It's not that my colleagues hate LGBTQ+ people, but they prefer not to know. It's easier for everyone if we just don't talk about it." These forms of silence can create an environment where queer individuals self-censor to avoid conflict, effectively making their lives invisible in public spaces.

8.4.2 Subtle Discrimination and the "Polite Closet"

Participants frequently distinguished between overt discrimination—such as violence or verbal abuse—and the more subtle, socially sanctioned forms of exclusion they encounter. One gay male respondent described this as "being tolerated but never truly accepted." Louis (FJ, 45–54) elaborated: "While there is little violent discrimination in Japan compared to other nations, discrimination here is prevalent and subtle. It is often disguised in patronizing terms or disinterest."

This observation aligns with what Ahmed (2012) describes as 'non-performativity,' where public gestures of tolerance or diversity fail to translate into genuine recognition or structural change. For example, several participants commented on how colleagues or acquaintances often assume heterosexuality by default, asking questions like "Do you have a girlfriend?" without considering other possibilities. These microaggressions, while not overtly hostile, reinforce heteronormative expectations and the need for LGBTQ+ individuals to either disclose or deflect.

8.4.3 Family Expectations and Social Roles

Family dynamics were also mentioned as a significant source of social pressure. In Japan, familial expectations around marriage, childbearing, and caretaking remain strong, and LGBTQ+ individuals often face implicit or explicit pressure to conform to these norms. Niran (FJ, 25–34) recalled, "My mother said she wanted a son, so when I came out she misunderstood and thought I wanted to be a girl. Over time she understood, but she still ignores my identity."

Others highlighted how these expectations intersect with cultural values of filial piety. For example, Yu (JJ, 18–24) noted, "Coming out is not just about me. It feels like I am betraying my family's expectations, and that makes it harder." Such familial silence reinforces what scholars like Kazama (2016) have observed: LGBTQ+ identities in Japan often exist in tension with traditional social roles, leading to a form of "quiet tolerance" that is conditional on discretion.

8.4.4 Intersectional Experiences of Indifference

The experience of indifference is not uniform. For non-Japanese participants, racial and linguistic differences compound the challenges of queer invisibility. Emma (FJ, 25–34) described feeling both safer and unseen: "As a queer woman, I feel much safer in Japan. I'm not worried about telling someone and getting an extremely negative or violent reaction. What's uncomfortable is feeling unseen, uncelebrated, and unimportant."

Similarly, Harry noted that while he does not face overt hostility, heteronormative assumptions are pervasive: "I do not face direct discrimination, however heteronormality is extremely prevalent, meaning most people I meet assume I like girls and will commonly ask me questions like 'Do you have a girlfriend?'"

Some transgender participants stressed that indifference can be as harmful as active discrimination because it denies their gender identity. One trans participant shared, "People think they are being kind by avoiding the topic, but it makes me feel like my identity is taboo."

8.4.5 Media, Visibility, and Misunderstanding

Several participants pointed to the role of Japanese media in shaping social attitudes. While LGBTQ+ characters and celebrities have become more visible in recent years, this visibility is often mediated through stereotypes or "trendy" portrayals. One participant commented: "On TV, being gay can be funny or trendy, but in real life, it's still something people avoid talking about. Another added, "Seeing celebrities come out didn't make my parents understand me any better. It feels like we are visible only when it's convenient for society."

This kind of conditional visibility aligns with the concept of precarious visibility discussed throughout this book: LGBTQ+ people are increasingly visible as media content, but this visibility rarely leads to substantive changes in law, policy, or everyday attitudes.

8.4.6 Religious and Cultural Narratives

Although Japan is less religiously conservative than many Western countries, some participants noted how cultural or spiritual beliefs still shape attitudes toward sexuality and gender. Niran explained how Buddhism in both Thailand and Japan can frame non-heteronormative identities as "in-between" or less valid: "In Thailand, for some strict Buddhism believers, it is wrong to be in between male and female. And I believe that this principle also applies to Japan… 'Minor diversity' tends to be awkward for the 'major diversity.'"

This "awkwardness" often translates into silence or avoidance rather than overt hostility, but its effects are equally profound, leaving queer individuals without affirmation or support.

8.4.7 Internalized Silence and Self-Policing

Some participants described how the culture of indifference leads them to self-regulate their behavior in order to avoid discomfort or scrutiny. Riku observed:

> "I can't explain to my family that I can't see my boyfriend, for example, and once I start thinking negatively, the situation then starts to spiral out of control. I worry that my being an LGBTQ+ person in this situation is causing me to feel inferior to his spouse."

Others admitted to withholding personal details even when there was no explicit threat of discrimination. One gay male participant shared, "I have not come out to my colleagues because I do not want to make things uncomfortable. It's easier for everyone if I keep it private."

This dynamic reflects Sedgwick's (1990) observation that the closet is not merely an individual choice but a socially enforced regime of silence, maintained through subtle cues and collective expectations.

8.4.8 Generational Differences and Hope for Change

A few participants expressed cautious optimism about younger generations being more open-minded. As Niran noted: "I have never experienced any discrimination, and I feel like new generations, not only in Japan but throughout the world, do not seem to judge other people's identity."

However, others argued that change remains slow, especially in rural areas where LGBTQ+ visibility is minimal. Emily commented,

> I do not find a lot of discomfort surrounding my treatment. Then again, I am not open with my sexuality in most settings where I encounter a majority of Japanese people... The assumption that because I am female I automatically want a husband and children is so frustrating and disheartening.

This ongoing tension between progress and persistence of normative expectations suggests that while societal attitudes may be shifting, the pace of change varies greatly across regions, social classes, and age groups.

8.4.9 Conclusion

The narratives in this section illustrate how indifference operates as both a shield and a barrier: while some LGBTQ+ individuals appreciate the lack of overt hostility in Japan, they also lament the absence of affirmation and engagement. Social attitudes are shaped by cultural norms of harmony, family obligation, and gendered expectations, all of which reinforce what I term a "polite closet"—a form of invisibility maintained through silence, avoidance, and subtle microaggressions. For many participants, this indifference is just as damaging as overt discrimination because it leaves them feeling unseen, unimportant, and unable to live authentically.

8.5 Diversity, Inclusion, and Internal Community Tensions

While participants often spoke about external discrimination from Japanese society, many also highlighted challenges within the LGBTQ+ community itself. Several respondents expressed frustration that certain voices—especially those of cisgender gay men—dominate public narratives, while bisexual, asexual, transgender, and non-binary individuals often feel sidelined. These dynamics reveal internal hierarchies that shape how "LGBTQ+ issues" are understood, represented, and addressed in both activism and media.

8.5.1 *Unequal Visibility of Sexual Identities*

One recurring theme was the unequal visibility of different sexual orientations. While gay men and lesbians are increasingly represented in mainstream media, bisexual and asexual individuals are often overlooked or misunderstood. Kiyoshi (JJ, 55–64), an asexual male, observed: "Because I am asexual, I sometimes feel that LGBT people do not include me in their group."

Similarly, Rui (JJ, 25–34) emphasized how bisexuality remains poorly understood: "The understanding of lesbians and gays is gradually spreading, but to be honest, the recognition and understanding of other sexualities is still lacking."

A bisexual female participant explained how invisibility is compounded by erasure within LGBTQ+ spaces: "When I'm with queer women, they assume I'm a lesbian. When I'm with straight friends, they assume I'm straight. There's rarely a space where I can just exist without having to explain myself."

This experience of being "in between" reflects what Yoshino (2006) calls the pressure to cover: bisexual individuals often feel compelled to downplay their sexuality or align with one side of the binary to be accepted. For asexual individuals, the challenge is even greater, as their identity is sometimes dismissed as a phase, naivety, or medical condition, as Emily noted:

> Finding someone in Japan who is not just LGBT friendly, but also ACE [asexual] friendly is quite difficult. It is a smaller label that is often overlooked, misunderstood, or ousted from the group because of people's assumption that it is either celibacy, naivete, or a lack of desire due to some medical condition.

8.5.2 *Transgender Experiences and Community Divides*

Transgender participants shared their struggles with both societal and internal community acceptance. While gay and lesbian narratives have gained some degree of cultural familiarity in Japan, transgender issues remain less visible and are often subject to misunderstanding or stigma—even within queer spaces. One transgender respondent explained: "Some gay and lesbian people don't understand why we fight for legal gender change or healthcare. They say it's not part of LGBT issues, which hurts."

Others pointed out that trans voices are often marginalized in media portrayals of LGBTQ+ people. Kei (JJ, 35–44) reflected: "When I see 'LGBT' on TV, I rarely see people like me. It feels like T is always left out. Or if we are included, it's just for shock value."

These dynamics echo what scholars like Bettcher (2009) describe as the "inclusion paradox": transgender individuals are nominally included in the LGBTQ+ acronym but are frequently sidelined in policy discussions, media representations, and activism that prioritize cisgender concerns.

8.5.3 Class, Race, and Intersectional Exclusion

Some participants noted that LGBTQ+ activism and community spaces tend to prioritize urban, middle-class voices, leaving out those with different social positions. Ryo critiqued this dynamic explicitly:

> If you are a cisgay, able-bodied, high-class person, you are probably the easiest of the sexes to live with. However, it is harmful for gay people who are unaware of their privilege to join the conservative discourse and play the role of an understanding minority.

Foreign residents also described a sense of exclusion within LGBTQ+ spaces. Chun-chieh, a Taiwanese gay man, shared: "In my experience, LGBTQ people do not treat foreigners in the same positive manner as ordinary Japanese people. There have been times in which our interactions have been cut off as soon as they realized that I am a foreigner."

This observation suggests that national and racial dynamics shape belonging in LGBTQ+ spaces, reinforcing a sense of "otherness" for non-Japanese queer individuals. Emily reflected on a similar experience, noting that some Japanese people assume being LGBTQ+ is "foreign":

> Perhaps because of our visibility as foreigners, and our comfortability with it, some Japanese people have implied that being LGBTQ+ is linked with being foreign more so than with being a part of someone's personhood. It is reductive, assumes quite a great deal about what it means to be Japanese, and harms Japanese LGBTQ+ people who are not foreign.

8.5.4 Community Expectations and Normativity

Participants also discussed internalized norms within LGBTQ+ spaces, such as expectations around masculinity and femininity. Harry commented on the "sports-minded" (tai'ikukaikei) atmosphere of some male-dominated queer groups: "My previous workplace was something you could call 'tai'ikukaikei' [sports-minded] so I would get comments like 'chimpo tsuiteruno?' [got a dick?] if I struggle to lift something heavy for example, so overall quite uncomfortable."

Others felt that queer communities can sometimes replicate heteronormative pressures, especially regarding relationships and gender presentation. One lesbian participant shared, "Even in lesbian circles, there's a strong expectation that someone must play the 'male' role. I don't fit that, so I often feel left out."

This mirrors what Rubin (1984) described as the "hierarchy of sexual value," where even within queer spaces, certain identities and expressions are privileged while others are marginalized.

8.5.5 Disagreements About Activism and Pride

Some participants criticized LGBTQ+ activism for failing to represent the breadth of queer experiences. As noted in Sect. 8.2, Pride events were particularly divisive. While some saw Pride as a positive expression of visibility, others believed it catered to a narrow, urban elite. One participant remarked: "Pride events are flashy but they don't represent me. I don't see people like me—ace, bisexual, or trans—in the spotlight. It feels like the same people are always on stage."

Another respondent voiced concern about Pride's commercialization: "Companies put rainbows on their ads for Pride month, but inside their offices, they don't even have proper anti-discrimination policies. It feels fake."

These criticisms suggest that even celebratory events can reproduce exclusionary dynamics if they fail to center the full range of LGBTQ+ experiences.

8.5.6 Quiet Belonging and Chosen Communities

Despite these tensions, some participants described finding support in smaller, more intimate networks rather than in formal LGBTQ+ organizations or events. These chosen communities often operate outside of public visibility, providing safe spaces for individuals who feel marginalized even within queer spaces. As one participant noted: "I feel more comfortable in small circles with friends who understand me, rather than big LGBT events. In small groups, I don't have to explain or justify my identity."

This echoes Weston's (1991) concept of "families we choose," where queer kinship is forged through mutual understanding and care, rather than through mainstream validation or institutional recognition.

8.5.7 Conclusion

The narratives in this section reveal that inclusion within the LGBTQ+ community is not automatic or uniform. While the acronym "LGBTQ+ " suggests a coalition of diverse identities, participants' testimonies highlight persistent hierarchies based on gender, sexuality, race, and class. Bisexual, asexual, transgender, and foreign participants often feel marginalized both by mainstream Japanese society and within queer spaces that claim to represent them. These internal dynamics underscore the importance of intersectional approaches to advocacy and community-building—ones that recognize the multiplicity of queer experiences rather than privileging a singular narrative.

8.6 Popular Culture and Media

Popular culture and media have played a crucial role in shaping public perceptions of LGBTQ+ individuals in Japan. Participants frequently referenced television shows, Boys' Love (BL) manga, celebrity "coming out" stories, and corporate Pride campaigns, noting how these forms of representation often create a paradox: while LGBTQ+ identities are increasingly visible in media, this visibility rarely translates into genuine understanding or systemic change. Instead, participants described such portrayals as "safe," "stylized," or even "entertainment-only," which can reinforce stereotypes rather than dismantle them.

8.6.1 Boys' Love and the Commodification of Queer Desire

One recurring theme was the popularity of BL (Boys' Love) manga and anime, which many participants felt created a distorted image of male homosexuality. While BL narratives have introduced same-sex romance to mainstream audiences, participants argued that these works are often written for heterosexual female readers and do not reflect real LGBTQ+ lives. Kira (JJ, 18–24) explained:

> I get the impression that male homosexuals are more accepted by society. On the other hand, with the popularity of BL and the like, I think there are many people who see it as just content. I would like to see more people understand that it is just love between human beings.

Another participant commented: "BL is not about real gay people. It's about fantasy, and it often shows toxic or unrealistic relationships. People who only know gay life through BL think it's just a cute or trendy thing, not something real."

These critiques resonate with scholarly debates about the fujoshi (female fan) culture, which often consumes male-male romance narratives without engaging with actual queer communities (Nagaike 2012). Participants expressed a desire for more nuanced, authentic depictions that move beyond fetishization.

8.6.2 Celebrity "Coming Out" and Conditional Visibility

Several participants reflected on the role of celebrities who have come out as LGBTQ+ or are widely perceived as queer. While some saw these public figures as paving the way for greater acceptance, others felt that celebrity coming-out stories remain highly curated and disconnected from the struggles of ordinary LGBTQ+ people. One participant remarked: "Seeing celebrities come out didn't make my parents understand me any better. It feels like we are visible only when it's convenient for society." A lesbian participant added: "TV shows have queer characters, but they are often used as jokes or sidekicks. It's not about real life, and it doesn't help people like me feel seen."

Such media visibility often amounts to a spectacle of queerness—one that showcases LGBTQ+ identities in public but fails to translate into actual rights or systemic change. Participants felt that while television and magazines might celebrate "fashionable" or "fun" LGBTQ+ figures, these same outlets rarely address issues like workplace discrimination, legal inequality, or mental health.

8.6.3 Media Stereotypes and Everyday Misunderstandings

Participants frequently described how media representations, particularly of gay men and transgender women, perpetuate stereotypes that affect how they are treated in daily life. As one gay male participant explained: "On TV, being gay can be funny or trendy, but in real life, it's still something people avoid talking about. People expect me to be like the comedians they see on variety shows." Another participant critiqued the shallow nature of this portrayal: "Media shows drag queens or 'okama' as if they represent all queer people. It's like we're entertainment, not real human beings."

These comments highlight a disconnect between media caricatures and the complex realities of LGBTQ+ identities. While queer representation is increasing, it is often restricted to narrow archetypes that fail to challenge the heteronormative status quo.

8.6.4 Corporate Pride and the Question of Authenticity

Corporate involvement in LGBTQ+ visibility—particularly during Pride events—was another area where participants expressed ambivalence. Some acknowledged that corporate sponsorship helps fund large-scale events and campaigns, but others criticized such efforts as performative or profit-driven. One participant remarked: "Companies put rainbows on their ads for Pride month, but inside their offices, they don't even have proper anti-discrimination policies. It feels fake."

This observation reflects broader critiques of "rainbow capitalism" and "pinkwashing," where LGBTQ+ imagery is used for marketing rather than genuine social progress (Puar 2007). Participants urged that corporate engagement should be paired with internal policy changes, such as workplace protections and inclusive benefits.

8.6.5 Media Silence on Transgender Issues

While gay and lesbian identities receive some level of representation in mainstream media, transgender issues remain largely invisible or sensationalized. Kei, a transgender woman, shared: "When I see trans women on TV, they're often portrayed as comedians or weirdos. It's hard to feel respected when that's the image people have of you."

Others noted that transgender men are rarely represented at all. As one participant put it, "People don't even know we exist. There are no stories about trans men, and that invisibility makes life harder." These accounts underline the need for media representation that is both diverse and respectful, rather than relying on outdated tropes or sensationalist framing.

8.6.6 The Role of Social Media

Social media emerged as a double-edged sword in participants' reflections. For some, online platforms provided a space for authentic LGBTQ+ representation and community-building that mainstream media failed to offer. A bisexual participant explained: "I feel more connected to queer people online than in real life. On Twitter or Instagram, I see people like me sharing real experiences, not just TV stereotypes."

However, others warned that social media can also amplify harassment and gatekeeping within the LGBTQ+ community itself. Makoto commented: "There is too much peer pressure online, even among gay people. If you don't fit a certain image, people judge you. It's exhausting."

8.6.7 Pride, Media, and Misrepresentation

The relationship between media and Pride events was another point of critique. Some participants felt that media coverage of Pride tends to focus on flashy costumes or corporate sponsorships rather than the political roots of the event. Isamu noted: "Pride events used to be useful for getting the word out, but now they are not useful because they engage in inappropriate activities that lead to misunderstandings." Another participant observed: "Media always shows the same images—rainbows, parades, happy couples—but never the struggles we face every day. It's like our pain doesn't exist for them."

8.6.8 Theoretical Reflections on Media Visibility

The participant narratives echo theoretical critiques of visibility politics. While representation in media can increase awareness, scholars like Ahmed (2012) and Berlant (2011) remind us that visibility does not automatically lead to equality or safety. In fact, certain forms of visibility—such as comedic portrayals or token celebrity figures—can reinforce marginalization by reducing complex identities to consumable images.

This ongoing tension is especially evident in the commodification of LGBTQ+ identities in Japan. While queer aesthetics have become "trendy" in fashion and entertainment, participants noted that this cultural embrace has not translated into legal protections or broad social acceptance. As one participant succinctly put it: "We are visible when it's fun for society, but invisible when it comes to our rights."

8.6.9 Conclusion

While media visibility is an important factor, participants emphasize that real change requires structural reform and cultural transformation, as discussed in the concluding section.

The voices in this section reveal a critical awareness of the gap between media visibility and lived reality. While participants acknowledged that popular culture has played a role in raising awareness, they also critiqued its tendency to flatten, exoticize, or trivialize queer experiences. Corporate Pride campaigns and BL narratives may offer symbolic recognition, but they often fail to engage with the structural inequalities faced by LGBTQ+ individuals in Japan. Participants called for more authentic and diverse media representations—ones that do not simply portray queer life as entertainment but as a spectrum of real, lived experiences deserving of respect and rights.

8.7 Conclusion: Participant Calls for Change

The voices gathered in this chapter offer a rich and sometimes contradictory map of how LGBTQ+ individuals in Japan understand rights, representation, and recognition. While participants spoke with passion about the need for legal reform, many also highlighted the subtler forms of discrimination—silence, indifference, and tokenization—that persist even as queer visibility increases in media and popular culture. Their reflections underscore that progress cannot be measured solely by symbolic gestures or corporate allyship. Instead, meaningful change requires the alignment of legal protections, cultural understanding, and inclusive activism that centers diverse voices.

8.7.1 Legal Reform as a Foundation

A clear consensus among participants was that legal recognition is the bedrock of equality. Same-sex marriage, adoption rights, and anti-discrimination laws were cited as essential to both symbolic and practical validation. Nana voiced a frustration shared by many: "I want to have a child, but I can't get [a child] in a safe way, including through a hospital. I can't even adopt a child."

Others emphasized that without legal recognition, LGBTQ+ people remain second-class citizens, regardless of how visible or "fashionable" queer culture becomes. Vincente summarized this sentiment: "Until Japan recognize same-sex marriage and provide adoption rights to the LGBT + community, there won't be any visible space in society for our community to develop and thrive."

Some participants expressed cautious hope that ongoing marriage equality lawsuits, combined with growing public support, might eventually lead to legislative reform. Yet others were skeptical, pointing to the slow pace of political change. "Court rulings may declare discrimination unconstitutional, but politicians do nothing to act on them," one respondent remarked. For these participants, legal reform is not only about equal treatment under the law but also about sending a broader cultural message that queer lives are valid and worthy of respect.

8.7.2 Education and Awareness

Several participants stressed that legal change must be accompanied by public education and awareness campaigns. Without deeper understanding, they feared that legal recognition would remain superficial. One participant observed: "We need to start teaching about LGBTQ+ people in schools. Right now, there's no information, and that means kids grow up thinking we don't exist."

Emily echoed this need for structural awareness: "In order to make progress, there needs to be support from outside of the queer community, and people need to actually vote. I haven't seen either yet."

Participants suggested that comprehensive sex education, workplace diversity training, and public service campaigns could help combat the pervasive indifference they encounter. As one noted, "It's not hatred that we face most of the time, it's ignorance. People just don't think about us."

8.7.3 The Struggle Against Indifference

The concept of indifference emerged as a powerful theme throughout the RL and GI responses. Unlike overt homophobia or transphobia, which participants felt was relatively rare, indifference manifests as a refusal to engage with LGBTQ+ issues at all. This form of exclusion is difficult to challenge because it is rooted in silence rather than hostility. A bisexual participant remarked: "People won't attack me for being queer, but they also won't acknowledge it. It's as if my life is something private or irrelevant."

As noted in Sect. 8.3, this "polite closet" operates through cultural norms of discretion, group harmony, and the avoidance of controversial topics. Yet, as Ayumi powerfully stated, "The opposite of love is indifference. I want people to separate it from politics and think of it as a human rights issue."

This call to treat LGBTQ+ rights as fundamental human rights, rather than as a "special interest," was echoed across participant narratives.

8.7.4 Rethinking Activism and Representation

While many participants valued the visibility brought by activists and Pride events, others felt that current strategies are too focused on urban, cisgender, and middle-class experiences. Shun noted: "Only a few LGBTQ+ people who are convenient for some leftist activists are given the opportunity to appear in public."

Similarly, Kaede criticized the tone of certain activist campaigns: "Japan's LGBT activists are getting too carried away. Shame on them."

These critiques do not diminish the importance of activism but rather call for more inclusive, intersectional approaches. Ryo emphasized the need for awareness of privilege:

> If you are a cisgay, able-bodied, high-class person, you are probably the easiest of the sexes to live with. However, it is harmful for gay people who are unaware of their privilege to join the conservative discourse and play the role of an understanding minority.

Participants suggested that activism should focus not only on legal reforms like marriage but also on less "glamorous" issues such as healthcare access, mental health support, and protections for transgender individuals.

8.7.5 Media as Both Ally and Obstacle

The role of media was another recurring theme in participants' visions for change. While they acknowledged that television dramas, BL manga, and celebrity coming-out stories have increased visibility, they felt that these forms of representation often trivialize or distort LGBTQ+ experiences. "On TV, being gay can be funny or trendy, but in real life, it's still something people avoid talking about," one respondent commented.

Some participants called for more diverse and realistic portrayals, particularly of bisexual and transgender individuals. "We are visible when it's fun for society, but invisible when it comes to our rights," remarked another participant. They urged that media representation should not only entertain but also challenge societal norms and promote empathy.

8.7.6 *Visions for the Future*

When asked about the future of LGBTQ+ rights and acceptance in Japan, participants were cautiously hopeful but realistic. Emily reflected: "In order to make progress, there needs to be support from outside of the queer community, and people need to actually vote. I haven't seen either yet."

Others felt that societal change will be gradual, shaped by generational shifts and international pressure. As Daisuke (JJ, 35–44) put it: "I believe that if same-sex marriage is recognized, it will become more and more widely accepted."

Another respondent highlighted the importance of intersectional solidarity: "Queer rights cannot be separated from issues of gender equality, immigrant rights, and disability rights. We need to work together to make society fairer for everyone."

8.7.7 *Toward Legal and Cultural Transformation*

Taken together, these narratives suggest that achieving equality in Japan will require both legal and cultural transformation. Legal recognition—through marriage equality, adoption rights, and anti-discrimination protections—provides a critical foundation, but it must be complemented by shifts in social attitudes, educational practices, and media representation. As scholars like Ahmed (2006) and Berlant (2011) argue, rights are not just formal entitlements but part of an ongoing struggle for recognition, belonging, and livable lives.

Participants' calls for change underscore that visibility alone is insufficient. As one respondent powerfully noted, "We don't just want to be seen. We want to live without fear, with the same rights as everyone else." This demand resonates across the diverse voices in this chapter, reminding us that the struggle for LGBTQ+ rights in Japan is as much about transforming cultural logics of silence and conformity as it is about passing new laws.

The final chapter synthesizes these findings and reflects on the pandemic's broader implications for the future of LGBTQ+ rights and recognition in Japan.

References

Ahmed, S. (2006). *Queer phenomenology: Orientations, objects, others*. Duke University Press.

Ahmed, S. (2012). *On being included: Racism and diversity in institutional life*. Duke University Press.

Berlant, L. (2011). *Cruel optimism*. Duke University Press.
Butler, J. (2004). *Undoing gender*. Routledge.
Bettcher, T. M. (2009). Trans Identities and First-Person Authority. In L. Shrage (Ed.), *You've changed: Sex reassignment and personal identity* (pp. 98–120). Oxford University Press.
Crenshaw, K. (1989). Demarginalizing the intersection of race and sex: A Black feminist critique of antidiscrimination doctrine, feminist theory, and antiracist politics. *University of Chicago Legal Forum*, 1989(1), 139–167.
Duggan, L. (2003). *The twilight of equality? Neoliberalism, cultural politics, and the attack on democracy*. Beacon Press.
Halberstam, J. (2005). *In a queer time and place: Transgender bodies, subcultural lives*. New York University Press.
Kazama, T. (2016, March 18). "'Kanyō' na bunka ni okeru dōseiai ken'o" [Homophobia in Japanese "Tolerant" Culture]. *Kokusai Kyōyō-gaku-bu Ron-sō*, 8(2), 1–16.
Nagaike, K. (2012). *Fantasies of cross-dressing: Japanese women write male-male erotica*. Brill.
Puar, J. K. (2007). *Terrorist assemblages: Homonationalism in queer times*. Duke University Press.
Rubin, G. (1984). Thinking sex: Notes for a radical theory of the politics of sexuality. In C. S. Vance (Ed.), *Pleasure and danger: Exploring female sexuality* (pp. 267–319). Routledge & Kegan Paul.
Sedgwick, E. K. (1990). *Epistemology of the closet*. University of California Press.
Weston, K. (1991). *Families we choose: Lesbians, gays, kinship*. Columbia University Press.
Yoshino, K. (2006). *Covering: The hidden assault on our civil rights*. Random House.

Chapter 9
Conclusion—Lessons from the Pandemic and Future Directions

Masami Tamagawa

Abstract This chapter synthesizes the key findings of this book, illustrating how the COVID-19 pandemic both magnified structural inequalities and catalyzed new forms of resilience for Japan's LGBTQ+ communities. Using the lens of precarious visibility, the chapter highlights how legal exclusion, workplace discrimination, and healthcare barriers intersected with personal experiences of isolation, family tensions, and digital activism. It draws on themes from earlier chapters to show how visibility could offer recognition and solidarity but also heightened risks of stigma and exclusion.

The chapter also situates domestic narratives alongside transnational perspectives, revealing how border closures, visa insecurity, and racialized discrimination compounded challenges for migrants and non-Japanese queer residents. Section 9.5 highlights the rise of digital worldmaking, where online platforms became crucial sites of activism, mutual aid, and storytelling. Section 9.6 revisits the momentum around marriage equality, anti-discrimination protections, and transgender healthcare reform. Concluding reflections emphasize the need for sustained advocacy, hybrid community networks, and cultural transformation to ensure that the lessons of the pandemic translate into lasting inclusion and justice.

9.1 Introduction: Reassessing LGBTQ+ Lives in a Time of Crisis

Building on the lens of precarious visibility, this section revisits the central questions that have guided this study: How did the COVID-19 pandemic shape the everyday lives of LGBTQ+ individuals in Japan? In what ways did Japan's legal and social frameworks exacerbate or mitigate these challenges? What strategies of resilience and community-building emerged in response to a period of profound uncertainty and isolation? And how might these lessons inform future advocacy, policy reform, and scholarship?

M. Tamagawa, *Japanese LGBTQ+ Lives, Diasporic Voices, and Resilience*,
https://doi.org/10.1007/978-981-95-3105-9_9

The chapters leading up to this conclusion have revealed a nuanced landscape of vulnerability, resilience, and resistance. While the pandemic magnified long-standing inequalities—such as legal exclusion, barriers to healthcare, and pervasive social stigma—it also catalyzed new forms of activism, digital solidarity, and public discourse around LGBTQ+ rights. Rather than being solely defined by loss or invisibility, this period became an opportunity for communities to mobilize, demand recognition, and confront structural barriers with renewed urgency. Chapter 8, focusing on rights and recognition, amplifies participants' voices on legal precarity, activism, and cultural representation, bridging the personal narratives of Chapters 2, 3, 4, 5, 6 and 7 with broader structural and political debates.

This concluding chapter synthesizes these insights, drawing attention to the pandemic's long-term implications for Japan's LGBTQ+ community. It highlights how grassroots initiatives and digital networks sustained communal ties in the absence of physical spaces, how advocacy efforts around marriage equality and anti-discrimination protections gained momentum, and how public perceptions of LGBTQ+ rights have begun to shift—though unevenly. Finally, this chapter calls for a sustained commitment to legal reform, healthcare equity, and cultural change to ensure that the hard-won lessons of the pandemic translate into lasting progress.

9.2 Precarious Visibility and Everyday Vulnerabilities

Building on the broader synthesis in Sect. 9.1, this section takes a closer look at how precarious visibility shaped the everyday realities of Japanese LGBTQ+ individuals during the pandemic. The narratives explored throughout the book reveal how visibility was never neutral: it could bring recognition, connection, and solidarity, but it also carried the risk of social exclusion, workplace discrimination, or familial tension. The pandemic heightened these dynamics by forcing individuals to negotiate new boundaries between private and public life—especially within digital spaces where visibility was often both empowering and precarious. These patterns underscore how structural inequalities intersected with intimate experiences of self-expression, safety, and community, making visibility a constant balancing act.

9.2.1 Structural Inequalities Exposed

The pandemic served as a stress test for Japan's legal and social systems, revealing the extent to which LGBTQ+ individuals remain marginalized. For same-sex couples, the lack of marriage equality became an acute issue during emergencies, with some partners denied hospital visitation or unable to make medical and financial decisions on behalf of their loved ones. Transgender individuals experienced interruptions in essential healthcare, including delays in hormone therapy and gender-affirming procedures, which were deemed "non-essential" by some medical institutions. These disruptions not only jeopardized physical health but also had profound mental health repercussions.

Economic vulnerabilities intensified as LGBTQ+ workers—particularly those in non-regular or service-sector employment—were disproportionately affected by layoffs and reduced hours. Participants' testimonies underscored how workplace discrimination, already pervasive, intersected with pandemic-related job insecurity. For many, government relief policies failed to account for diverse family structures, leaving queer individuals without the safety net provided to legally recognized families.

9.2.2 Social Isolation and Community Resilience

Social distancing measures disrupted the physical spaces that have historically served as sanctuaries for queer connection and self-expression—bars, community centers, Pride events, and other public gatherings. Many participants described a profound sense of isolation, exacerbated by living with unsupportive families or being unable to visit partners across prefectural or national borders. For transgender and queer youth, who often relied on informal community networks for affirmation, the closure of these spaces was particularly damaging.

Yet, out of these challenges emerged remarkable forms of resilience. Online platforms—ranging from social media groups to virtual Pride parades—became vital hubs for connection, activism, and mutual aid. Digital spaces allowed for new forms of solidarity, enabling community members to share information, organize petitions, and support mental health initiatives. Some participants noted that online interactions made activism more accessible, particularly for those living in rural areas or those who had previously felt disconnected from urban LGBTQ+ scenes.

9.2.3 Visibility and Shifting Public Awareness

The pandemic also brought increased visibility to the structural disadvantages faced by LGBTQ+ individuals. Stories of same-sex partners being excluded from emergency benefits or denied recognition during medical crises circulated widely in the media, sparking renewed debates over marriage equality and legal protections. Court cases challenging the constitutionality of Japan's ban on same-sex marriage gained traction during this period, illustrating how moments of crisis can generate both public empathy and political momentum. Similarly, advocacy groups intensified campaigns for national anti-discrimination laws and the removal of medical and legal barriers affecting transgender communities, framing these issues as matters of public health and human rights rather than "special interests."

These shifts in public discourse, coupled with grassroots campaigns and legal challenges, highlight how the pandemic became both a magnifier of inequalities and a catalyst for change. The following Sect. (9.3) draws together insights from Chapters 2, 3, 4 and 5 to further examine how these dynamics unfolded across domestic contexts, including family, work, and digital communities.

9.3 Lessons from Domestic Narratives

Drawing on the domestic narratives presented in Chapters 2, 3, 4 and 5, this section synthesizes key findings related to family, work, healthcare, and digital spheres.

The domestic Chapters (2, 3, 4 and 5) reveal how precarious visibility shaped everyday life for LGBTQ+ individuals in Japan, particularly within family, work, healthcare, and digital spheres. Social isolation and entrenched legal and cultural stigmas created conditions where visibility often brought heightened vulnerability, while invisibility required suppressing identity and forgoing critical support. Chapters 2 and 3 examined how familial silence and domestic tensions intensified during lockdowns, while Chapters 4 and 5 highlighted workplace challenges, digital activism, and intersectional struggles faced by marginalized queer communities. These narratives show that visibility during the pandemic was not merely a matter of public recognition but a daily negotiation of safety, belonging, and self-expression. Three key themes—marriage equality and family rights, anti-discrimination protections, and transgender healthcare reform—emerged as particularly urgent during this period.

9.3.1 Marriage Equality and Family Rights

The pandemic underscored the urgent need for legal recognition of same-sex partnerships in Japan. Same-sex couples faced heightened vulnerability due to their lack of access to spousal benefits, inheritance rights, and hospital visitation privileges—issues that became starkly visible during medical emergencies caused by COVID-19. Participants shared stories of being unable to advocate for hospitalized partners or being excluded from government-issued pandemic relief programs designed exclusively for legally recognized families. These lived experiences reinforced the necessity of marriage equality not only as a symbolic affirmation of rights but as a matter of basic legal and economic security.

Marriage equality lawsuits across Japan gained renewed public attention during this period. Grassroots groups and advocacy organizations leveraged pandemic-related hardships to push for constitutional challenges and local partnership ordinances. While progress at the national level has remained slow, the legal momentum and public discourse generated by these efforts have begun to shift mainstream perceptions, positioning marriage equality as a fundamental civil rights issue rather than a niche demand of the LGBTQ+ community. These struggles underscore how legal invisibility translates into real-life vulnerability, making marriage equality central to both recognition and survival.

9.3.2 Anti-Discrimination Protections

The absence of comprehensive anti-discrimination laws for sexual orientation and gender identity remains one of Japan's most glaring legal gaps. The pandemic amplified this deficiency, particularly in the workplace. Non-regular workers—disproportionately represented among LGBTQ+ individuals—were often the first to face layoffs or reduced hours. Several participants reported subtle but persistent biases from employers who assumed heteronormative family structures, leaving single queer employees with fewer protections or benefits.

Advocates have called for a national anti-discrimination framework that would extend to employment, housing, and healthcare, arguing that the pandemic revealed the life-and-death consequences of systemic exclusion. The failure to pass even a non-binding "LGBT Understanding Promotion Bill" before the 2021 Tokyo Olympics further illustrated the government's reluctance to implement substantive change. However, public frustration with the slow pace of reform has strengthened calls for legal measures comparable to those in other G7 nations. The absence of legal protections perpetuated a climate where queer individuals remained selectively visible—recognized as workers but denied equal rights as citizens.

9.3.3 Transgender Healthcare Reform

Transgender participants in this study consistently emphasized the structural barriers that limit access to gender-affirming care in Japan—barriers that became even more pronounced during the pandemic. Legal requirements for gender marker changes, including forced sterilization and invasive psychiatric evaluations, reflect outdated and harmful medical norms. Interruptions in hormone therapy and gender-affirming procedures during the pandemic deepened mental health struggles for many transgender individuals.

Activists have highlighted how these legal and medical barriers are fundamentally at odds with international human rights standards. Organizations such as Nijiiro Diversity and trans-led advocacy groups have intensified efforts to dismantle these restrictions, framing transgender healthcare access as a matter of bodily autonomy and public health rather than elective or cosmetic treatment. The pandemic made clear that visibility for transgender individuals is often mediated by gatekeeping institutions that restrict bodily autonomy, further illustrating the tension at the heart of precarious visibility.

The domestic narratives from Chapters 2, 3, 4 and 5 illustrate how the pandemic both exposed and intensified the vulnerabilities embedded in Japan's legal and social structures, while also highlighting the creative strategies of resilience that emerged in response. However, these experiences cannot be fully understood in isolation from transnational dynamics, as border restrictions, visa insecurity, and legal recognition shaped the lives of both Japanese LGBTQ+ migrants abroad and non-Japanese queer residents in Japan. The following Sect. (9.4) turns to these transnational and legal dimensions, drawing on Chapters 6 and 7 to examine how visibility, precarity, and activism intersect across national boundaries.

9.4 Diasporic and Transnational Dimensions

While the domestic narratives illuminate how precarious visibility shaped everyday life within Japan, the experiences of Japanese LGBTQ+ migrants abroad and non-Japanese queer residents reveal how these dynamics were intensified by border regimes, legal exclusions, and racialized barriers. Border restrictions, visa insecurity, and the absence of legal recognition for same-sex partnerships compounded the vulnerabilities of those living across or between national boundaries. For some, the inability to reunite with partners or return home during the pandemic magnified feelings of isolation, while others faced compounded discrimination due to intersecting factors of race, language, and immigration status. Chapters 6 and 8 trace these transnational dynamics, showing how the pandemic disrupted intimate relationships, exposed systemic legal gaps, and forced individuals to renegotiate their sense of belonging both within and beyond Japan. This section synthesizes those findings, highlighting the intertwined struggles for recognition, mobility, and rights in a global context.

9.4.1 Border Closures and Separation

The pandemic's strict border controls exposed the fragility of legal recognition for queer relationships, particularly for binational couples. Same-sex partners were often excluded from emergency travel exemptions and family reunification policies, leaving many separated for extended periods. Stories from participants like Shufen (FJ, 35–44) and Aanan (FJ, 45–54) reveal how these restrictions not only strained intimate relationships but also highlighted the lack of formal protections for LGBTQ+ families under Japanese law. For migrants and expatriates, the inability to return home or navigate complex entry requirements further deepened feelings of isolation and dislocation.

9.4.2 Legal Invisibility and Mobility

Alongside border restrictions, visa and residency rules compounded the challenges faced by queer individuals during the pandemic. Non-Japanese LGBTQ+ residents encountered difficulties renewing visas or accessing spousal benefits due to the absence of marriage equality. Japanese LGBTQ+ migrants abroad also reported how Japan's lack of legal recognition for same-sex partnerships hindered their ability to claim rights in foreign jurisdictions. This legal invisibility left many individuals in precarious positions, forcing them to navigate their identities strategically in contexts where visibility could mean both recognition and risk, further reinforcing the need for both domestic and international policy reforms.

9.4.3 Intersectional Challenges and Racialized Experiences

Non-Japanese LGBTQ+ individuals living in Japan often navigated layered forms of discrimination, shaped by race, nationality, and language barriers. The pandemic heightened these intersectional challenges, as misinformation, xenophobia, and cultural stigma amplified social exclusion. Testimonies from participants like Emma (FJ, 25–34), Alejandro (FJ, 25–34), and Fenhua (FJ, 18–24) highlight how these intersecting identities shaped their access to healthcare, housing, and community support. Despite these barriers, many forged transnational networks and online communities that offered solidarity and mutual aid, further illustrating how community-building transcended national borders during times of crisis.

These transnational narratives reveal that precarious visibility operates not only within Japan but also across borders, where legal invisibility, restricted mobility, and intersecting forms of discrimination create additional layers of vulnerability. At the same time, these accounts highlight the resilience and adaptability of LGBTQ+ individuals who forged new networks of solidarity—often in digital or diasporic spaces—despite structural and geographical barriers. The pandemic thus underscored how struggles for recognition and rights are simultaneously local and global, shaped by both national policies and transnational flows of information and activism. The following Sect. (9.5) turns to the role of community resilience and digital world-making, examining how online spaces became crucial sites of support, advocacy, and visibility during this period of crisis.

9.5 Community Resilience and Digital Worldmaking

As physical spaces for queer connection—such as bars, community centers, and Pride events—were shuttered during the pandemic, online platforms emerged as crucial lifelines for LGBTQ+ individuals. Digital environments became spaces not only for social interaction but also for activism, mutual aid, and creative forms of visibility that transcended geographical boundaries. From virtual Pride parades to grassroots crowdfunding campaigns, these initiatives demonstrated how communities could reimagine solidarity in times of crisis. Building on the domestic and transnational narratives discussed earlier, this section highlights how digital networks provided both refuge and a catalyst for renewed activism.

9.5.1 Virtual Pride and Activism

The cancellation of in-person Pride events and community gatherings led to the rapid expansion of online activism. Virtual Pride parades, live-streamed panel discussions, and social media campaigns became platforms for LGBTQ+ voices to challenge invisibility and share stories during lockdowns. These events allowed participants from rural areas, as well as those who were closeted or unable to attend physical events, to engage with queer communities in new ways. Online activism also facilitated the rapid spread of petitions and policy advocacy efforts, amplifying calls for marriage equality and anti-discrimination protections.

9.5.2 Online Mental Health and Mutual Aid

Digital networks became essential for mental health support during the pandemic, especially for individuals who were isolated from affirming social circles. Community organizations and informal peer groups hosted online counseling sessions, support groups, and workshops tailored to LGBTQ+ needs. Crowdfunding initiatives and mutual aid networks were also launched to support those facing economic hardship, particularly non-regular workers and migrants. These digital responses highlighted how technology could mitigate the isolation caused by both the pandemic and systemic social exclusion.

9.5.3 Digital Storytelling and Visibility

The pandemic fostered an outpouring of digital storytelling, with individuals using blogs, YouTube, podcasts, and social media to share personal experiences of being LGBTQ+ in Japan. These narratives provided both visibility and solidarity, creating a collective archive of pandemic-era queer life. Influencers, activists, and community members used these platforms to counter mainstream narratives, raising awareness about legal and social inequalities while celebrating queer resilience. Such digital expressions played a crucial role in shaping public discourse and fostering a sense of belonging during a period of widespread uncertainty.

The digital initiatives and networks that emerged during the pandemic illustrate how precarious visibility can be both a risk and a resource, while also serving as a powerful driver of resilience. Online spaces offered opportunities for connection, activism, and storytelling that transcended physical limitations, yet they also exposed individuals to surveillance, harassment, and the pressure to perform authenticity in public forums. These dynamics underscore the dual-edged nature of digital visibility—while it can empower marginalized communities, it also reinforces the need for structural protections and inclusive policies. The following Sect. (9.6) examines how these digital forms of resilience intersect with ongoing legal and policy debates, particularly the renewed push for marriage equality, anti-discrimination laws, and transgender healthcare reforms in Japan.

9.6 Legal and Policy Horizons Post-Pandemic

The pandemic brought renewed urgency to Japan's ongoing struggles over legal recognition, workplace equity, and healthcare access for LGBTQ+ individuals. While digital activism and community resilience created new forms of visibility (as discussed in Sect. 9.5), these efforts also underscored the limitations of symbolic recognition in the absence of substantive legal and policy reform. The gaps in marriage equality, anti-discrimination measures, and transgender healthcare became starkly visible during the crisis, as queer individuals faced systemic exclusion from rights and benefits afforded to heterosexual and cisgender counterparts. In this context, precarious visibility becomes a useful lens for understanding how visibility during the pandemic both illuminated injustices and fueled momentum for advocacy and reform. The following subsections examine key legal and policy debates that have gained traction in the wake of COVID-19, highlighting both the progress made and the challenges that remain. Insights from Chapter 8, which foreground participants' reflections on marriage equality, workplace discrimination, and media representation, further underscore how these legal and cultural struggles intersect with everyday experiences of visibility.

9.6.1 Momentum for Marriage Equality

The legal exclusion of same-sex couples remains one of the most urgent issues. As one gay participant noted, "My partner was hospitalized, and I wasn't allowed to see him. His family—who doesn't accept us—made decisions without me" (Kenta, JJ, 25–34). This is not an isolated case but emblematic of a system that denies queer couples the basic rights afforded to heterosexual spouses. Marriage equality is not merely symbolic—it is vital for healthcare decision-making, inheritance rights, and access to emergency relief. The increasing number of lawsuits filed across Japan and the expansion of local partnership certificates show that change is possible, but national legislation remains the ultimate goal. This struggle underscores how legal invisibility directly shapes the vulnerability of queer relationships, reinforcing the urgency of structural recognition.

9.6.2 Anti-Discrimination and Workplace Equity

The pandemic also highlighted workplace discrimination and economic precarity. A queer educator in the JET program commented, "As a queer woman, I feel safer here than in the United States, but I feel unseen, uncelebrated, and unimportant" (Emma, FJ, 25–34). Her statement illustrates how "safety" can coexist with structural erasure and a lack of validation. National anti-discrimination laws, particularly in employment and housing, are urgently needed to ensure that LGBTQ+ workers are protected from both overt harassment and systemic neglect. The absence of such protections forces many individuals to remain selectively visible, weighing the benefits of disclosure against potential social and economic penalties.

9.6.3 Transgender Healthcare and Mental Health

The pandemic revealed serious gaps in transgender healthcare, as many gender-affirming procedures were delayed or deprioritized. Participants like Ryo (JJ, 35–44) described feeling "suspended in time" as their medical transitions were halted, leading to significant mental health challenges. Expanding LGBTQ+ -inclusive healthcare—particularly mental health services that are culturally sensitive and accessible—must be a policy priority. The pandemic exposed how transgender individuals' visibility is mediated by restrictive medical systems, where access to care is both a right and a contested terrain.

9.6.4 Hybrid Activism and Grassroots Strength

Grassroots networks adapted impressively during the pandemic, combining digital tools with mutual aid. Virtual Pride events, online counseling sessions, and crowd-funding initiatives not only filled critical gaps but also broadened participation, allowing rural and international LGBTQ+ individuals to connect. The challenge ahead is to sustain these hybrid models while rebuilding physical spaces for connection, which remain crucial for visibility and belonging. This hybrid activism highlights how visibility—though precarious—can also be reimagined as a collective force for empowerment and solidarity.

9.6.5 International Collaboration and Human Rights Advocacy

Japan's LGBTQ+ movement has much to gain from global solidarity. Collaborations with activists in Taiwan, South Korea, and beyond provide models for effective lobbying and public education. At the same time, Japan's unique cultural and legal context offers valuable lessons for other nations, particularly in navigating the tension between privacy, visibility, and collective activism. These exchanges underscore how precarious visibility is both a local and global phenomenon, shaped by interconnected struggles for rights and recognition.

The legal and policy struggles intensified by the pandemic reveal how precarious visibility is inseparable from structural power and the pursuit of rights. While court cases, advocacy campaigns, and grassroots activism have sparked important conversations, tangible reforms—such as national marriage equality and comprehensive anti-discrimination legislation—remain incomplete. Transgender healthcare reforms, though increasingly recognized as urgent, continue to face resistance rooted in outdated legal frameworks and cultural stigma. The pandemic demonstrated that visibility alone is insufficient; without systemic changes, queer communities remain vulnerable to both institutional neglect and social exclusion. These dynamics set the stage for the final reflections in Sect. 9.7, which consider how the lessons of the pandemic can inform a more inclusive and sustainable future for Japan's LGBTQ+ communities.

9.6.6 Queer Theoretical Reflections on Visibility and Future Directions

These legal and policy debates resonate with broader theoretical insights, which offer critical tools for understanding visibility, recognition, and resilience during the pandemic.

The lessons drawn from this book resonate strongly with the insights of queer theory, which interrogates how visibility, recognition, and vulnerability are constructed within power-laden social and legal frameworks. Butler's (1993, 2009) work on performativity and precarity underscores how the pandemic highlighted the fragility of queer lives in Japan. Participants' struggles for legal recognition and healthcare access reveal how identity is continuously enacted and contested in spaces where heteronormative expectations dominate.

Sedgwick's (1990) epistemology of the closet further illuminates the tension between being "seen" and being "protected." As this book has shown, pandemic-era visibility often meant being recognized only as exceptions—excluded from legal benefits or treated as anomalies within policy frameworks. Visibility, in this context, was precarious because it did not equate to safety or rights.

Ahmed's (2006) concept of queer orientation also helps explain + the spatial and emotional navigation of LGBTQindividuals during the pandemic. Digital platforms, online communities, and mutual aid networks allowed participants to "reorient" themselves toward spaces of care and belonging when physical environments remained unwelcoming or unsafe.

Finally, Muñoz's (2009) vision of queer futurity offers a hopeful frame for interpreting the resilience documented across these chapters. The grassroots activism, digital worldmaking, and personal strategies of survival described here are not simply reactive measures—they are gestures toward imagined futures where queer lives are affirmed. Similarly, Berlant's (2011) notion of "cruel optimism" reminds us that the pursuit of recognition—such as marriage equality—can be both sustaining and constraining, necessitating critical reflection on the forms of life we strive to protect and nurture.

9.7 Concluding Reflections: Toward Inclusive Futures

The COVID-19 pandemic has revealed that the struggles of Japan's LGBTQ+ communities are not temporary disruptions but deeply rooted in structural inequities that persist across legal, cultural, and social spheres. Throughout this book, the concept of precarious visibility has served as a lens to understand how queer lives are simultaneously rendered visible and vulnerable—seen in moments of activism and resilience, yet often overlooked or excluded in policy and practice. As we move beyond the immediate crisis, the challenge is to ensure that the lessons learned during the pandemic do not fade into silence but are translated into lasting systemic change. This concluding section reflects on three critical areas that demand ongoing attention: building sustainable community networks, advancing legal reforms, and fostering cultural transformation.

9.7.1 Building Sustainable Community Networks

The pandemic underscored the importance of grassroots and digital initiatives that sustained LGBTQ+ individuals when physical spaces were closed. Online activism, virtual Pride events, and mutual aid networks proved vital, but these must now be integrated with physical community spaces to ensure long-term resilience. Hybrid models—combining digital accessibility with in-person solidarity—can offer a more inclusive approach, particularly for individuals living in rural areas or those who remain closeted. These networks must also prioritize mental health resources and intersectional inclusivity to address the diverse needs of Japan's LGBTQ+ population.

9.7.2 Advancing Legal and Policy Reforms

The momentum for marriage equality, anti-discrimination protections, and transgender healthcare reform gained unprecedented visibility during the pandemic, but progress remains incomplete. Court cases and local ordinances have pushed the national conversation forward, yet systemic change requires sustained advocacy at both grassroots and institutional levels. Policy reforms must not only address formal recognition but also tackle economic precarity, workplace discrimination, and healthcare barriers. Legal visibility must go hand-in-hand with tangible protections that secure the rights and well-being of all queer individuals.

9.7.3 Fostering Cultural Transformation

Beyond legal change, cultural attitudes toward gender and sexuality play a decisive role in shaping the lived realities of LGBTQ+ people in Japan. The pandemic highlighted both the resilience and fragility of queer communities as they navigated familial silence, heteronormative expectations, and public discourse. Storytelling—through media, literature, and personal narratives—remains a powerful tool to challenge stereotypes and foster empathy. A more inclusive society will depend on sustained efforts to shift public understanding, making queer lives visible not as exceptions but as integral to Japan's social fabric.

9.7.4 Final Thoughts: Precarious Visibility Revisited

This book complements my forthcoming volume, *Queer Intimacies and Cultural Dissent in Japanese Life: Quiet Subversion* (Routledge, 2025), which examines broader cultural and aesthetic practices of quiet resistance in Japanese queer life. While that work focuses on literary, artistic, and performative expressions of dissent, the present volume foregrounds the lived realities of LGBTQ+ individuals during the COVID-19 pandemic. Together, these two books offer a multi-layered perspective on Japanese queer experiences—one tracing the cultural politics of representation, the other capturing voices of resilience and survival amid crisis.

The notion of precarious visibility has threaded together the diverse experiences presented in this book—from domestic challenges in family and work to transnational struggles across borders. The pandemic made visible the vulnerabilities that have long been embedded in Japan's social and legal systems, while also highlighting the creative forms of resilience and solidarity that emerged in response. As Japan moves forward, the task is not only to address the structural gaps exposed by this crisis but also to build a future where visibility no longer carries such profound risks. Ultimately, this book calls for a vision of inclusivity grounded in both legal recognition and cultural transformation, where the lives and voices of LGBTQ+ individuals are celebrated rather than silenced.

Taken together, Chapters 2 through 8 reveal a continuum of experiences—from intimate narratives of isolation, family, and resilience to collective struggles over rights, recognition, and cultural representation—underscoring that the fight for LGBTQ+ equality in Japan is both deeply personal and profoundly structural. The lessons of these chapters point toward a future where individual stories and collective advocacy converge, transforming precarious visibility into sustainable forms of inclusion and justice.

These reflections also point toward future research agendas that consider how crises like the pandemic can deepen our understanding of queer life at the intersection of local and global dynamics (Table 9.1).

Table 9.1 Select participants (Narrative & Case Studies) (N = 137)

ID*	Name**	LGBTQ+ identity	Age group	Highest level of education	Occupation	Relationship status	Living situation	Area of residence	Race/ ethnicity
1JJ	Yu	Transgender FtM/X	18–24	High school or equiv	Student	In a relationship, not living together	Alone	Suburban	Japanese
4JJ	Mayumi	Pansexual female	45–54	Bachelor's degree	Employed full-time	Partnership	w/a spouse or partner	Urban	Japanese
5JJ	Shinji	Gay	45–55	Bachelor's degree	Self-employed	Divorced/ separated	w/a spouse or partner & a parent(s)	Urban	Japanese
8JJ	Kumiko	Lesbian	35–44	Master's degree	Employed full-time	Single	w/a parent(s)	Suburban	Japanese
9JJ	Misaki	Lesbian	25–34	Bachelor's degree	Employed full-time	Living with a partner	w/a spouse or partner	Urban	Japanese
10JJ	Hiroshi	Gay	55–64	Bachelor's degree	Employed part-time	Single	Alone	Urban	Japanese
13JO	Daisuke	Gay	35–44	Doctorate degree	Student	Single	Alone	Urban	Japanese
14JO	Ai	Q + (Others) female	25–34	Master's degree	Employed full-time	In a relationship, not living together	w/a parent(s)	Suburban	Japanese
15JJ	Aya	Bisexual female	25–34	Master's degree	Self-employed	Married (opposite-sex)	Alone	Urban	Mixed/ multiple ethnic groups
16JJ	Hitomi	Transgender MtF/X	25–34	Some grad school	Employed full-time	Married (opposite-sex)	w/a spouse or partner	Urban	Japanese
17JO	Makoto	Gay	45–54	High school or equiv	Home maker	Married (same-sex)	w/a spouse or partner	Rural	Japanese

(continued)

Table 9.1 (continued)

ID*	Name**	LGBTQ+ identity	Age group	Highest level of education	Occupation	Relationship status	Living situation	Area of residence	Race/ethnicity
18JJ	Junko	Lesbian	45–54	Doctorate degree	Employed full-time	Living with a partner	w/a spouse or partner	Urban	Japanese
21JO	Shu	Transgender FtM/X	35–44	Bachelor's degree	Home maker	Married (opposite-sex)	w/a spouse or partner	Suburban	Japanese
28JJ	Shun	Gay	18–24	Bachelor's degree	Employed full-time	Single	w/a parent(s)	Rural	Japanese
32FJ	Bill#	Bisexual male	45–54	Master's degree	Employed full-time	Married (opposite-sex)	w/a spouse or partner	Suburban	White/European
33JO	Sho	Transgender FtM/X	25–34	Bachelor's degree	Self-employed	Widowed	Alone	Urba	Mixed/Multiple ethnic groups
35FJ	Louis#	Gay	45–54	Bachelor's degree	Self-employed	Living with a partner	w/a spouse or partner	Urban	Mixed/Multiple ethnic groups
37JJ	Jun	Transgender FtM/X	18–24	High school or equiv	Student	Single	Alone	Suburban	Japanese
39JO	Tsuyoshi	Gay	35–44	Bachelor's degree	Employed full-time	Partnership	w/a spouse or partner	Urban	Japanese
42FO	Michael#	Gay	25–34	Master's degree	Student	Single	Alone	Urban	White/European
46FO	Chia-hao#	Gay	25–34	Bachelor's degree	Employed full-time	Single	w/someone else	n/a	Southeast Asian

(continued)

Table 9.1 (continued)

ID*	Name**	LGBTQ+ identity	Age group	Highest level of education	Occupation	Relationship status	Living situation	Area of residence	Race/ ethnicity
47FJ	Vicente#	Bisexual male	25–34	Doctorate degree	Employed part-time	Living with a partner	w/a spouse or partner	Urban	Mixed/ Multiple ethnic groups
53JJ	Ryo	Transgender FtM/X	35–44	Doctorate degree	Dispatched employee	Living with a partner	w/a spouse or partner	Urban	Japanese
54FJ	Niran#	Gay	25–34	Bachelor's degree	Student	In a relationship, not living together	Alone	Urban	Southeast Asian
55JJ	Tom#	Bisexual male	45–54	Bachelor's degree	Employed full-time	Married (opposite-sex)	w/a spouse or partner	Urban	White/ European
56JJ	Yohei	Gay	35–44	Master's degree	Self-employed	Living with a partner	w/a spouse or partner	Urban	Japanese
59JJ	Tetsuya	Gay	45–54	Master's degree	Self-employed	Living with a partner	w/a spouse or partner	Urban	Japanese
60JO	Toru	Gay	35–44	Master's degree	Employed full-time	Living with a partner	w/a spouse or partner & a parent(s)	Rural	Japanese
61JJ	Ren	Gay	18–24	Vocational school	Employed full-time	In a relationship, not living together	with a parent(s)	Suburban	Japanese
62FJ	Alexandre#	Gay	25–34	Associate degree	Employed full-time	Single	Alone	Urban	White/ European
65JJ	Kaito	Gay	35–44	Vocational school	Employed part-time	Single	w/ someone else	Suburban	Japanese
67JJ	Kentaro	Pansexual male	35–44	n/a	Dispatched employee	Single	Alone	Suburban	Japanese

(continued)

Table 9.1 (continued)

ID*	Name**	LGBTQ+ identity	Age group	Highest level of education	Occupation	Relationship status	Living situation	Area of residence	Race/ethnicity
69JJ	Tsubasa	Transgender MtF/X	35–44	Bachelor's degree	Unable to work	Single	w/a parent(s)	Suburban	Japanese
70JJ	Yusuke	Gay	45–54	Bachelor's degree	Employed full-time	Living with a partner	w/a spouse or partner	Urban	Japanese
72JJ	Koichi	Gay	55–64	Associate degree	Employed full-time	Single	w/a parent(s)	Suburban	Japanese
75JJ	Aoi	Lesbian	18–24	Bachelor's degree	Dispatched employee	Single	w/ someone else	Urban	Mixed/Multiple ethnic groups
77JJ	Rin	Lesbian	18–24	Bachelor's degree	Student	Single	w/a parent(s)	Urban	Korean
78FJ	John#	Gay	35–44	Doctorate degree	Employed full-time	Living with a partner	w/a spouse or partner	Urban	White/European
80JJ	Kei	Transgender MtF/X	35–44	Bachelor's degree	Unable to work	Single	Alone	Suburban	Japanese
81FJ	Olivia#	Lesbian	35–44	Some grad school	Employed full-time	Living with a partner	w/a spouse or partner	Suburban	White/European
83FJ	Emma#	Q + (Others) female	25–34	Bachelor's degree	Employed full-time	Single	Alone	Suburban	White/European
84FJ	Shufen	Lesbian	35–44	Bachelor's degree	Employed full-time	In a relationship, not living together	Alone	Urban	Other Northeast Asian
85JJ	Ken'ichi	Gay	25–34	Bachelor's degree	Employed full-time	Single	w/a parent(s)	Suburban	Japanese

(continued)

Table 9.1 (continued)

ID*	Name**	LGBTQ+ identity	Age group	Highest level of education	Occupation	Relationship status	Living situation	Area of residence	Race/ ethnicity
86JJ	Takumi	Transgender FtM/X	18–24	Associate degree	Student	Single	Alone	Suburban	Japanese
89JJ	Ayano	Asexual female	25–34	Some college	Employed part-time	Single	Alone	Rural	Japanese
93JJ	Daichi	Gay	18–24	Vocational school	Self-employed	Living with a partner	w/a spouse or partner	Urban	Japanese
95JJ	Chihiro	Transgender MtF/X	35–44	Bachelor's degree	Employed part-time	Single	Alone	Urban	Japanese
100JJ	Mirai	Pansexual female	18–24	Bachelor's degree	Employed part-time	Single	w/a parent(s)	Rural	Japanese
101JJ	Kazuki	Gay	35–44	n/a	Employed full-time	Living with a partner	w/a spouse or partner	Urban	Japanese
102FJ	James#	Bisexual male	25–34	Bachelor's degree	Employed full-time	In a relationship, not living together	Alone	Urban	White/ European
104FJ	Chun-chieh	Gay	35–44	Master's degree	Employed full-time	Single	Alone	Urban	Other Northeast Asian
105JJ	Kazuya	Gay	25–34	Vocational school	Employed part-time	Single	Alone	Rural	Japanese
107JO	Naoki	Gay	35–44	Bachelor's degree	Employed full-time	Married (same-sex)	w/a spouse or partner	Suburban	Japanese
110JJ	Kenta	Gay	25–34	Bachelor's degree	Employed full-time	Single	w/a parent(s)	Rural	Japanese
111JJ	Satoshi	Gay	35–44	Bachelor's degree	Employed full-time	Living with a partner	w/a spouse or partner	Urban	Japanese

(continued)

Table 9.1 (continued)

ID*	Name**	LGBTQ+ identity	Age group	Highest level of education	Occupation	Relationship status	Living situation	Area of residence	Race/ ethnicity
112JJ	Naoto	Bisexual male	25–34	Master's degree	Self-employed	In a relationship, not living together	Alone	Urban	Japanese
114JJ	Ken	Transgender FtM/X	25–34	Master's degree	Employed full-time	Single	w/a parent(s)	Urban	Mixed/ multiple ethnic groups
115JJ	Haru	Transgender FtM/X	18–24	High school or equiv	Student	Single	Alone	Urban	Japanese
120JJ	Isamu	Q + (Others) male	45–54	Bachelor's degree	Other	Single	w/a parent(s)	Urban	Japanese
122FJ	Harry#	Gay	25–34	Bachelor's degree	Self-employed	Living with a partner	w/a spouse or partner	Suburban	Mixed/ multiple ethnic groups
123JJ	Ayumi	Transgender MtF/X	25–34	Bachelor's degree	Employed part-time	Single	w/a parent(s)	Urban	Japanese
131JJ	Susumu	Gay	55–64	Bachelor's degree	Employed full-time	Single	Alone	Urban	Japanese
135JJ	Yutaka	Transgender FtM/X	45–54	High school or equiv	Self-employed	Partnership	Alone	Rural	Japanese
136JJ	Yusei	Transgender FtM/X	25–34	Vocational school	Self-employed	Single	Alone	Urban	Japanese
149JJ	Tatsuya	Gay	45–54	Some college	Employed full-time	In a relationship, not living together	w/a parent(s)	Urban	Japanese

(continued)

Table 9.1 (continued)

ID*	Name**	LGBTQ+ identity	Age group	Highest level of education	Occupation	Relationship status	Living situation	Area of residence	Race/ ethnicity
155JJ	Yuka	Bisexual female	18–24	Some grad school	Student	Other	w/a parent(s)	Suburban	Japanese
158JJ	Mai	Pansexual female	18–24	Bachelor's degree	Student	Single	w/a parent(s)	Urban	Japanese
160JJ	Chinatsu	Q + (Others) female	25–34	Bachelor's degree	Employed full-time	Single	Alone	Urban	Japanese
163JJ	Mayu	Pansexual female	18–24	Bachelor's degree	Student	Single	Alone	Suburban	Japanese
165JJ	Hinata	Transgender FtM/X	18–24	High school or equiv	Student	In a relationship, not living together	w/a parent(s)	Rural	Japanese
168JJ	Nana	Bisexual female	25–34	Some college	Employed part-time	Married (same-sex)	w/a parent(s)	Urban	Korean
175JJ	Taka	Transgender FtM/X	35–44	High school or equiv	Self-employed	Single	Alone	Urban	Japanese
177JJ	Tadashi	Gay	55–64	Bachelor's degree	Self-employed	Divorced/ Separated	w/a parent(s)	Urban	Japanese
179FJ	Fenhua	Gay	18–24	Master's degree	Student	Single	Alone	Urban	Other Northeast Asian
180JJ	Aki	Transgender MtF/X	18–24	Some college	Student	Single	w/a parent(s)	Rural	Japanese
186JJ	Yuma	Gay	35–44	High school or equiv	Employed full-time	Living with a partner	w/a spouse or partner	Urban	Japanese
189JJ	Oto	Pansexual female	18–24	Some college	missing	In a relationship, not living together	w/a parent(s)	Rural	Japanese

(continued)

Table 9.1 (continued)

ID*	Name**	LGBTQ+ identity	Age group	Highest level of education	Occupation	Relationship status	Living situation	Area of residence	Race/ethnicity
193JJ	Toma	Gay	45–54	n/a	Employed full-time	Living with a partner	w/a spouse or partner	Urban	Japanese
194JJ	Rui	Bisexual female	25–34	Some college	Dispatched employee	Single	w/a parent(s)	Suburban	Japanese
195JJ	Hiroto	Gay	35–44	Bachelor's degree	Employed full-time	Living with a partner	w/a spouse or partner	Urban	Japanese
197JJ	Haku	Transgender FtM/X	18–24	High school or equiv	Student	Single	w/a parent(s)	Suburban	Japanese
200JJ	Masa	Transgender FtM/X	25–34	Some college	Employed part-time	Single	Alone	Urban	Japanese
202JO	Himari	Bisexual female	18–24	High school or equiv	Student	Single	Alone	Urban	Japanese
203JJ	Koki	Gay	45–54	Master's degree	Self-employed	Living with a partner	w/a spouse or partner	Urban	South Asian
208JJ	Yuzuru	Q + (Others) male	45–54	Bachelor's degree	Employed part-time	Divorced/Separated	w/a parent(s)	Suburban	Japanese
209JJ	Hikaru	Asexual female	18–24	Vocational school	Employed part-time	Single	w/a parent(s)	Rural	Japanese
213JJ	Sota	Gay	45–54	High school or equiv	n/a	Single	w/a parent(s)	Urban	Japanese
217FJ	Emily#	Asexual female	25–34	Bachelor's degree	Dispatched employee	Single	Alone	Urban	White/European
220JJ	Jiro	Gay	35–44	Bachelor's	Employed full-time	Living with a partner	w/a spouse or partner	Urban	Japanese

(continued)

Table 9.1 (continued)

ID*	Name**	LGBTQ+ identity	Age group	Highest level of education	Occupation	Relationship status	Living situation	Area of residence	Race/ ethnicity
221JJ	Kira	Lesbian	18–24	Vocational school	Employed full-time	Single	w/ someone else	Urban	Japanese
223JJ	Saori	Pansexual female	45–54	High school or equiv	Dispatched employee	Living with a partner	w/a spouse or partner	Suburban	Japanese
224JJ	Soma	Gay	35–44	Bachelor's degree	Employed full-time	Living with a partner	w/a spouse or partner	Urban	Japanese
233JJ	Shizu	Q + (Others) female	18–24	High school or equiv	Student	Single	w/a parent(s)	Suburban	Japanese
234JJ	Kaede	Q + (Others) female	25–34	Bachelor's degree	Employed full-time	Single	w/a parent(s)	Suburban	Japanese
239JJ	Kiyoshi	Asexual male	55–64	Doctorate degree	Employed full-time	Single	Alone	Suburban	Japanese
241FJ	Diego#	Gay	18–24	High school or equiv	Student	Partnership	Alone	Urban	Latinx
242JJ	Kotoha	Pansexual female	18–24	High school or equiv	Student	In a relationship, not living together	w/a parent(s)	Urban	Korean
243JJ	An	Transgender MtF/X	65–74	High school or equiv	n/a	Married (opposite-sex)	w/a spouse or partner	Urban	Japanese
244JJ	Mio	Pansexual female	25–34	Bachelor's degree	Employed part-time	In a relationship, not living together	w/a parent(s)	Urban	Japanese
246JJ	Masaru	Bisexual male	35–44	Some college	Home maker	Single	w/a parent(s)	Urban	Japanese
247FJ	Riku	Gay	55–64	Master's degree	Employed part-time	In a relationship, not living together	w/a parent(s)	Urban	Japanese
249JJ	Yamato	Gay	25–34	High school or equiv	Employed part-time	Single	w/a parent(s)	Urban	Japanese

(continued)

Table 9.1 (continued)

ID*	Name**	LGBTQ+ identity	Age group	Highest level of education	Occupation	Relationship status	Living situation	Area of residence	Race/ethnicity
252JJ	Kaho	Transgender MtF/X	45–54	Vocational school	Self-employed	Married (opposite-sex)	w/a spouse or partner	Suburban	Japanese
253JJ	Koharu	Q + (Others) female	25–34	n/a	Employed full-time	In a relationship, not living together	w/a parent(s)	Rural	Japanese
256JJ	Kaiya	Gay	18–24	High school or equiv	Student	Single	w/a parent(s)	Suburban	Japanese
265JJ	Hirotaka	Gay	45–54	Doctorate degree	Employed part-time	In a relationship, not living together	Alone	Suburban	Japanese
270JJ	Hiro	Transgender FtM/X	35–44	n/a	Employed full-time	Single	w/a parent(s)	Urban	Japanese
271FJ	Charlotte#	Bisexual female	35–44	Master's degree	Self-employed	Married (opposite-sex)	w/a spouse or partner	Suburban	White/European
272FJ	Amelie#	Bisexual female	25–34	Master's degree	Employed full-time	Married (opposite-sex)	w/a spouse or partner	Suburban	White/European
273JJ	Hideki	Gay	35–44	High school or equiv	n/a	Single	Alone	Urban	Japanese
274JJ	Gaku	Gay	25–34	High school or equiv	Employed part-time	Single	Alone	Suburban	Japanese
277JJ	Tomo	Transgender FtM/X	25–34	Bachelor's degree	Employed full-time	In a relationship, not living together	w/a parent(s)	Urban	Japanese
279JJ	Nao	Lesbian	18–24	Vocational school	Student	Single	w/a parent(s)	Urban	Japanese
284FJ	Aranya	Transgender MtF/X	25–34	Some grad school	Employed full-time	Living with a partner	w/a spouse or partner	Urban	Southeast Asian

(continued)

Table 9.1 (continued)

ID*	Name**	LGBTQ+ identity	Age group	Highest level of education	Occupation	Relationship status	Living situation	Area of residence	Race/ ethnicity
285JJ	Yuna	Q + (Others) female	25–34	Bachelor's degree	Employed full-time	Single	Alone	Suburban	Japanese
286JJ	Rio	Transgender FtM/X	25–34	Bachelor's degree	Employed full-time	Single	Alone	Rural	Japanese
287JJ	Itsuki	Transgender FtM/X	35–44	Master's degree	Dispatched employee	Single	w/a parent(s)	Suburban	Japanese
288JJ	Honoka	Pansexual female	18–24	Vocational school	Student	Single	Alone	Urban	Japanese
289JJ	Hajime	Gay	35–44	Bachelor's degree	Self-employed	Living with a partner	w/ someone else	n/a	Japanese
290JJ	Ryu	Gay	25–34	High school or equiv	Employed full-time	Single	Alone	Urban	Japanese
292JJ	Aimi	Asexual female	35–44	Vocational school	n/a	Living with a partner	w/a spouse or partner	Urban	Japanese
294JJ	Yoshio	Gay	45–54	Bachelor's degree	Employed full-time	Living with a partner	w/a spouse or partner	Urban	Japanese
298JJ	Sora	Lesbian	18–24	Bachelor's degree	Student	Living with a partner	w/a spouse or partner	Suburban	Japanese
300JJ	Nanami	Lesbian	18–24	Bachelor's degree	Student	In a relationship, not living together	w/a parent(s)	Rural	Japanese
301JJ	Masato	Gay	25–34	Middle school or equiv	Employed full-time	Living with a partner	w/a spouse or partner	Urban	Japanese
306JJ	Go	Gay	25–34	n/a	Employed full-time	Single	Alone	Suburban	Japanese

(continued)

Table 9.1 (continued)

ID*	Name**	LGBTQ+ identity	Age group	Highest level of education	Occupation	Relationship status	Living situation	Area of residence	Race/ethnicity
307JJ	Katsutoshi	Gay	55–64	Bachelor's degree	Employed full-time	In a relationship, not living together	w/a parent(s)	Urban	Japanese
309JJ	Sento	Gay	25–34	Master's degree	Employed full-time	In a relationship, not living together	Alone	Suburban	Japanese
310JJ	Kazuto	Gay	35–44	Bachelor's degree	Self-employed	In a relationship, not living together	Alone	Urban	Japanese
312JJ	Ichiro	Gay	35–44	Bachelor's degree	Employed full-time	In a relationship, not living together	Alone	Urban	Japanese
313JJ	Taiga	Bisexual male	18–24	High school or equiv	Student	Single	w/a parent(s)	Suburban	Japanese
316FJ	Skyler#	Q + (Others) female	25–34	Bachelor's degree	Employed full-time	Single	Alone	Urban	White/European
320FJ	Alejandro#	Gay	25–34	Bachelor's degree	Employed full-time	In a relationship, not living together	Alone	Urban	Latinx
321JJ	Riko	Q + (Others) female	18–24	Bachelor's degree	Student	Single	Alone	Suburban	Japanese
328FJ	Aanan#	Gay	45–54	Doctorate degree	Employed full-time	Living with a partner	w/a spouse or partner	Urban	South Asian
336JJ	Tsumugi	Pansexual female	18–24	High school or equiv	Student	Single	w/a parent(s)	Urban	Japanese
337JJ	Hana	Asexual female	18–24	High school or equiv	Student	Single	w/a parent(s)	Suburban	Japanese

* JJ = Japanese nationals in Japan; FJ = non-Japanese nationals in Japan; JO = Japanese nationals or immigrants overseas; FO = non-Japanese nationals overseas
** All names are pseudonyms
#Participants responded/corresponded in English. All translations are mine unless otherwise noted

References

Ahmed, S. (2006). *Queer phenomenology: Orientations, objects, others.* Duke University Press.
Berlant, L. (2011). *Cruel optimism.* Duke University Press.
Butler, J. (1993). *Bodies that matter: On the discursive limits of "sex."* Routledge.
Butler, J. (2009). *Frames of war: When is life grievable?* Verso.
Muñoz, J. E. (2009). *Cruising utopia: The then and there of queer futurity.* New York University Press.
Sedgwick, E. K. (1990). *Epistemology of the closet.* University of California Press.

Index

M. Tamagawa, *Japanese LGBTQ+ Lives, Diasporic Voices, and Resilience*, https://doi.org/10.1007/978-981-95-3105-9

MIX
Papier aus verantwortungsvollen Quellen
Paper from responsible sources
FSC® C105338

If you have any concerns about our products, you can contact us on
ProductSafety@springernature.com

In case Publisher is established outside the EU, the EU authorized representative is:
Springer Nature Customer Service Center GmbH
Europaplatz 3, 69115 Heidelberg, Germany

Printed by Libri Plureos GmbH
in Hamburg, Germany